HUGO GROTIUS
MELETIUS
SIVE
DE IIS QUAE INTER CHRISTIANOS
CONVENIUNT EPISTOLA

STUDIES IN THE HISTORY
OF
CHRISTIAN THOUGHT

EDITED BY

HEIKO A. OBERMAN, Tucson, Arizona

IN COOPERATION WITH
HENRY CHADWICK, Cambridge
JAROSLAV PELIKAN, New Haven, Conn.
BRIAN TIERNEY, Ithaca, N.Y.
E. DAVID WILLIS, Princeton, N.J.

VOLUME XL

HUGO GROTIUS

MELETIUS
SIVE
DE IIS QUAE INTER CHRISTIANOS
CONVENIUNT EPISTOLA

Portrait of Grotius by M. J. Mierevelt, 1608

HUGO GROTIUS
MELETIUS

SIVE

DE IIS QUAE INTER CHRISTIANOS CONVENIUNT EPISTOLA

CRITICAL EDITION WITH TRANSLATION,
COMMENTARY AND INTRODUCTION

BY

GUILLAUME H. M. POSTHUMUS MEYJES

E.J. BRILL
LEIDEN • NEW YORK • KØBENHAVN • KÖLN
1988

BT
1100
.G69513
1987

Library of Congress Cataloging-in-Publication Data

Grotius, Hugo, 1583-1645.
  Meletius, sive, De iis quae inter Christianos conveniunt epistola.

  (Studies in the history of Christian thought, ISSN 0081-8607; v. 40)
  In English and Latin, with a commentary in English.
  Bibliography: p.
  Includes index.
  1. Apologetics—17th century. 2. Religion—early works to 1800. 3. Theology—Early works to 1800.
  I. Posthumus Meyjes, G. H. M. (Guillaume Henri Marie) II. Title. III. Title: Meletius. IV. Title: De iis quae inter Christianos conveniunt epistola. V. Series.
  BT1100.G69513 1987   239   87-33809
  ISBN 90-04-08356-1

ISSN 0081-8607
ISBN 90 04 08356 1

© Copyright 1988 by E. J. Brill, Leiden, The Netherlands

All rights reserved. No part of this book may be reproduced or translated in any form, by print, photoprint, microfilm, microfiche or any other means without written permission from the publisher

PRINTED IN THE NETHERLANDS BY E. J. BRILL

To the memory of
Alexander Emile Marie van der Does de Willebois
(† 12 July 1987)

CONTENTS

List of illustrations	IX
Preface	XI
Abbreviations	XV
a) The Bible	XV
b) Classical and patristic authors	XV
c) The works of Grotius	XVII
d) Other abbreviations	XVIII
Introduction	1
1. Discovery	1
2. Manuscript and transmission, marginalia	6
a) Manuscript and transmission	6
b) Marginalia	8
3. Dating	10
4. Title	15
5. Purpose, composition, mode of thought, structure	22
a) Purpose	22
b) Composition	26
c) Mode of thought	26
d) Structure	31
6. Analysis of the contents	41
7. Reception	44
8. Commentary: justification and explanation	61
9. Sources	67
10. Explanatory remarks on textual form and translation	71
Text	75
Translation	103
Commentary	137
List of marginalia	163
List of underlinings	165
Appendix I: From the Prolegomena of Stobaeus' *Dicta Poëtarum* (1623)	167
Appendix II: The correspondence of Grotius and his friends about the *Meletius* (1611/12)	169
Index of biblical references	183
Index of proper names	185
Index of subject matters and terms	188

LIST OF ILLUSTRATIONS

Portrait of Grotius by M. J. Mierevelt, 1608 — (Private collection, Stockholm), frontispiece.

1. The manuscript of Grotius' *Meletius*, fol. 1^r. Illustration of the hand of copyist *a* — (Remonstrant collection, ms. G 90, *University Library* Amsterdam), page 2.

2. The manuscript of Grotius' *Meletius*, fol. 3^v. Illustration of the hand of copyist *a*, marginal annotations in the hand of Grotius — (Remonstrant collection, ms. G 90, *University Library* Amsterdam), page 9.

3. The manuscript of Grotius' *Meletius*, fol. 10^r. Illustration of the hand of copyist *b*, marginal annotations in the hand of Grotius — (Remonstrant collection, ms. G 90, *University Library* Amsterdam), page 11.

4. Facsimile of Patriarch Meletius' letter to Janus Dousa, 23 October 1597 — (Collection Dupuy, ms. 490, fo. 62^r, *Bibliothèque Nationale* Paris), page 16.

5. Title page of *Epistola Meletii ... ad Dousam* (1598) — (*Royal Library* The Hague), page 19.

6. Portrait of Johannes Boreel. 18th century's drawing by D. Vlietland from an older copy — (*Zelandia Illustrata, State Archives* Middelburg), page 21.

7. Patriarch Meletius' signature from his letter to Janus Dousa, 23 October 1597 — (Collection Dupuy, ms. 490, fo. 65^r, *Bibliothèque Nationale* Paris), page 22.

8. Portrait of Antonius Walaeus — (J. Meursius, *Athenae Batavae*, 1625), page 47.

9. Facsimile of the minute of Grotius' letter to [Apollonius Schotte], [3 April 1612] — (Remonstrant collection, ms. III C 5, *University Library* Amsterdam), page 58.

10. Portrait of Petrus Cunaeus — (J. Meursius, *Athenae Batavae*, 1625), page 60.

PREFACE

Colloquia and conferences devoted to the commemoration of historical events or figures are intended to encourage the progress of scholarship. The commemoration means that the event or figure in question receives concentrated scholarly attention, that a connection is established with recently developed views on kindred subjects, that new information is revealed, new questions are formulated, and so on. In short, the old image is renewed and comes into focus, the event or figure in question moves out of the dark and is inserted in the stream of contemporary research. Such commemorations often lead to new initiatives, like the publication of critical editions, and sometimes to new discoveries.

The discovery of Hugo Grotius' *Meletius* is an example. When the Royal Netherlands Academy of Arts and Sciences decided to organise an international colloquium in 1983 in order to commemorate the 400th anniversary of Grotius' birth I had the honour of being invited to read a paper. As I was preparing it I immersed myself in Grotius' letters and works and it then occurred to me that, at the beginning of the Twelve-Year Truce, he had composed a theological treatise entitled *Meletius* which was believed to have been lost. I therefore experienced a 'shock of recognition' when I came across the title in an old manuscript catalogue early in 1984. After some strenuous weeks spent transcribing and comparing I could conclude that the manuscript was indeed by Grotius and that I had discovered his earliest theological treatise.

As a theologian and church historian I did not feel particularly qualified to edit such a work. Grotius himself had a peculiar, not to say wayward, quality as a theologian and a religious thinker. A typical Christian humanist, he was an 'irregular' theologian who sought out and followed a path of his own. His approach to the subject was conditioned by classical antiquity which he regarded as the normative period and of which he possessed an unparalleled knowledge owing both to his education and his genius. For these and other reasons I soon had to rely on the assistance of professional classicists in preparing an edition of the *Meletius*, and I now take the opportunity of thanking them for their ready support at all stages of my labours.

With his already legendary precision, knowledge, and severity my colleague H. J. de Jonge read the first draft of my work and rightly made a large number of remarks, some of them highly critical. He provided me with important supplementary information and elucidations, and, in a word, showed me how a text should be edited. For this, and the promptness of his help, I am deeply grateful.

When the newspapers reported the discovery of Grotius' *Meletius* my colleague J. H. Waszink spontaneously offered me his assistance, for which I am most grateful. I have made good use of his learned comments, his technical advice, and his practical help in preparing the Latin text and the commentary. I hope that what the work has now become will give him more satisfaction than my mediocre performance when I had the privilege of being taught Classics by him at the Municipal Grammar School in Utrecht during the war.

I gratefully acknowledge the valuable assistance on various levels I have received from the staff of the Grotius Institute in The Hague, H. J. M. Nellen, E. Rabbie and A. C. G. M. Eyffinger, now staff-member of the Library of the Peace Palace in The Hague. I also want to thank my friends and colleagues C. H. Beelaerts van Blokland, J. A. H. G. M. Bots, S. Dresden, R. Feenstra, R. A. V. van Haersolte and J. Trapman. They all read the whole, or parts, of my manuscript and I am indebted to them for their comments and suggestions.

As to the numerous scholars who have assisted in the English translation, the first to be mentioned is Mrs Therese Heesterman-Visser of the Theological Institute in Leiden. After having supported me at all stages of my labours she finally translated the entire work into English with the utmost dedication. Her work in this respect was much facilitated by the meticulous Dutch translation of the Latin text by A. J. van Duyvendijk, former rector of the Gymnasium Haganum. For his selfless contribution, now hidden in the English translation, I take the opportunity to thank him warmly. The English translation of the notes and the introduction was further improved by A. G. H. Bachrach and A. Hamilton, while the English translation of the Latin text was thoroughly checked by J. M. van Ophuysen of the Department of Classics in Leiden, by the Patristic scholar J. S. Alexander and the Church historian James K. Cameron, both of St Mary's College at St Andrews. To all these fine scholars I extend my profound thanks.

I gladly recognize the assistance of members, and former members, of the Department of Ecclesiastical History in Leiden: Mrs Joke Spaans, Miss Marthe de Vries, Mrs Ernestine van der Wall, J. van der Meij and J. P. Heering (who was particularly helpful in compiling the indexes).

Finally, I wish to record my thanks to the Leids Universiteits-Fonds for providing a subsidy for the translation, to my friend Heiko A. Oberman for inviting me to publish this book in his prestigious series, and to the firm of Brill for the pleasant cooperation and the great care taken of the edition.

This book is dedicated to the memory of a dear friend of my youth whose good humour, noblemindedness and wisdom I shall never forget.

Theologisch Instituut, Leiden G. H. M. Posthumus Meyjes
September 1987

When this book was already in the press I discovered in the Remonstrant collection of *Grotiana*, deposited with the University Library in Amsterdam, a number of autographic items (drafts, sketches, annotations etc.) which, apparently, belong to an earlier stage of the *Meletius*. Being unable to make use of this interesting material for this edition I intend to devote a separate publication to it in the near future.

ABBREVIATIONS

a) THE BIBLE

Vetus Testamentum

Gn.	Genesis
Ex.	Exodus
Deut.	Deuteronomium
Eccl.	Ecclesiastes

Novum Testamentum

Mt.	Matthaeus
Lc.	Lucas
Ioh.	Iohannes
Act.	Acta Apostolorum
Rom.	Ad Romanos
1. Cor.	1. ad Corinthios
Gal.	Ad Galatos
Phil.	Ad Philippenses
Col.	Ad Colossenses
1., 2. Tim.	1., 2. ad Timotheum
Tit.	Ad Titum
Hebr.	Ad Hebraeos
Ap. Ioh.	Apocalypsis Iohannis

b) CLASSICAL AND PATRISTIC AUTHORS

Ael. L.	Aelius Lambridius
Aeschyl.	Aeschylus
Amm. Marc.	Ammianus Marcellinus
Aristoph.	Aristophanes
Equ.	*Equites*
Plut.	*Plutus*
Aristot.	Aristoteles
Eth. Eud.	*Ethica Eudemia*
Eth. Nic.	*Ethica Nicomachea*
Metaph.	*Metaphysica*
Phys.	*Physica*
Pol.	*Politica*
Arnob.	Arnobius
Adv. nat.	*Adversus nationes*
Athen.	Athenaeus
Aug.	Augustinus
Civ.	*De civitate Dei*
Conf.	*Confessiones*
Doctr. chr.	*De doctrina christiana*
Epist.	*Epistulae*
Cass. Dio	Cassius Dio
Cens.	Censorinus
Cic.	Cicero
Ac. 1	*Lucullus sive Academicorum priorum libri*
Ac. 2	*Academicorum posteriorum libri*
Att.	*Epistulae ad Atticum*
Div.	*De divinatione*
Fin.	*De finibus*
Inv.	*De inventione*
Nat.	*De natura deorum*
Off.	*De officiis*
Rep.	*De republica*
Sest.	*Pro P. Sestio*
Tusc.	*Tusculanae disputationes*
Vatin.	*In P. Vatinium testem interrogatio*
Clem. Al.	Clemens Alexandrinus
Prot.	*Protrepticus*
Strom.	*Stromateis*
Demosth.	Demosthenes
Dig.	*Digesta*
Dio Chrys.	Dio Chrysostomus
Diod.	Diodorus Siculus
Diog. Laert.	Diogenes Laertius
Epic.	Epicurus
Epict.	Epictetus
Ench.	*Enchiridion*
Diss.	*Dissertationes*
Eur.	Euripides
Andr.	*Andromache*
Eus.	Eusebius

H.E.	*Historia Ecclesiastica*	Plin.	Plinius maior et minor
P.E.	*Praeparatio Evangelica*	*Nat.*	*Naturalis historia* (Plinius maior)
Gal.	Galenus	*Epist.*	*Epistulae* (Plinius minor)
Nat.fac.	*De naturalibus facultatibus*	Plut.	Plutarchus
Hes.	Hesiodus	*Aud.*	*De audiendis poetis*
Op.	*Opera*	*Mor.*	*Moralia*
Hom.	Homerus	*Num.*	*Vita Numae*
Od.	*Odyssea*	Pomp. Trog.	Pompeius Trogus
Hor.	Horatius	Ps. Long.	Pseudo Longinus
Ars	*Ars poetica*	*Subl.*	*De sublimitate*
Epist.	*Epistulae*	Publil.Syr.	Publilius Syrus
Sat.	*Satirarum libri*		
		Rutil.Nam.	Rutilius Namatianus
Isoc.	Isocrates		
Iuv.	Iuvenalis	Salv.	Salvianus
Sat.	*Saturnalia*	*Gub.Dei*	*De gubernatione Dei*
Ios.	Iosephus	Sen.	Seneca
Ant.Iud.	*Antiquitates Iudaicae*	*Ag.*	*Agamemnon*
Ap.	*Contra Apionem*	*Benef.*	*De beneficiis*
Iust.M.	Iustinus Martyr	*Epist.*	*Epistulae*
1., 2. Apol.	*1., 2. Apologia*	*Herc.f.*	*Hercules furens*
		Ira	*De ira*
		Nat.	*Naturales quaestiones*
Lact.	Lactantius	Sent. Varr.	Sententiae Varronis
Inst.	*Institutiones divinae*	Soph.	Sophocles
Liv.	Livius	*Ant.*	*Antigone*
Lucan.	Lucanus		
Phars.	*Pharsalia*		
		Tac.	Tacitus
		Germ.	*Germania*
		Hist.	*Historiae*
M. Aur.	Marcus Aurelius	Ter.	Terentius
Martial.	Martialis	*Andr.*	*Andria*
Max. Tyr.	Maximus Tyrius	*Hec.*	*Hecyra*
Diss.	*Dissertationes*	Tert.	Tertullianus
		Apol.	*Apologia*
		Spec.	*De spectaculis*
Ov.	Ovidius	Theoph.Ant.	Theophilus Antiochenus
Ars	*Ars amatoria*	*Autol.*	*Ad Autolycum*
Phil.	Philo Alexandrinus	Val.Max.	Valerius Maximus
Spec.leg.	*De specialibus legibus*	Verg.	Vergilius
Philostr.	Philostratus	*Aen.*	*Aeneis*
Vit.Apollon.	*Vita Apollonii*		
Plato	Plato		
Alc. 1, 2	*Alcibiades 1, 2*	Xen.	Xenophon
Apol.	*Apologia*	*Apol.*	*Apologia*
Crit.	*Crito*		
Phaed.	*Phaedo*		
Phaedr.	*Phaedrus*	Zos.	Zosimus
Rep.	*De republica*	*Hist.*	*Historia nova*

c) THE WORKS OF GROTIUS

AE	*Adamus Exul* in *Sacra in quibus Adamus Exul* (= *TMD* no. 21), reprinted, translated into Dutch and commented in *Dichtwerken* I 1a and 1b
Annot. in NT	*Annotationes in Novum Testamentum* (= *TMD* no. 1148) in *OT* II & III
Annot. in VT	*Annotationes in Vetus Testamentum* (= *TMD* no. 1148) in *OT* I
Bewijs	*Hugo de Groot's Bewijs van de ware godsdienst met zijne overige Nederduitsche gedichten*, (ed.) J. de Vries, Amsterdam 1844 (= *TMD* no. 151) 1-167
BW	*Briefwisseling van Hugo Grotius* I, 's-Gravenhage 1928 and ff.
CP	*Tragoedia Christus Patiens*, text, translation into Dutch and commentary in *Dichtwerken* I 2a/b 5
Def.	*Defensio decreti Ordinum Hollandiae pro pace Ecclesiae* (= *TMD* 911) in *OT* IV 195-200.
Dichtwerken	*De dichtwerken van Hugo Grotius. Oorspronkelijke dichtwerken*, (tekst, vertaling, toelichting), (ed.) B. L. Meulenbroek (e.a.), I 1a; I 1b; I 2a 1; I 2b 1; I 2a 2; I 2b 2; I 2a/b 5, Assen 1971-78.
Dogm.	*De dogmatis quae reipublicae noxia sunt aut dicuntur* (= *TMD* no. 907) in *OT* IV 754-55
Euch.	*Eucharistia* in *Dichtwerken* I 2a 2 (111-23)
Excerpta	*Excerpta ex tragoediis et comoediis Graecis*, Paris 1626 (= *TMD* no. 468)
Fruin, *Verhooren*	R. Fruin, *Verhooren en andere bescheiden betreffende het rechtsgeding van Hugo de Groot*, Werken Hist. Genootschap NR 14, Utrecht 1871
Imp.	*De imperio summarum potestatum circa sacra* (= *TMD* no. 901) in *OT* IV 202-92
Iur.	*De iure belli ac pacis libri tres in quibus ius naturae & gentium*, (ed.) B. J. A. De Kanter-Van Hettinga Tromp, Lugd. Bat. 1939 (= *TMD* no. 617)
Orat.	*Oratio ... habita in senatu Amstelredamensi...* , (= *TMD* no. 854) in *OT* 75-94
Onderwijsinge	*Onderwijsinge der gedoopte kinderen door vragen en antwoord*, in *Bewijs* (= *TMD* no. 151) 168-93
OT	*Opera Theologica* I-IV, Basil. 1732 (= *TMD* no. 921, reprinted Stuttgart 1972)
Par.	*Parallelon rerumpublicarum liber tertius: De moribus ingenioque populorum Atheniensium, Romanorum, Batavorum. — Vergelijking der gemeenebesten ... Derde boek: Over de zeden en den inborst der Athenieseren, Romeinen en Hollanderen*, (ed.) Johan Meerman, I-IV, Haarlem 1801-03 (= *TMD* no. 750)
Pietas	*Ordinum Hollandiae Pietas ab calumniis vindicata* (= *TMD* no. 822) in *OT* IV 97-125
Rem.	*Remonstrantie nopende de ordre dije in de Landen van Hollandt ende Westvrieslandt dijent gestelt op de Joden*, (ed.) J. Meijer, Amsterdam 1949 (= *TMD* no. 816)
Rep. emend.	*De Republica emendanda. A juvenile tract by Hugo Grotius on the emendation of the Dutch polity*, in *Grotiana* NS 5 (1984)
Sacra	*Sacra in quibus Adamus Exul*, see above *AE*
Satisfact.	*Defensio fidei catholicae de satisfactione Christi adversus Faustum Socinum Senensem* (= *TMD* no. 931) in *OT* IV 293-348
Sent. de fato	*Philosophorum sententiae de fato, et de eo quod in nostra est potestate* (= *TMD* no. 527) in *OT* 377-453
Stob. *Dicta*	*Dicta poëtarum quae apud Io. Stobaeum exstant*, Paris. 1623 (= *TMD* no. 458)
TMD	J. ter Meulen & P. J. J. Diermanse, *Bibliographie des écrits imprimés de Hugo Grotius*, La Haye 1950
Ver.	*De veritate religionis Christianae* (= *TMD* no. 980), in *OT* IV 1-96

d) OTHER ABBREVIATIONS

abl.	*ablativus*
add.	*addunt*
afl.	aflevering/*issue*
annot.	*annotatio*
App.	*Appendix*
BLGNP	*Biografisch Lexicon voor de Geschiedenis van het Nederlandse Protestantisme*, I, Kampen 1978 and ff.
cf.	confer
DNB	*Dictionary of National Biography from the earliest times to 1900*, 1-63, London 1885-1900
e.a.	et alii
ed.	edidit/ediderunt
edd.	*editiones*
ff.	*following*
fo.	*folio*
FV	H. Diels, *Fragmente der Vorsokratiker, Griechisch und Deutsch*, [6] I-III, Berlin 1951-56
Grotiana	*Vereeniging voor de uitgave van Grotius*, I-IX, s'-Gravenhage 1928-1942
Grotiana NS	A Journal under the auspices of the *Grotiana Foundation*, I, Assen 1980 and ff.
Grotius, Proceedings	The World of Hugo Grotius (*1583-1645*). Proceedings of the International Colloquium organized by the Grotius Committee of the Royal Netherlands Academy of Arts and Sciences, Rotterdam 6-9 April 1983, Amsterdam/Maarssen 1984
Haentjens	A. H. Haentjens, *Hugo de Groot als godsdienstig denker*, Amsterdam 1946
i.a.	*inter alia/alios*
i.e.	id est
JKNAW	*Jaarboek van de Koninklijke Nederlandse Akademie van Wetenschappen*, Amsterdam
JTS	*Journal of Theological Studies*, London
lib.	liber
libr.	libri
LS	Charlton T. Lewis & Charles Scott, *A Latin Dictionary*, Oxford [1958]
LThK	*Lexikon für Theologie und Kirche*, [2] I-X, Freiburg i.B. 1957-1965
M[K]NAW	*Mededelingen van de [Koninklijke] Nederlandse Akademie van Wetenschappen*, Amsterdam
ms.	manuscript
n.	note
NAKG	*Nederlands(ch) Archief voor Kerkgeschiedenis*, NS 's-Gravenhage/Leiden
Nauck[2]	A. Nauck, *Tragicorum graecorum fragmenta*. Supplementum ... adiecit B. Snell,[2] Hildesheim 1964
NNBW	*Nieuw Nederlandsch Biographisch Woordenboek*, I-X, Leiden 1911-1937
no.	number
nos.	numbers
NS	Nieuwe Serie/New Series
o.c.	*opus citatum*
Op. Omn.	*Opera Omnia*
Op. Theol.	*Opera Theologica*
p.	page
PRE	*Realencyklopädie für protestantische Theologie und Kirche*, [3] 1-24, Gotha 1896-1913
prol.	prolegomena

RAC	*Reallexikon für Antike und Christentum*, I, Stuttgart 1950 and ff.
RQ	*Renaissance Quarterly*, New York
reg.	register
RGP	*Rijks Geschiedkundige Publicatiën*, 's-Gravenhage
RHPR	*Revue d'Histoire et de Philosophie Religieuses*, Strasbourg
sq.	sequens
sqq.	sequentes
SR	*Studia Rosenthaliana*, I, Amsterdam 1967 and ff.
s.v.	sub voce
SVF	H. von Arnim (- M. Adler), *Stoicorum Veterum Fragmenta*, I-IV, Leipzig 1903-1924 (Stuttgart 1968)
TLL	*Thesaurus Linguae Latinae*, München
TW	*Theologisch Wörterbuch zum Neuen Testament*, I-X, Stuttgart 1933-1979
Univ. Libr.	University Library
Vg.	*Vulgata*
Vives, *Ver.*	L. Vives, *De veritate fidei christianae*, Basil. 1543
Wolf	D. Wolf, *Die Irenik des Hugo Grotius*, ² Hildesheim 1972

INTRODUCTION*

> "Sententiam meam de editione huius tui qua docti qua pii scripti equidem non libenter pronuncio, quia fructum quidem, si eo, quo aequum est, studio excipiatur, non exiguum ecclesiae Christi ex eo oriturum plane mihi persuadeo; tamen nostrorum temporum et ecclesiarum ratio, medicam hanc manum, ut vereor, vix feret."
>
> Antonius Walaeus in a letter to Grotius (*App.* II no. 8.4-9)

1. *Discovery*

Early in 1984, I chanced upon a hitherto virtually unknown work by Hugo Grotius. Thumbing through a catalogue of manuscripts deposited with the Amsterdam University Library (which I had requested for different purposes), I came across a title which looked vaguely familiar to me. It was of an unpublished and practically forgotten text by Grotius, his *Meletius sive de iis quae inter Christianos conveniunt epistola*. The title as such had been known from his correspondence and an apologetic treatise, but, curiously enough, this had never led anybody, in all those years since Grotius' death, to search for the work in the Dutch archives, rich though they are in *Grotiana*. The reason for this remarkable omission may well be that the work had already passed into oblivion in Grotius' time. Not only does he himself never mention it in his letters after 1612, but even Caspar Brandt, his first biographer, remains silent about it. Whether or not as a consequence, no later biographers record that Grotius had once composed a work with this title either,[1] and we know of only one author who paid any attention at all to the *Meletius*: the eminent P. C. Molhuysen.

---

* Parts of this Introduction have been published earlier in the following articles: 'Het vroegste theologische geschrift van Hugo Grotius herontdekt, zijn *Meletius* (1611)', in *Bestuurders en Geleerden*, opstellen ... aangeboden aan Prof. Dr. J. J. Woltjer, [Dieren/Amsterdam 1985] 75-84, and 'De receptie van Hugo de Groots *Meletius*', in *Kerkhistorische Opstellen aangeboden aan Prof. Dr. J. van den Berg*, Kampen 1987, 30-44.

[1] Cf. P. C. Molhuysen in *BW* I no. 215, 184 n. 2: "Brandt [= Caspar Brandt/A. van Cattenburgh, *Historie van het leven des heeren Huig de Groot*, Amsterdam/Dordrecht 1727], Lehmann's Manes, Burigny [= J. Levesque de Burigny, *Vie de Grotius...*, ²Amsterdam 1754)] do not so much as mention the title [i.e. *Meletius*]." (transl.) Cf. also *BW* I, Inleiding, XXII. Since Molhuysen called attention to the *Meletius*, the treatise is mentioned more than once in secondary literature. See for instance, W. J. M. van Eysinga, *Huigh de Groot. Een schets*, Haarlem 1945, 54-5, and J. den Tex, *Oldenbarnevelt* III, Bestand 1609-1619, Haarlem 1966, 287.

1. The manuscript of Grotius' *Meletius*, fol. 1ʳ. Illustration of the hand of copyist *a*

Molhuysen (1870-1944) studied classics at Leiden. In 1897 he was appointed head of the manuscript department of the Leiden University Library, and in 1913 librarian of the Peace Palace Library (The Hague). In 1921 came his appointment as librarian of the Royal Library in The Hague, a post he held until 1937.[2] Leaving aside other important scholarly initiatives and editions with which his name is linked, I shall restrict myself to his concern with Grotius.

It was Molhuysen who, when in charge of building up the Peace Palace Library, found the time to publish a new edition of Grotius' *De iure belli ac pacis*.[3] It appeared in 1919 and, for twenty years, was the standard edition, only to be replaced in 1939 by the so-called *editio major* by Mrs B. J. A. de Kanter-van Hettinga Tromp.[4] Molhuysen was also closely connected, ever since its foundation, with the 'Vereeniging tot Uitgave van Grotius'.[5] For years he acted as its secretary, under the chairmanship of the Leiden professor of International Law, C. van Vollenhoven. The latter is to be credited with having first promoted the publication of Grotius' correspondence.

"In the course of 1917", Molhuysen declared, "Van Vollenhoven wrote to me about the desirability of preparing a complete edition of Grotius' works in view of the renewed interest he, the father of modern international law, had attracted. We soon agreed that to this end the moral as well as the financial support of the national authorities was indispensable, and without much delay the 'Vereeniging tot Uitgave van Grotius' was founded. Its members undertook to provide a certain amount of money for some years for the purpose of preparing that edition. Without wishing to specify the details of the plans for the time being, we were still of the opinion that the letters to and from Grotius ought to be given priority, because they show us how his works originated."[6]

At a later stage this plan was taken up by the Koninklijke Nederlandse Akademie van Wetenschappen (Royal Netherlands Academy of Arts and Sciences), which, in its turn, succeeded in interesting the Union

---

[2] A biographical note on Molhuysen is given by A. G. Roos in *JKNAW* (1944-1945), 161-175; for his bibliography, see A. J. de Mare, *Herinneringen aan Dr. P. C. Molhuysen. Feiten en geschriften*, 's-Gravenhage 1948.

[3] *TMD* no. 615.

[4] *TMD* no. 616.

[5] Communications about the activities of the *Vereeniging tot uitgave van Grotius* appeared regularly in the periodical *Grotiana*. See *Grotiana* I (1928) 10 ff.; II (1929) 11 ff.; III (1930) II ff.; IV (1931) 10 ff.; V (1932) 10 ff.; VI (1933-1935) 10 ff.; VII (1936-1939) 10 ff.; VIII (1940) [10]; IX (1941-1942) 10.

[6] *BW* I, Inleiding [VII] (transl.)

Académique Internationale in the venture.⁷ By 1928 the first volume of the correspondence could appear in the series *Rijks Geschiedkundige Publicatiën*, to be followed by the second volume eight years later. In editing both volumes, Molhuysen laid the foundations, and at the same time set the tone, for the edition in its entirety. It comprises twelve volumes to date, covering the period to 1641 and is now approaching its completion.⁸ In his Introduction Molhuysen apologises for the fact that the first volume had taken so long.⁹ Yet there is nothing to warrant such an apology in view of the quantity of material which had to be selected, examined, and organized, also on an international level, before an ambitious project of this scope could bear fruit.

Apart from these two volumes of correspondence Molhuysen published over many years a number of shorter articles on Grotius, all well worth reading. Suffice it to mention "De bibliotheek van Hugo de Groot in 1618" ("Grotius' library in 1618"), which, like most of his contributions in this field, appeared as a communication of the Royal Academy.¹⁰

In the Introduction to the first volume of the correspondence covering the years 1597 to 1618 Molhuysen, prompted by the reference to this work in some of the letters of that period, broaches the subject of the *Meletius*. He points out that once the Truce (1609-1611) had been settled, Grotius followed the controversies between Remonstrants and Counter-Remonstrants with growing concern, and that he saw only one way in which to avert the danger threatening the young Republic: to appeal for tolerance. To quote Molhuysen: "At the end of 1611, he (Grotius) had completed a treatise on this subject, the ... *Meletius*, probably so named after two schismatics from the fourth century.¹¹ The work is lost, and even its name almost forgotten." Pointing out the letters and other works mentioning the *Meletius*, he continues: "It is not impossible that fragments of this treatise, or *adversaria* used for its composition, are hidden among the *Grotiana* of the Amsterdam University Library or among those of the Remonstrant Church in Rotterdam, but the illegible handwriting of the author, especially in his annotations and *collectanea*, is not conducive to a (successful) search. Yet it would be of great importance to discover this *Meletius*, both because it is Grotius' earliest theological

---

⁷ Cf. *Grotiana* I (1928) 17 ff.; II (1939) 13 ff. III (1930) 13 ff.; V (1932) II ff.; VI (1933-1935) II ff.; VII (1936-1939) II ff.; VIII (1940) [11] ff.; IX (1941-1942) [10].

⁸ Vol. 12, containing letters dating from 1641, appeared January 1987 (*RGP* 197).

⁹ *BW* I, Inleiding [VII].

¹⁰ P. C. Molhuysen, 'De bibliotheek van Hugo de Groot in 1618', *M[K]NAW* afd. lett. NR no. 3, Amsterdam 1943, (= Molhuysen 'Bibliotheek'), 45-63.

¹¹ Molhuysen is referring to Meletius of Lykopolis and Meletius of Antioch respectively. See about these K. Baur s.v., in *LThK* 7, 256-258.

work and because it would enable us to determine whether his opinions remained unaltered after his English voyage.''[12]

Molhuysen, then, was hot on the trail when he referred to the Amsterdam collections of *Grotiana* as a possible location for (fragments of) the *Meletius*, for it is indeed among these papers that the manuscript is preserved. The documents concerned are all owned by the Remonstrant Church of Amsterdam, which decided at the end of the last century to deposit these and other valuable manuscripts and books with the Amsterdam University Library where they have been held up to the present day.

It is not in the least surprising that so many *Grotiana* should be found in Remonstrant collections. Grotius strongly sympathized with the Remonstrants and, conversely, they always greatly admired him; they studied his life and works, and collected letters and other autographic documents which often sooner or later found their way to the Amsterdam and Rotterdam Remonstrant collections, either by inheritance, purchase or donation. For this reason both collections contain numerous *Grotiana* which have hitherto only been examined cursorily or superficially.[13]

In his search for unknown letters by Grotius and his correspondents, Molhuysen is bound to have consulted the Amsterdam documents more than once. How, then, can the *Meletius* have escaped his attention? The reason is presumably that he restricted himself to the voluminous bundles of *Grotiana* which in most cases had been arranged by Grotius himself, and later came into the hands of professor A. van Cattenburgh, who transferred them to the Remonstrant Library.[14] Now the manuscript we are concerned with never formed part of the two collections just mentioned, but was transmitted anonymously. So it did not get to the Remonstrant Library via Van Cattenburgh, but arrived there in quite a different way as we shall see.

As a disconnected item the *Meletius* was catalogued under its own number in the various printed Remonstrant catalogues which have appeared since the 19th century. In the first catalogue of 1849, composed by P. Scheltema, it occurs both on p. 11 under no. 86.1, and, in the register s.v. 'Meletius' (p. 18).[15] Unfortunately, this useful practice of incorporating the *incipit* of anonymous writings in a register was discon-

---

[12] *BW* I, XXII; cf. X (transl.) The treatise is also mentioned in P. C. Molhuysen, 'De briefwisseling van Hugo Grotius', *MKNAW* afd. lett. 66, serie B (1928), 22.

[13] A very useful though unpaginated survey was prepared by A.[C.G.M.] Eyffinger, *De handschriftelijke nalatenschap van Hugo de Groot. Inventaris van de papieren in Nederlandse openbare collecties*, Den Haag 1985, unpublished. (*Grotius Instituut*, Royal Library, The Hague).

[14] Remonstrant collection (*Univ. Libr.* Amsterdam), mss. III C 5 and III C 6.

[15] P. Scheltema, *Catalogus van de handschriften en boeken, behoorende tot de bibliotheek der Remonstrantsch-Gereformeerde Kerk te Amsterdam*, Amsterdam 1849.

tinued by the compilers of subsequent catalogues, J. H. Tideman (1877)[16] and M. B. Mendes da Costa (1923)[17], with the result that the work could easily pass unnoticed. This may well be why it eluded the attention of so thorough an investigator as Molhuysen.

Be that as it may, at one point I laid hands on the old catalogue by Scheltema. My attention was caught by the title 'Meletius', which I vaguely remembered from the correspondence. It had remained in my mind because I had been surprised that Grotius should name an irenic writing after a schismatic. It should be understood that neither Molhuysen, nor I at the time, knew of any 'Meletius' other than the two schismatics from the early period of the Church. It was only when I saw the manuscript that I realised that other bishops of that name had existed. Had I known this earlier and had my erudition been more profound, the title would not have aroused my curiosity; but in that case the discovery might never have been made.

2. *Manuscript and transmission, marginalia*

a) *Manuscript and transmission*

How and when the manuscript of Grotius' *Meletius* came to the Remonstrant Library in Amsterdam cannot be traced with any certainty. The shelfmarks it bears — one in purple ink, the other in red — unmistakably date back to the 19th century. I could not find it in the handwritten catalogues previous to the printed ones. From both these circumstances it might be inferred that the manuscript had not yet been incorporated in the library in the 18th century. I consider it likely that until the 19th century it was in private hands, probably in those of the descendants of Philippus van Limborch (1633-1712), the famous professor at the Remonstrant Seminary in Amsterdam and a friend of Locke.

An undated, autographic list of manuscripts in his possession which forms part of the same Remonstrant collection shows that he owned the *Meletius*. Page 1 of his list gives the full title: *Meletius, sive de his quae inter Christianos conveniunt epistola.*[18]

---

[16] [Joh. Tideman], *Catalogus der boeken en handschriften van de bibliotheek der Remonstrantsche Gemeente te Amsterdam*, Amsterdam 1877. Our ms. appears as no 86, (81).

[17] M. B. Mendes da Costa, *Bibliotheek der Universiteit van Amsterdam. Catalogus der handschriften, VII. De handschriften krachtens bruikleencontract in de Universiteitsbibliotheek berustende.* Amsterdam 1923. Our ms. appears as no. 130, (18) and is described as "17th century ms. in two (?) hands. — 20 pp. fo. [shelfmark] G 90." (transl.)

[18] Mendes da Costa, *Catalogus* VII 3, no. 17: "Limborch (Ph.) van, [Lijst der hem toebehoorende handschriften]. Eigenhandig geschreven, — 6 blz. 4° [shelfmark] Z 42."

Although we cannot rule out that this concerned a different copy from the one in question, it seems highly improbable. In the first place the title entered on the list is totally consonant with what our manuscript gives on fol. 1r.[19] Secondly, it is an established fact that in the course of the 18th and 19th centuries numerous other documents from the property of Van Limborch were transferred to the Remonstrant Library by his descendants.[20] The most obvious conclusion would therefore be that our manuscript came to this library in the same way. We thus have hardly any choice but to assume that this and the manuscript owned by Van Limborch are one and the same.

More difficulties are raised by the question of how Van Limborch obtained the manuscript. In principle, of course, there are many possibilities, but the first answer that comes to mind is transmission within the family. In that case there are only two possible channels: either it came from Grotius via his friend Simon Episcopius to Van Limborch, or it reached Van Limborch through the intermediary of Grotius' son Pieter. In both cases it has been handed on within the family, for Episcopius was a great-uncle of Van Limborch, while Van Limborch was related to the Grotius family through his first wife's brother, and was also an intimate friend of Pieter de Groot.[21]

The manuscript in question consists of eleven *diplomata*, the first four of which are arranged in a row, and the last seven inserted into each other and subsequently joined together. The folios bear a contemporary numbering, 1-20. Fol. [21r] and [21v] are unmarked; fol [22r] bears the indication *Meletius Gr[otii]* in unfamiliar handwriting (*d*), and fol. [22v] repeats the full title, with one minor alteration, in the handwriting of Grotius himself. The manuscript is written in three different hands, *a*, *b* and *c*. Fol 1r-9v are in hand *a*; fol. 10r-20v in hand *b*, while additions and corrections in the margin are written by hand *c*. Hands *a* and *b* are easy to read. Possibly they are those of students of the *Statencollege* in Leiden. Petrus Bertius, a subregent of this college and a friend of

---

It comes as a surprise to see the following title before the *Meletius* in this list: "Different tusschen de Joden en Christenen. Authore H. Grotio. Gallice." It is far from clear to which treatise of Grotius this refers. Research among the manuscripts formerly belonging to Van Limborch and nowadays incorporated in the Amsterdam Remonstrant collection, has so far been fruitless.

[19] See below 137, note to *Mel.* 1 on the *Title*.
[20] Cf. for instance Remonstrant Collection (*Univ. Libr.* Amsterdam), mss. B 57 and Z 42, and the survey by Eyffinger mentioned above (n. 13).
[21] P. J. Barnouw, *Philippus van Limborch*, (thesis Groningen), 's-Gravenhage 1963, 10 and 18 n. 15.

Grotius, occasionally rendered him assistance in copying manuscripts by putting students with a legible handwriting on the job.[22]

Hand *c*, though sometimes less easy to decipher, is far more interesting, because it is undoubtedly that of Grotius himself. One envisages him scrutinizing the copied text at leisure, here and there adding corrections in the margin or in the text — his own or those advised by others.

b) *Marginalia*

The marginalia are of two kinds. They partly summarize, in one or more words, the content of the text; and they partly give the Latin translation of Greek terms and quotations occurring in the text. In places these quotations are not given in full, and in those cases the manuscript has some blank lines. In the subsequent edition of the manuscript the marginal translations are inserted in the text in italics and between round brackets according to Grotius' habit in the works printed under his auspices. When the text does not give the full Greek quotation I have added it between square brackets.

I have compiled a separate list of those *marginalia* that contain a summary of the text, giving an exact record of the paragraph and line the marginal note refers to.[23] Would it not have been preferable, we may ask, to give these summaries in the margin of the printed text, since they were made by Grotius himself? I have indeed considered this alternative but ultimately rejected it. In the first place these *marginalia* are incomplete; they no longer occur after fol. 16^v. In the second place, they are very uneven; to some passages Grotius added them in profusion, while in others he only noted them very summarily. They therefore provide little insight into the segmentation of the text. For this reason I preferred not to burden the printed text with these *marginalia* but to put them in a separate list and to clarify the composition of the treatise with the help of an independently made and more detailed content-analysis, to be found in § 6 of this introduction.

With regard to the manuscript it should be remarked that it has a running text; in other words there are no paragraphs, chapters or subdivisions. The caesuras and the corresponding numbers are all mine. Finally the manuscript has a number of underlinings in an uncertain hand: was it that of Grotius himself or of the friends to whom he had sent it for

---

[22] Molhuysen, *BW* I, Inleiding, XIX. This is purely hypothetical however. It is also possible that Grotius ordered his secretary in The Hague to copy the text. The care shown by hand *a* in particular might be an indication to that effect.

[23] See below, 163.

2. The manuscript of Grotius' *Meletius*, fol. 3ᵛ. Illustration of the hand of copyist *a*, marginal annotations in the hand of Grotius

perusal? The latter possibility seems the least plausible. What is certain is that they cannot have been applied by the one man who went into the *Meletius* most thoroughly, the Middelburg minister and later professor at Leiden Antonius Walaeus. That this is not the copy he set eyes on can be proved by the fact that, in one of his letters to Grotius, he not only cites quotations from the *Meletius* to the letter — which conclusively corroborates the authenticity of our work if any corroboration were still needed —, but also accompanies them with accurate page indications. Now none of these indications correspond to the foliation of our manuscript, which means that Walaeus must have received another copy of the *Meletius*.[24] We may therefore conclude that a second copy must have existed which may turn up again in the future.

The manuscript in question was presumably Grotius' own copy. The corrections, the *marginalia*, and the 'second' title on fol. [22ᵛ], all of them added by Grotius himself, indicate as much.[25] From this we may infer that the underlinings are also his. These underlinings serve two purposes: they are partly applied to terms and basic notions in the argumentation and as such recur more than once in the marginal summaries, and they occur partly under Latin quotations and should thus be regarded as italicizations. All underlinings, save the underscored quotations, are also recorded in a separate list.

3. Dating

In his *Memorie van mijne Intentiën* (*Statement of my intentions*), an apology composed in Loevestein, Grotius writes as follows: "As to Toleration ... my opinion on this can partly be understood from an unprinted work, entitled Meletius ...".[26] Apart from this personal testimony from 1620, the work is mentioned in a number of letters written by Grotius himself as well as by others, all dating back to the last months of 1611 and the first months of 1612.[27] Over against the latest date thus given, April 1609 can be posited as the earliest date. And, indeed, from the Introduction to the work it appears that the Twelve-Year Truce was already in force.

---

[24] Walaeus devoted three letters to the *Meletius*: *App.* II nos 1, 3 and 8. In nr. 8 he refers to pages of Grotius' treatise four times: p. 3 = fo. 2ᵛ; p. 5 = fo. 4ʳ; p. 16 = fo. 11ʳ and p. 18 = fo. 12ʳ.

[25] See *Mel.* 1, note to the *Title*.

[26] R. Fruin, *Verhooren en andere bescheiden betreffende het rechtsgeding van Hugo de Groot*, Werken Hist. Genootschap NR 14, Utrecht 1871, (= Fruin, *Verhooren*) 3-4.

[27] Besides the letters mentioned in n. 24, there are two letters from Grotius written to Walaeus in reply. Three further letters concerning the *Meletius* have survived: one from Grotius to Apollonius Schotte; one from Schotte to Petrus Cunaeus; and one from Cunaeus to Schotte. For all these letters see *App.* II.

3. The manuscript of Grotius' *Meletius*, fol. 10ʳ. Illustration of the hand of copyist *b*, marginal annotations in the hand of Grotius

Grotius speaks about "the recollection of the War (with Spain) which is hardly over" (*belli vixdum sopiti memoria*).[28] Would it be possible to narrow the span still more — April 1609 to the end of 1611 —, and even further pinpoint the moment when the work was composed and completed? I for one have not been able to trace any decisive evidence. I have, for instance, vainly searched for remarks indicating that Grotius was engaged in writing this particular work in his letters to intimate friends before the end of 1611. So the more precise date which I venture to propose is necessarily conjectural.

It seems plausible that the work was completed around August/September 1611. The grounds for this assumption are the following:

1. A fact telling against an earlier dating — 1610 — is that at that time Grotius was strenuously working on his *De antiquitate Reipublicae Batavicae*, the Latin version and a translation into Dutch of which were published in the beginning and at the end of 1610 respectively.[29] Although it cannot in principle be excluded that he was working at both writings simultaneously, it is hardly likely in this case. Indeed the *Meletius* gives too strong an impression of having been started and completed uninterruptedly, and besides, the limited size of the work does not suggest a long-term labour. Grotius himself speaks of a "rudimentary and hastily composed work" (*opus rude et subitarium*).[30]

2. The fact that, until 1612, the *Meletius* is mentioned more than once in the letters is due to Grotius' habit of allowing manuscripts to circulate among his friends, most of whom let him have their reactions in writing.[31] He valued their opinion and wanted to have their remarks and suggestions for correction before considering publication. Because the subject of his treatise entailed a certain urgency, and also because he himself is bound to have been eager to learn the opinion of his friends, it is highly unlikely that he would have kept his work to himself for long after its completion. He would therefore have circulated it as soon as it was finished. Now the earliest written reaction he received from one of his friends is dated 1 November 1611.[32] Counting back from this established date, and assuming that one or two months were required for the copying, dispatch and the perusal of it by the recipient, we reach August/September 1611 as the date of its completion.

---

[28] *Mel.* 1.11.
[29] *TMD* nos. 691 and 698.
[30] *App.* II no. 2.5.
[31] See above n. 24 en 27.
[32] *BW* I no. 214, 184-185.

How long Grotius had been working at the text can only be guessed. Considering his fabulous creative capacity, his miraculous memory, and the swiftness with which he usually finished whatever he was doing, I suggest that he would have needed one, or at the most two, months, in between his routine tasks. If this is so, we may assume that he started working on the *Meletius* in June or July 1611.

Taking this as an established fact, one may suppose that the immediate occasion for the composition of the treatise was provided by the conclusion of the so-called 'Haagse conferentie' (The Hague Conference) on 20 May 1611. By resolution of the States General it was then decided that Remonstrants and Counter-Remonstrants had to respect each other's religious persuasions, and that the churches should be exhorted to toleration.[33]

Nothing in Grotius' biography seems to contradict this suggestion. If it is correct it implies that he wrote his tract at the age of 28. By that time he had been married to Maria van Reigersberch for three years, and for four years had held the post of Advocate General of the States of Holland and Zealand, stationed in the Hague. As such it was his task to watch over the proprietary and other rights of the States. The religious quarrels that were to disrupt the Republic during the years of the Truce were on the increase in this period. This greatly alarmed Grotius, and, as was to be his life-long habit, he employed the little spare time his exacting function allowed him to launch an appeal for reflection and reconciliation. The *Meletius* is the earliest expression of this appeal. It shows us Grotius at the very moment when he first ventured into the field of theology and religious politics. Up till then he had kept aloof from these domains, and the Counter-Remonstrants still took it for granted that he was on their

---

[33] The Hague Conference represented a colloquium of Remonstrant and Counter-Remonstrant theologians organized under the auspices of the States General. It was closed with the resolution that both parties should sum up the state of the controversy and should send their summary to the States General, including all the documents exchanged. The question of the Five Articles of the Remonstrants remained "in statu quo", while from the pulpit these had to be treated only "soberly and moderately". Cf. H. C. Rogge, *Johannes Wtenbogaert en zijn tijd* II, Amsterdam 1875, 92 ff. and J. den Tex. *Oldenbarnevelt* III, Bestand 1609-1619, Haarlem 1966, 148 ff. Ten years later, looking back to the Hague Conference, Grotius wrote (Fruin, *Verhooren*, 4): "Specialick wat aengaet de tolerantie van de leerstucken verhandelt in de Haegsche Conferentie, heb ick altydt geoordeelt, dat deselve tolerantie was conform Godes woort, alsoo 't verschil nyet en was fundamenteel, maer oock van alle tyden bevonden onder geleerde ende godtsalige luyden van één gemeenschap, Calvinus, Wittakerus, Perkins, Paraeus, Piscator, Molinaeus hebben selve soo geoordeelt, ende de gantsche vergadering van Hollant (soo ick mene) nae de Conferentie." Grotius got acquainted with most of these theologians only after 1611. They are all used and cited abundantly in his *Pietas* (1613), composed after his stay in England.

side. They were only disillusioned in 1613, when his *Pietas Ordinum* appeared.[34]

In the Introduction to the *Meletius* Grotius sketches a desolate picture of the general situation in the Republic. Having pointed out the curious phenomenon that meeting one's compatriots in a foreign country is a greater delight than meeting them at home, he continues:

> "Likewise we ourselves who live in these parts not only consider the other Europeans as foreigners, but even we as Germans are differentiated as High and Low Germans (= Dutch). Firstly, the Low Germans are kept divided by the recollection of a war which is hardly over; next, some are Guelders and others Frisians; and would that the peoples of Holland and Zealand, who always used to be so closely connected, differed only in name and not also in sympathy! Not to mention at this point the cities — rival centres rather —, the quarrels between city districts or the enmity between the great families. When we take all this into consideration, there is no doubt that neighbours and relatives seem more alien to one another than Italians or even Spaniards seemed to you (= Johan Boreel) when you sojourned in Syria."[35]

This lament about the rivalry between the provinces and the cities, and the absence of any form of unanimity, has a striking parallel in the report on the situation in the Republic which Grotius had sent not long before, on 18 September 1609, to Pierre Jeannin, the French envoy at the Truce negotiations. In it he wrote:

> "The situation in the Republic is the same as when you left us: the mutual understanding between the various provinces leaves much to be desired. There is an incessant quarrelling with the Zealanders. I was in Zealand recently, and was amazed at there being people so injudicious, shameless even, that they publicly proclaim that Zealand will not fare well until and unless it has broken off all relations with the other provinces and become wholly independent. Nor does this madness restrict itself to words, but in every possible manner the authority of the States General is being held in contempt and the common bond jeopardized. It is not difficult to guess what all this will lead up to. The fact, however, that the cities of Zealand are involved in a fierce struggle with one another and that even within the cities there are greater quarrels and factionalisms than ever, justifies the expectation that even they will not reach agreement among themselves towards a good end in a negative direction, as often they have not towards a good end in a positive direction."[36]

---

[34] C. van der Woude, *Hugo Grotius en zijn "Pietas Ordinum Hollandiae ac Westfrisiae vindicata"*, Kampen 1961, 6 ff.

[35] *Mel.* 1.9-17.

[36] *BW* I no. 170 (18 sept. 1609). See the article by the scholar who discovered these and other letters of Grotius: A. Eekhof, 'Grotiana in Noord-Amerika', *NAKG* NS 17 (1923-'24), 127 ff.

This picture of the situation in the Republic is strongly coloured by the circumstances Grotius had encountered in Zealand. Nor is this very surprising, since he is known to have had close ties with this province: his wife Maria was of Zealand origin and he had many friends there. What is remarkable is his choice of the friends to whom he sent his *Meletius* for perusal. From the correspondence it is clear that only Johan Boreel, Antonius Walaeus, Apollonius Schotte, and Petrus Cunaeus were sent the manuscript.[37] What did these four men have in common, apart from the fact that all had studied at Leiden and were mutual friends? Every single one of them had been born in Zealand and either maintained close relations with that province or worked there. Boreel, to whom I shall return, was the son of the mayor of Middelburg, the city in which Walaeus was a minister until 1619. Apollonius Schotte, from 1610 onward a member of the Supreme Court, was also the son of a Middelburg mayor. The father was a wealthy man, at whose expense Apollonius and Walaeus made a 'grand tour' to France, Switzerland and Germany. And Petrus Cunaeus, from 1612 onward extraordinary professor of Latin at Leiden, came from Flushing.[38]

Taking all this into account, we can justifiably conclude that, when writing in his Introduction to the *Meletius* about the quarrels disrupting the Republic, Grotius had Zealand foremost in mind, for it was there, in his opinion, that the quarrels raged most violently. Probably assuming that they were concerned about the situation in Zealand and were suffering on account of it, he chose his friends as the men best suited to comment critically on his appeal for reconciliation.

4. *Title*

Molhuysen, as we have seen, believed that the title 'Meletius' must refer to one of the homonymous bishops of the early Church, involved in the

---

[37] See for all these, P. J. Meertens, 'De Groot en Heinsius en hun Zeeuwse vrienden', in *Archief Zeeland* (1949-'50), 53-99 and the same author's masterly *Letterkundig leven in Zeeland in de zestiende en de eerste helft van de zeventiende eeuw*, (thesis Utrecht), Amsterdam 1942 (= *Letterkundig leven*). That Grotius restricted himself to dispatching his manuscript to his Zealand friends only, seems to be confirmed by what he says to Walaeus (*App*. II no. 2. 7-8): ''Nam postquam misso in Zelandiam exemplo, meum ipse scriptum relegere coepi...''

[38] For bibliographical data concerning Petrus Cunaeus, see Margreet Ahsmann and Robert Feenstra, *Bibliografie van hoogleraren in de rechten aan de Leidse Universiteit tot 1811*, Geschiedenis der Nederlandse Rechtswetenschap, VII afl. 1, Amsterdam/Oxford/New York 1984 (= Ahsmann/Feenstra, *Bibliografie*), 85-102. Cunaeus stayed for one year at Schotte's home in The Hague probably to get acquainted with law practice. So Meertens, *Letterkundig leven*, 375, following A. Vorstius, *Oratio funebris D. Petri Cunaei*, Lugd. Bat. 1638. See also n. 146 below.

4. Facsimile of Patriarch Meletius' letter to Janus Dousa, 23 October 1597

so-called Meletian schism.[39] In this he was wrong. The treatise itself clearly shows that it was not one of the 'Meletii' from the fourth century that Grotius had in mind, but a namesake from the sixteenth century, Meletius Pegas (1549-1601).

The latter's life offers many parallels with that of Cyril Lukaris (1572-1638), younger by a generation and far better known to us.[40] Grotius' Meletius was born in 1549 in Herakleion on Crete, studied at Padua and then became a monk in the Ankarathos monastery on Crete. He stayed from 1585 to 1588 with the patriarch Jeremias II in Constantinople and was in 1590 himself appointed patriarch of Alexandria. From 1597 to 1598 he also deputized for the patriarch of Constantinople. Meletius was a learned man, who called forth all his talents to defend the Eastern orthodoxy against the unification policy of Rome in general and of the Jesuits in particular. He was familiar with the Western theological tradition, especially with Augustine, and of this he made use in his polemics against the primacy of the pope and his claims to absolute power which he qualified as 'anti-Christian'. This seems to point to Protestant influence, for the older Greek theologians coupled the term 'Antichrist' solely with Islam.[41]

That Meletius was not an altogether unknown figure among the scholars in the Netherlands must be attributed in the first place to Georgius (Joris) Dousa (1574-99), a son of Janus Dousa the famous humanist. Georgius travelled in the East from 1593 to 1597. For seven months he stayed at the Sublime Porte, at the house of Queen Elisabeth's legate Edward Barton, through whose intermediary he was introduced to the patriarch Meletius. The young Dousa kept his friends at home

---

[39] See above n. 11.

[40] Cf. B. Kotter in *LThK* 7, 258, s.v. 'Meletios Pegas', and particularly the work mentioned there of Ph. Meyer, *Die theologische Literatur der griechischen Kirche im sechzehnten Jahrhundert*, Leipzig 1899, 4, 6, 53-69, 132-33; furthermore E. Legrand, *Bibliographie Hellénique ou description raisonnée des ouvrages publiés en Grec par les Grecs au XVe et XVIe siècles* II and IV, Paris 1885, 1906; by the same, *Bibliographie Hellénique... dix-septième siècle* I-V, Paris 1894-1903, by the same, *Bibliographie Hellénique... dix-huitième siècle* I-II, Paris 1918, 1928, in all cases reg. s.v. Pigas (Mélétius); by the same, *Lettres de Mélétius Pigas*, [= *Lettres*], Paris 1902; Steven Runciman, *The Great Church in Captivity*. A Study of the Patriarchate of Constantinople from the Eve of the Turkish Conquest to the Greek War of Independence, Cambridge 1968, 190, 214, 234, 261-66, 280, 333 and A. H. de Groot, *De betekenis van de Nederlandse Ambassade bij de Verheven Porte voor de studie van het Turks in de 17de en 18de eeuw*, Voordracht gehouden voor het Oosters Genootschap in Nederland op 20 Nov. 1978, Leiden 1979, 26 sq. For a 'uniated' and therefore very negative judgement on Meletius, see Leo Allatius, *De ecclesiae occidentalis atque orientalis perpetua consensione libri tres*, Colon. Agripp. 1648, lib. III, VII 11 (996) and VIII 1 (1000-03), where the 'calvinicola' Georgius Dousa is also mentioned.

[41] Meyer, *o.c.*, 63. For Meletius' treatise about the papal primacy, see Legrand, *Bibliographie Hellénique... dix-septième siècle*, I 168.

informed of his experiences by dispatching letters and reports which were soon printed. Meletius' name having thus become known in the Netherlands, his reputation was enhanced by a personal and elaborate letter of condolence to Dousa senior on the death of his son Jan, of which Georgius had apprised him.[42]

The death of his elder brother was the immediate cause of Georgius' breaking off his journey and returning to the Netherlands. Along with many other literary treasures, to which the patriarch had added as a present a valuable manuscript from the physician Actuarius in the hope of getting it printed, the letter of condolence was taken home by Georgius and printed soon after. Already in 1598, a few months after his return, Meletius' *Epistola consolatoria* to Janus Dousa was published by Aelbrecht Hendriksz. in The Hague.[43] Besides an interesting list of the books which Dousa junior had brought from Constantinople the editor added a

---

[42] J. J. Scaliger maintained over the years a probably indirect relationship with Patriarch Meletius, as can be seen from his letter, dated 12 May 1602, to Marcus Velserus (in I. Scaliger, *Epistolae omnes...*, Francf. 1628, no. 157, 349-50), cited by Ph. Meyer in *PRE* 12, 562-63 s.v. 'Meletius Pegas' and by Legrand, see below: "Exemplaria multa Arabica ope Meletii Patriarchae Alexandrini sperabam me nacturum, quod ei magna cum iis Hollandis qui istic negotiantur familiaritas intercedebat. Sed ante paucos menses optimus doctissimusque vir, magno meo et negotiatorum Batavorum dolore, quos ille semper summa comitate exceperat, discessit... si ille nunquam satis laudatus vir diutius vixisset, magna facultas mihi omnia Arabica, Aethiopica et Aegyptiaca, quaecunque optassem, habendi suggerebatur... Ante annos enim viginti ... reginae Navarrae pyxidem instructam gemmis cum epistola graeca misit, qua petebat ut Basilii, Chrysostomi, Naziazeni exemplaria, quae aliunde nancisci non poterat, sibi mitteret. Epistolae exemplum adhuc penes me habeo." This letter is not identical with the undated one, written to the Queen of Navarra, which has been edited by Legrand, *Lettres*, nr. 50, see preface, XI-XIII. — For Georgius Dousa (Joris van der Does), see Regt in *NNBW* VI 418-19, where his travel-stories are also mentioned. Present in *Univ. Libr.* Leiden are: a letter from G. Dousa to Bon. Vulcanius (June 1598) (= *Vulc.* 106¹); copies of two letters from Maximus Archidiakonus of Alexandria to G. Dousa (*Vulc.* 62¹, fo 36-7). A copy of Meletius' inscription in G. Dousa's *Album Amicorum*, dated July 1597, is inserted in J. J. Scaliger, *Scaligerana*, Amsterdam 1740. See also n. 40 towards the end, and Legrand, *Bibliographie Hellénique... XVe et XVIe siècles* IV, reg. s.v. Dousa (Georges). Georgius Dousa figures more than once in Grotius' poems, see *Dichtwerken* I 2B 1, reg. s.v.

[43] *Epistola Meletii Papae ac Patriarchae Alexandrini... ad Janum Dousam Nordovici Dominum super obitu filij, consolatoria...*, Hagae-Comitis, Ex officina Alberti Henrici, MDXCVIII (= W. P. C. Knuttel, *Catalogus van pamfletten berustende in de Koninklijke Bibliotheek*, I, 's-Gravenhage 1889, (= Knuttel, *Pamfletten*) no. 1004; see next page; also H. C. Rogge, *Beschrijvende catalogus van de pamflettenverzameling der Remonstrantsche Kerk te Amsterdam*, II, Amsterdam 1865, (= Rogge, *Catalogus*) no. 2, 136, and Legrand, *Bibliographie Hellénique... XVe et XVIe siècles* IV, no. 853, 345-47. The autograph of this letter is in the Collection Dupuy, no. 490, fo. 62 sqq. (*Bibl. Nat.* Paris), see above, 16. A translation into Dutch of the letter without the annexes is given by Bor, *Oorspronk, begin ende vervolgh der Nederlandscher oorlogen*, IV, Amsterdam 1684, fol. 442-43, referred to by G. Brandt, *Historie der Reformatie* I, Amsterdam 1677, 836-37. The Latin version of the *Epistola consolatoria* is also to be found in *Praestantium ac eruditorum virorum epistolae*, ed. tert., Amsterdam 1704, no. 25. For Edward Barton (1562?-1597), Queen Elisabeth's second ambassador at the Sublime Porte, see *DNB* III, 342-43.

EPISTOLA
MELETII
PAPAE AC PATRI-
ARCHAE ALEXANDRINI, &c. PRAE-
SIDIS CONSTANTINOPOLITANI AD IA-
num Dousam Nordovici Dominum
super obitu filij,

CONSOLATORIA;

*Quam Georgius, defuncti Dousae frater, post continuam quinquennij
peregrinationem, una cum festiua codicum manuscriptorum
copia hactenus ineditorum Domum secum Con-
stantinopoli redux attulit Prid. Idus
Majas, Anni 1598.*

HAGÆ-COMITIS,
Ex officinâ Alberti Henrici.
CIƆ.IƆ.XCVIII.

5. Title page of *Epistola Meletii ... ad Dousam* (1598)

number of documents about Meletius obviously intended to accentuate his greatness.

In view of the circles in which Grotius moved, and taking into consideration his friendship with Georgius Dousa, it stands to reason that Meletius' letter would not have escaped him, yet he acquired his knowledge about the patriarch via a different route. He got it from an unnamed scholar mentioned in the Introduction to his *Meletius*, who can easily be identified with his friend Johannes Boreel (1577-1629), the later Grand Pensionary of Zealand, together with whom he had studied at Leiden.[44] He speaks about Boreel with great reverence, points out his proficiency in law and theology — Boreel had studied both disciplines —, praises his thorough knowledge of languages, particularly Greek and Hebrew, and concludes by saying that he was eminently well informed about the "old and new enemies of Christianity" and had a thorough knowledge of the factions within the Eastern Church.

Boreel, too, knew the East from personal experience. Around the turn of the century this son of a Middelburg burghomaster had travelled in Asia Minor, Syria, and Palestine, and, like the young Dousa, had brought home a great number of valuable books and manuscripts. He had repeatedly told Grotius about his experiences in those regions — conceivably when both men were practising law in The Hague and saw each other frequently.[45] On those occasions Boreel had evinced deep admiration for Meletius, whom he had come to know personally in the course of his journey. Grotius refers to this in the conclusion of his Introduction:

> "But now that distance as well as professional duties do not allow us to meet, I shall write down what you told me the Patriarch Meletius often used to express to you; on condition however, that you, who have the more accurate knowledge, will make the necessary emendations and corrections.

---

[44] For J. Boreel, see Meertens, *Letterkundig leven*, 443, 469 n. 223 and his article mentioned (n. 36), 67 ff.; furthermore *Secunda Scaligerana*, ed. P. Des Maizeaux, Amsterdam 1740, 241, where P(aul) C(olomiés) refers to "Vossius dans sa Harangue sur la mort d'Erpenius, et... Cunaeus dans la Preface de sa République des Hébreux", for biographical details on Boreel. Cf. also A. C. G. M. Eyffinger, 'De Republica Emendanda. A juvenile tract by Hugo Grotius on the emendation of the Dutch polity', *Grotiana* NS 5 (1984), 30 ff.; Alastair Hamilton, *William Bedwell, the Arabist 1536-1632*, Leiden 1985 and P. T. van Rooden, *Constantijn l'Empereur (1591-1648). Professor Hebreeuws en Theologie te Leiden*. Theologie, bijbelwetenschap en rabbijnse studiën in de zeventiende eeuw, (thesis Leiden), Leiden 1985, reg. s.v. 'J. Boreel'. In a letter to Grotius (20 July 1629, *BW* IV no. 1412, 77) Wtenbogaert refers to Boreel's acquaintance with Patriarch Meletius: "Wat gevoelen had Meletius, als de heer Boreel met hem confereerde?"

[45] See R. Fruin, 'Een onuitgegeven werk van Hugo de Groot. Naschrift', in *Robert Fruin's Verspreide Geschriften* (ed. P. J. Blok, P. L. Muller, S. Muller) III, 's-Gravenhage 1901, 365-445, 443: "Around 1608 Mr. Johannes Boreel was among Hugo Grotius' closest friends." (transl.)

6. Portrait of Johannes Boreel. 18th century's drawing by D. Vlietland from an older copy

I have no doubt but that you, too, will take delight in recalling this, and that it will be profitable to me to learn about them more accurately from you.
Now this Meletius was Patriarch of Alexandria and at the same time ruler of the church of Constantinople, a man of venerable sanctity and highly proficient in every kind of learning — for he even spoke Latin, which is unusual for Greeks and he had also read all the most famous authors in that language. He furthermore loved peace among Christians so much that he could not refrain from tears when execrating our dissensions, as he often did, and he used to beg us at long last to turn our eyes, made fierce by contemplating one another, on the Turks and the riff-raff society of uncivilised peoples. But above all he emphasized the points of consensus between the

Christians. That, he used to say, was so much more universal and momentous than was commonly thought. At the same time his one concern was to point out that what was shared by all Christians contained everything that is held to be best in any philosophical school or among national institutions, and apart from this many specific points of its own unknown to all the others. All this he extolled in a remarkably eloquent way; we, for our part, can only try to expound it as meticulously as possible."[46]

These words clearly show why Grotius named his tract after Meletius. Although he had never personally met the Eastern patriarch about whom Boreel had told him so much, he recognized in him a kindred spirit, a man who suffered under the religious quarrels as much as he did himself, and who was no less than Grotius convinced that the evil could only be remedied by reflecting on what the factions had in common. When doing this they would acknowledge that what united them by far surpassed the issues dividing them.

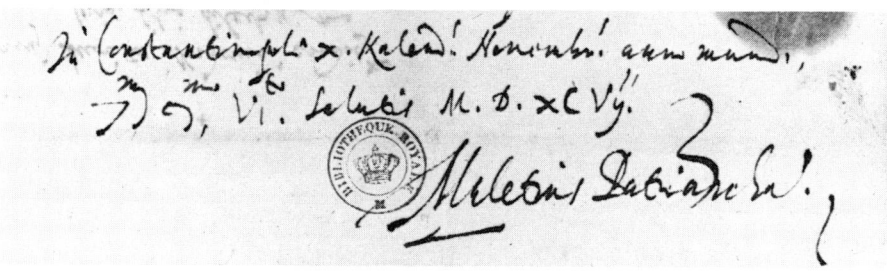

7. Patriarch Meletius' signature from his letter to Janus Dousa, 23 October 1597

5. *Purpose, composition, mode of thought, structure*

a) *Purpose*

Just as the 16th- and 17th-century authors used to give an elaborate exposition in their Prefaces and Epilogues of why and for what purpose they brought out a particular work, so Grotius described his object in writing the *Meletius* in his Introduction and Epilogue. He did so elsewhere, too, for his contemporary correspondence also reveals, and sometimes elucidates, his aims. Let us first turn to the Introduction.

We have already noticed that he was seriously alarmed at the progressively increasing tensions between Remonstrants and Counter-Remonstrants. We have also seen that he was no less anxious about the political and regional rivalries which were partly bound up with the

---

[46] *Mel.* 5.55-72.

religious ones. In his Introduction he sets out by depicting the political conflicts. He then continues:

> "The same, I notice, has occurred in religion. For from the moment that the Christian name had become widespread and, once the strength of its antagonists had been broken, an opening had been created for them to differ first in opinion and then in conviction, different teachers and parties began to emerge alienating Christians from Christians in the same way as non-Christians had been strangers to Christians. That disease already started a long time ago. But in our age and that of our fathers it has grown to such an extent that it cannot possibly go on any further. For not only indifference or rivalry, but also implacable hatred and anger, indeed — something before unheard of — wars are started under no other pretext than that of the very religion whose purpose is peace. Yet, if we were willing to consider the people of the Indies, to whom we send our ships so successfully, or the Turks among whom you (= J. Boreel) have lived, or the Jews who are now settling among us, we should be obliged to remember our almost forgotten kinship, even if only by comparing ourselves with them. For are we not strongly united by the very issue that separates us all from them, regardless of whether we consider them as a body or individually?"[47]

The tenor of this passage, inspired equally by the classical, Hellenistic notion of origin and depravation and by the Renaissance ideal of the true *civitas*,[48] is unequivocal. What Grotius wants to convey to his readers is that the political as well as the religious differences are so strongly emphasized that much more fundamental issues are bound to be neglected, namely the awareness of consanguinity and of sharing one and the same religious persuasion. Except for the excursus in his Introduction he scarcely mentions the natural bond.[49] But he pays all the more attention to the religious aspect, his primary aim being to transcend the controversy on this point. He attempts to reach this goal by defining a sort of common denominator, a broad religious concept, based on the idea of *consensus*, on the assumption that by recognizing and acknowledging this concept as their shared conviction, the parties will be brought to a mutual rapprochement and to love. Following the example of the patriarch Meletius, he announces that he will, in his own way, put this common denominator into words. For the time being I shall leave aside the question as to how he goes about it, and first turn to the Epilogue where, according to the rules of rhetoric, he again summarizes and exhortatorily accentuates his purpose. The patriarch Meletius is once more brought to the fore:

---

[47] *Mel.* 2.18-22.
[48] Note to *Mel.* 2.18-22, and to *Mel.* 3.44.
[49] *Mel.* 68-69.

"When that venerable Patriach had expounded the essentials of the Christian religion along these lines, he went on to say that it was amazing that people who agreed on so many points yet seemed so diverse and out of harmony. Wondering what could be the cause of this evil, he said, "It seems to me that the principal cause is that the dogmas are declared to be the most essential part of the religion, whereas the ethical precepts are disregarded. Now this is altogether wrong, for dogmas generally subserve precepts and lead to them." Indeed Seneca was right when he said, "everybody prefers discussing to living". And since ethical rules are mostly plainer and less complicated, it stands to reason that people most readily agree on precepts. We therefore choose rather to think piety has to do with dogmas, for over dogmas we fight with others, while the battle over ethical rules takes place in ourselves. Now violating one's own conscience is more difficult than quarrelling with others. Because he is least inclined to discharge his obligations man has turned religion into a matter of controversy and transferred to life what has been a matter for discussion in the schools."[50]

The Epilogue ends with an exhortation in which the author gives priority to right actions, considering dogmatic quarrels to be as meaningless as they are unavailing, and states that it would therefore be wise for Christians to keep the number of dogmas as limited as possible.

Thus, on the basis of the Introduction and the Epilogue, a twofold answer is given to the question of Grotius' purpose in writing his *Meletius*. In the first place, he wants to drive his Christian contemporaries to reflect on what they have in common. Secondly, he wants to impress on them that acting rightly is more important than doctrine and dogma, that practice, in short, outweighs theory.

Still more than the Introduction and the Epilogue the letters show that, even though the Arminian controversy was the immediate cause of his work, Grotius wanted to do more than clear up this particular controversy. Indeed from the letters he wrote at the time it is evident that he also had the Roman Catholics in mind, and that he therefore observed a certain restraint in his formulations, without however totally concealing his adherence to the *religio repurgata*.[51] Far from wanting to repel his Roman Catholic readers with an unequivocal, typically Protestant concept of religion, he was bent on offering them a picture of the common religious belief in which they could easily recognize their own faith. On the other hand he expected his concept of religion to express a sufficiently

---

[50] *Mel.* 89.1-13.
[51] *App.* II no. 2.24-32: "Inter alia profanissimum morem Deum effingendi per simulachra, *ne scripto quidem meo dissimulare potui, in quo tamen proposueram a controversiis abstinere* (italics PM)... Ea autem ipsa quae apud pontificios sunt periculosissima, *puto etiam ex illis principiis, quae ut confessa pono, posse convelli ac labefactari* (italics PM)." See also n. 54.

critical attitude to objectionable Roman Catholic doctrines on iconolatry, free will, and merits.⁵²

But his scope was wider still. We can go one step further and ascertain that it was not only Christians — Protestants and Catholics — whom he had in mind, but, more universally, believers in general. He consequently addresses Jews and pagans, as he was to do in his later *De veritate religionis christianae*.⁵³ Even if, in his *Meletius*, he does not elaborate on this universal intention as emphatically as in his later work, both writings nevertheless have the same starting-point. As we shall see presently, this typically Grotian pursuit of comprehensiveness emerges from the way in which he defines his concept of religion in the *Meletius*. Furthermore he pronouncedly expresses the universality of his intention. In one of his letters he says in so many words that it is his avowed object to define a consensus to which not only Christians, but also "the others" could agree.

> "It was my intention", he writes, "both to stimulate Christians to love one another for what they have in common, and to induce the others (*caeteris*) to embrace the common Christian confession as well".⁵⁴

In conclusion we can say that Grotius, in his *Meletius*, addressed not only Christians but believers in general. Occasioned by the dissensions surrounding the Truce, the book aims primarily at overcoming these quarrels; but, transcending this aim, Grotius equally sought to contribute to religious peace in general. It follows naturally from this intention that he could also call his *Meletius* an "Introduction to the Christian religion".⁵⁵ As such it can be viewed as a harbinger of the much more consummate work he created a couple of years later, his *Proof (Bewijs)*, which, in the Latin version entitled *De veritate religionis christianae*, was to contribute so enormously to his fame.

---

⁵² See above n. 51. For Grotius's feelings about the Roman Catholic Church in these years, see the present author's 'Hugo Grotius as an Irenicist', in *The World of Hugo Grotius (1583-1645)*, Proceedings of the International Colloquium organized by the Grotius Committee of the Royal Netherlands Academy of Arts and Sciences, Rotterdam 6-9 April 1983, Amsterdam/Maarssen 1984 (= *Grotius, Proceedings*), 58-9, and the literature there mentioned. For his ideas concerning a protestant world council under King James' leadership, see Van der Woude's oration (mentioned n. 34), 9 ff., and, for its links with foreign policy, A. Th. van Deursen, 'Honni soit qui mal y pense? De Republiek tussen de mogendheden (1610-1612)', *MKNAW* NR 28 no. 1, Amsterdam 1965, 91 sq.

⁵³ *TMD* nr. 994 sq. Contrary to *Ver.* (VI), Grotius does not pay attention to Islam in his *Meletius*.

⁵⁴ *App.* II no. 4. 21-29: "Quanquam autem ego ea quae inter Christianos controversa sunt... quam sint gravia... facile intelligo, tamen eam gravitatem... ante oculos ponere non erat eius instituti, in quo et *Christianos, ob ea quae sunt inter ipsos communia, ad charitatem hortari volui et caeteris auctor esse, ut... ea quae inter Christianos confessa sunt ipsi quoque amplectantur* (italics PM)."

⁵⁵ *App.* II no. 2. 47-50: "cum εἰσαγωγὴν quandam vellem scribere et me velut aptare iis quoque qui ad christianismum invitandi adhuc sunt..."

b) *Composition*

The treatise is divided into four chapters, each of which can be subdivided into smaller units and paragraphs. The four chapters deal with the following themes:
I. Evidence of religion.
II. The purpose of religion: the supreme good.
III. The theoretical content of religion.
IV. The practical content of religion.

The first two chapters are very short, no more than two pages each. In these chapters Grotius attempts first of all to define the 'Commonalty', i.e. his concept of religion as announced in the Introduction, then to indicate what the Christian religion regards as the supreme good. Chapters III and IV are more circumstantial, covering 12 and 10 pages respectively. This proportion already gives an indication of what mattered most to him — to clarify the relationship between doctrine and life in the perspective of religion. This is the cardinal point of the treatise. The tenor of these pivotal chapters is that theory should be subservient to practice, and that doctrine must be limited to what is the foundation and the stimulation of ethics. This point is again emphatically enjoined on the reader in the Epilogue.

c) *Mode of thought*

In the first place the *Meletius* is conspicuous for its abundance of quotations from poets and philosophers from Antiquity. Here too the doors of the treasure chambers of Antiquity are flung open and Grotius moves in and out of them with sovereign ease. It is above all the Ancients who contribute the material for discussion, just as it is their influence which can be seen in the terminology as well as in the arrangement of the treatise. This is in no way surprising, considering that Grotius was a classicist — he had been the most brilliant student of Josephus Justus Scaliger —, but even so one is amazed at his profuse knowledge and the virtuosity he applies to it. We may also wonder how he defines the relationship between the classical and the Christian material in his *Meletius*, a work which, after all, purported to be Christian.

Grotius believed that the wisdom and perceptions of the greatest minds of pagan Antiquity were to be regarded as a preparation for, and an anticipation of, the truth that Christ was to reveal. In the *Prolegomena* to one of his later works — the edition of Stobaeus' *Dicta Poëtarum* of 1623[56] — he expresses this conviction in unmistakable terms. In a perfect

---

[56] *TMD* no. 458.

analogy with the discussions held on the subject in Antiquity itself — both in classical Antiquity (Plato) and in early Christian Antiquity (the Apologists) —, he expounds how, in the course of history, wisdom and knowledge had progressively grown into certainty. The process had been started tentatively by the poets — by Homer in particular. Even though they had cleared the way for deeper perception on many points their main concern had been the intensification of emotions, and they had thereby frequently violated the canons set by wisdom, the very tenet of which is that emotions should be kept under control. Indeed Plutarch very aptly remarked that the pronouncements of the poets should be tested against the judgment of sterner teachers — philosophers. But even they had not always been able to avoid fallacies. They often contradicted each other or defended false opinions. Plutarch himself gave an example of this by teaching an erroneous view of Providence and the hereafter.

To this blend of true and untrue, certain and uncertain knowledge, the result of what pagan poets and thinkers had devised, the Jews had added new certainties, which had not originated in their own minds but which they owed directly to God. Grotius then continues:

> "... even more (than the Hebrews owed to God) do we as Christians owe to Him, we to whom everything that is of any moment towards a just arrangement of life has been revealed with such certainty that in upright minds no place is left for doubt. For that God is the source of what the Prophets and Apostles have handed down to us, is an established fact in the only way in which this can be established, and to the full extent that it can be established, by the provision of miracles and by the testimony of those very men who command belief by the innocence of their lives, by their having nothing to gain by lying, and by the many evils, including death, that they endured on account of this testimony."

With this reference to Christ, by whom the supreme certainty had been given, and to the example of the Apostles, Grotius concludes his survey, inferring the following lesson:

> "It follows that, just as we have to appeal from the poets to the philosophers, so there is a third tribunal to which we have to appeal above both the poets *and* the philosophers. It is that of the Prophets and the Apostles; and we should consider no sentences ratified but those which are capable of being upheld before this court (*ea demum dicta rata habenda quae in hoc auditorio stare possunt*)."[57]

The idea expressed by Grotius in the prologue to his edition of Stobaeus is continuously applied in his *Meletius*. The numerous statements by authorities from Antiquity which he adduces on each page of this work

---

[57] Stobaeus, *Dicta poëtarum*, see *App.* I, 167-68. Grotius summarises here what he developed much more elaborately in *Ver.* II 4-6 (IV 33b 25-36a 18).

are tested time and again against the 'true' and 'certain' testimony of the Old and, in particular, the New Testament. It is remarkable that this appearance before the court of Prophets and Apostles should usually occur peaceably and goodhumouredly. Although he does draw lines and never fails to criticize the opinion of someone or other, he almost invariably succeeds in digging up a poet or thinker from Antiquity whose tentatively worded perception refers to Christian revelation or is concordant with it. This shows his conviction that human wisdom and divine revelation have an eminently harmonious relationship. They merge with one another smoothly and organically, since, in Grotius' view, rationality is their common feature.

The roots of this attitude can be traced back to the first centuries of the Christian era, to the period of the Apologists and the early Church Fathers. These were the ones who, in the wake of Jewish-Hellenistic apologetics, developed the notion that Greek wisdom originated in Jewish wisdom and that the pagan philosophers owed their perceptions to Moses and the Prophets. By means of this 'historical' theory they expressed their conviction that the truth of Old Testament revelation and pagan philosophical views were very closely connected, indeed that they could, to a certain extent, be identified with each other. For both streams had sprung from the same source, and this origin remained discernible, however much polluted the pagan stream might have become in the course of time, influenced as it was by demons or otherwise. The more Stoically orientated theory of the λόγος σπερματικός, especially connected with the name of Justin Martyr, also shows a like tendency to identify pagan and Jewish-Christian concepts of truth. According to Justin Martyr, 'seeds' were to be found among the pagans, but only the Christians had been granted the revelation of the λόγος in all its fullness. Finally, a third theory, developed in particular by Eusebius of Caesarea, tried to establish proof positive of the confirmation of the truth of sacred history by profane history.[58]

The fact that Grotius was intimately acquainted with this early Christian complex of apologetical theories, which invariably aimed at

---

[58] For this matter see the excellent study of Fr. Laplanche, *L'Evidence du Dieu Chrétien. Religion, culture et société dans l'apologétique protestante de la France classique (1576-1670)*, Association des Publications de la Faculté Protestante de Strasbourg 1983, 69 ff. To the literature there mentioned we may add, for the early Church, Ragnar Holte, *Béatitude et sagesse. Saint Augustin et le problème de la fin de l'homme dans la philosophie ancienne*, Paris/Worcester (Mass.) 1962, 111 ff., for the Middle Ages, A. Lang, *Die Entfaltung des apologetischen Problems in der Scholastik des Mittelalters*, Freiburg/Basel/Wien [1962], and for the Renaissance, P. O. Kristeller, *Renaissance Thought* II, Papers on Humanism and Arts, New York/Evanston/London [1965], chapter IV 'The Platonic Academy of Florence', 89-101.

demonstrating the antiquity and reasonableness of the Jewish-Christian revelation as against the pagan world, may well be one of the reasons why he reached his harmonious attitude towards the relationship between reason and revelation.

The strong emphasis in Grotius' thought on 'reason' and 'rationality' inevitably raises the question of the relationship between his attitude and that of the 18th-century rationalists and deists, who, as we know, frequently referred to him. The answer to this question is more difficult. Nowhere in his work does Grotius give a precise definition of what '*ratio*' means to him, anymore than he ever ventures into the field of epistemology. Without any further ado, almost naively, he simply starts from the principle that human reason has manifested itself in the thinking of the Ancients so powerfully and unequivocally that it would be entirely superfluous to specify its boundary or to think twice about the certainty it offers.[59] Summarizing his scattered statements on this issue, we can say that the way in which he defines reason and the way in which the later rationalists and deists do so differ so greatly because, for him, reason is not an autonomous entity. Any discrepancy between reason and revelation is out of the question, for revelation itself is to be considered eminently reasonable. It perfects the rationality of the Ancients and ultimately determines what is rational in those cases in which the Ancients either did not pronounce themselves at all, or did so vaguely or contradictorily. Grotius therefore sees no obligation for revelation to justify itself to reason. Reason, rather, should account for itself to revelation. In this respect there is a great distance between him and the later rationalists and deists. On the other hand, however, he is close to them in his conviction that revelation is rational in the best sense of the word, indeed that it literally epitomizes reason.

Our work offers more than one example of this belief. When, for instance, Grotius discusses the subject of the Holy Trinity, he attempts to demonstrate its rationality by referring to Aristotle and Plato, who in their respective conceptions of God had adduced distinctions which closely approximated the Christian doctrine of the divine hypostases.[60] Having explained this, he continues significantly:

"Even though human reason by itself has not been able to find out that God is like this, yet when it is told that this is so it finds it easy to agree."[61]

---

[59] Cf. J. Huizinga, 'Grotius' plaats in de geschiedenis van den menschelijken geest', in *Tien Studiën*, Haarlem 1926, 117-'25; reprinted in *Verzamelde Werken* II, Haarlem 1948, 382-'88.
[60] *Mel.* 22.
[61] *Mel.* 23.37-38: "Haec ita se in Deo habere, quanquam humana ratio reperire quidem per se non potuit, ubi tamen audit assentit facile."

In other words human reason is conditioned to accept truth and certainty which, complementarily, are offered from on high. That this acceptance is more than a mere acceptance as truth — *assensus* in its scholastic sense — appears from the use of the word 'easy'. It indicates that Grotius considers man capable of perceiving rationality, including the rationality of the insights given from on high. This is corroborated by a casual remark concerning belief in God, which occurs elsewhere in his *Meletius*. It runs as follows:

> "To believe in God is certainly difficult for others who do not know God's word, but for Christians who carefully observe God's word it is easy."[62]

The qualification 'easy', used again in this passage, demonstrates anew that his concept of belief is entirely rational. Consequently, the 'novelty' that man receives in belief and revelation is to be considered as a continuation of the perceptions which he, as a rational being, already possesses by nature. These perceptions are therefore not essentially new. If this is so, what is the purpose of the revelation? The answer must be: revelation not only enhances the quality of natural human perception,[63] but, above all, it is its guarantee. There is no more need to grope and seek, for certainty is pledged by heaven.[64] This is the first and most important result of revelation. Besides, it reveals what matters most in life, the hierarchy of values. Grotius says, for instance, that it is thanks to revelation that Christians consider the worship of God as the highest duty, something of which the Ancients had had scarcely any notion.[65]

The smooth connection between reason and revelation which Grotius uses again and again reflects his conviction that the world is rationally constructed, and that in this world imperishable harmony and order reign supreme, guaranteed by God as the Creator and Preserver. Like everything in created reality, man has his proper, fixed place in the harmonious world order. He is the crown of creation, and as a rational being, enlightened by heaven, he is able to comprehend the structure of that order, just as, as an ethical being, he is supposed to sustain it by his deeds. This certitude is so firmly anchored in Grotius' mind that he applies to this postulated rational structure everything that is relevant to

---

[62] *Mel.* 61-32-34: "Et credere quidem Deo difficile sane est aliis quid Deus dicat nescientibus; Christianis ipsam Dei vocem asservantibus id facile est..."

[63] Reason and revelation are in the proportion of free will to grace. Cf. Haentjens, *o.c.*, 77 sq.

[64] *Ibidem*, 19 n. 53 and *Mel.* 44.279-281: "...operae pretium est videre quomodo velut in tenebris palpitantes alii aliis propius ad verum accesserint."

[65] *Mel.* 60.16-20: "Officiorum quae Deo debentur prima esse debet ratio, ut est apud Christianos. Qua in parte non possunt satis culpari veteres prope omnes qui de officiis aut moribus scripsere..."

the relationship between God, man, and the world. He thus emerges as the typical exponent of classicism, the man who measures, designs, and builds, and whose idea of reason and rationality is the reflection of a preconceived conception of a harmonious and well-structured world-order.[66]

d) *Structure*

After these more general remarks on Grotius' method and mode of thinking we must now return to his *Meletius*. We already saw that in his Introduction he announced his intention of writing about the factor common to all Christians. Contrary to expectation, he does not define this by starting from the Apostolic Symbol, the confession subscribed to by all Christians through the centuries, but follows a quite different path. Instead of approaching the matter from the angle of the traditionally fixed creed, in chapter I he drafts very sketchily a generalized concept of religion which he assumes to be valid and recognizable for both Christians and other believers.[67] The point of departure for defining this general concept of religion is the passage from the Epistle to the Hebrews (11: 6): "For whoever would draw near to God must believe that He exists and that He rewards those who seek Him."

Starting with this apostolic and therefore absolutely true and certain principle, he first proves God's existence in a few words — in the light of the Stoic (*consensus*) as well as the Aristotelian philosophy (God as the Prime Mover) —, and then enters at greater length into the question about the nature of the suppositions and implications regarding God's being a Remunerator. He resolves this theme, as it were, into factors which he considers to be totally rational, each of which he takes from Ancient philosophy. In a running discussion with the Ancients he invariably determines the height and depth, the validity and invalidity, of the pronouncements in the light of the apostolic writings which in his view have an unimpeachable authority.[68] He infers from them that God

---

[66] Cf. J. Huizinga, 'Hugo de Groot en zijn eeuw', in *Tien Studiën*, Haarlem 1926, 99-116; reprinted in *Verzamelde Werken* II, Haarlem 1948, 389-403.

[67] This plan corresponds with that of *Ver.* books I and II. Cf. what Grotius writes to his Jesuit friend A. Schottus (8 July 1621), *BW* II no. 662, 102: "Is labor in libros sex fluit, quorum primus Deum esse probat, ac scitu maxime necessarias proprietates ei assignat, providentiam, et aliud post hoc, quod hic agitur, aevum; atque inde religionem generaliter adstruit. Secundus docet eam esse veram religionem, quam Christus Dominus noster in terras attulit."

[68] Cf. his very clear and revealing statement in *Iur.* II 20, 49, 1 (522): "Prius est veritatem christianae religionis, quatenus scilicet naturali ac primaevae religioni non pauca *superaddit* (italics PM), argumentis meris naturalibus persuaderi non posse, sed niti historia tum resurrectionis Christi tum miraculorum ab ipso et apostolis editorum; *quae*

is a *natura intelligens*, with a free will, Omnipotent and Good; that He is the Creator, Preserver and Legislator; and that He created man as a rational being.[69]

Having demonstrated the reasonableness of the notion that God rewards, he winds up his exposition with a lengthier, syllogistic argument intended to prove that man is also truly rewarded by God.[70] Finally, he states that Christianity has all the previously mentioned principles in common "with all religion, the false ones and the true but less perfect ones, such as, in the first place, natural religion, and, next, the Mosaic religion."[71]

The 'common factor' that he had promised to describe in the Introduction has thus been specified by means of these principles. In other words, Grotius assumes that all Christians — like all believers — acknowledge that God exists and remunerates, and that they all subscribe to the philosophical principles implied in this acknowledgement.

With the concept of religion as he develops it in his first chapter, Grotius wanted to give a rational, compelling description of religion in general. That he views Christianity as its logical sequel and its culmination, becomes evident in chapter II as soon as he inquires, according to Aristotelian principles, into the purpose (*finis*) of religion. Indeed he almost imperceptibly introduces notions from the Christian tradition, and weaves them into a seamless tissue with the concept of religion as developed by the Ancients. Positing, in keeping with their views, that the purpose of religion is to be sought in the highest good (*summum bonum*), he first defines it, following Augustine, as delighting in God (*frui Deo*),[72] and then specifies it as the afterlife of the soul and the resurrection of the body after death.[73] In a manner strongly reminiscent of the early Christian Apologists he further argues that the various values seen by various peoples as the *summum bonum* are all included in the highest good as it is known in the Christian religion.[74] He hereby confirms that the Christian religion is a continuation of the natural as well as the Mosaic religion in

---

res est facti (italics PM) aliis quidem irrefragabilibus testimoniis probata, sed olim ita ut et haec quaestio facti sit, et iam perantiqui." The same argumentation, but in a much more developed form in *Ver.* III 1-12 (IV 50a1-54a25).

[69] *Mel.* 7-10.
[70] *Mel.* 11.
[71] *Mel.* 12.58-60: "Haec illa sunt principia quae communia habet christiana religio et cum falsis omnibus, et cum veris quidem, sed minus perfectis, qualis est primum naturalis religio, inde Mosaïca."
[72] See note to *Mel.* 13.35-36.
[73] *Mel.* 18.
[74] *Mel.* 17. Cf Just. Mart. 2. *Apol.* 13,4: "Ὅσα οὖν παρὰ πᾶσι καλῶς εἴρηται, ἡμῶν τῶν Χριστιανῶν ἐστι.

the sense that Christianity preserves, corroborates, and perfects what is best in paganism and Judaism. In other words, in his eyes the Christian religion is the perfection, the completion, of religion in general. This thesis continues to be the basic principle which will repeatedly be elaborated in the course of the treatise in defence of Christianity.

Having thus proved religion to exist and Christianity to be its supreme manifestation, Grotius continues the argument with a description of the content of religion. This is the true theme of the treatise, to be developed first in its theoretical, and next in its practical aspect. His initial argument is essential for the correct understanding of the structure of these chapters. He says:

> "Now religion, since it concerns those actions which are prompted by free will, all of which, however, are pre-determined by (an act of) the intellect, necessarily consists of two parts, theoretical and practical. The former is made up of doctrines, the latter of ethical precepts. Seneca, following Cicero, renders these notions in Latin as *decreta* and *praecepta*, principles and rules, and they demonstrate that these two terms embrace all that is taught about customs and duties. Principles are sometimes also called tenets, decrees or opinions. Principles should be active in every field of science and not be irrelevant nor redundant, but should either incite to action or to some extent make clear what must be done and how it must be done."[75]

This is an important statement, extending beyond the structure of the *Meletius*. It has implications for the encyclopaedia as a whole, which give rise to the question of Grotius' conception of the relationship between the sciences. So before proceeding with the examination of the structure and content of the *Meletius*, I shall go more deeply into his views of the encyclopaedia of sciences in general.

He pronounces himself on this subject as clearly as can be in a famous and much published letter of May 1615, addressed to his friend Aubéry Dumaurier, the French ambassador to the Netherlands.[76] He introduces his exposition of the structure and the coherence of the sciences with the warning that, in those cases where a distinction should be made in philosophy between theoretical (*philosophia contemplativa*) and practical (*philosophia practica*) sciences, care should be taken that the theoretical sciences do not become autonomous but remain subservient to the practical ones. It is wholly in accordance with this aversion to anything remotely resembling abstract speculation that he hurries through his survey of the theoretical sciences (logics, physics, metaphysics), and

---

[75] *Mel.* 19.1-9.
[76] *BW* I no. 402, 384-87. For the different editions of this work, see *TMD* nos 482 sq. More information on his views of the encyclopaedia is to be found in *Par.* III 24.

discusses at far greater length all that concerns *philosophia practica*, i.e. ethics and political theory.

For both these disciplines he recommends Aristotle as the teacher *par excellence*.[77] It is not enough, however, merely to read Aristotle's *Nicomachean Ethics* and *Politics*; we should also be familiar with the ethical views of Pythagoras, the Stoics, the adherents of the old and the new Academy, and Epicurus, and further develop and refine our ethical judgement by delving into collections of proverbs (Jesus Sirach and Solomon), Theophrastus' *Characters*, and the ethical pronouncements of Euripides, Terence and Horace. To these works he adds Cicero's *De officiis*, a text, he says, too well known to get the appreciation it deserves.[78] In this connection he also mentions the letters and tragedies of Seneca and Plutarch's philosophical essays. Finally, for political theory he refers to Polybius, Cassius Dio, Sallust, Plutarch's *Lives* and Cicero's *Letters to Atticus*, in addition to Aristotle's *Politics*.

He then opens the discussion on rhetoric. Contrary to custom, he opines, this should only be studied after ethics and political theory. He continues:

> "Having come this far, there is nothing I could recommend to you more than the study of Law; not of that part of civil law which is only a means of subsistence for pettifoggers and devil's advocates, but the study of international law and public law. Cicero calls this an eminent science, because it bears upon treaties, alliances, and pacts between peoples, kings, and nations, and upon the law of war and peace."[79]

Finally, as regards the discipline of history he advises Dumaurier to start with historical works of recent date, and only afterwards to investigate historical writers from an earlier period.

What is the result of the comparison between Grotius' encyclopaedic views as expressed in his letter to Dumaurier on the one hand, and the passage from the *Meletius* which was our point of departure on the other? The most important conclusion is that for Grotius the main point of the encyclopaedia of sciences was apparently to be found in the *philosophia practica*; in other words, what he is concerned with is above all ethics and political theory. We can say without exaggerating that he views the place

---

[77] See also *Iur.* prol. 42 (21): "Inter philosophos merito principem obtinet locum Aristoteles, sive tractandi ordinem, sive distinguendi acumen, sive rationum pondera consideres."

[78] Cf. also *Iur.* prol. 40 (21): "Usus sum etiam ad iuris huius probationem testimoniis philosophorum," with, in annotation 1, the exclamation: "Quid ni, cum Alexander Severus Ciceronis de republica et officiis libros perpetuo lectitarit?" [add. edd. 1642, 1646].

[79] Of the recommended theological authors Thomas Aquinas is mentioned first, in particular his *S. Th.* IIa IIae q. 58 (and, probably, Ia IIae q. 91) (*BW* I no. 402, 386).

and function of the sciences exclusively from the point of view of their application to and use for the practice of individual and social life.[80] He is interested invariably and in all respects in furthering individual ethos and building up society according to the rational principles he finds in the Ancients and in Scripture. Acknowledging the primacy of practice, he selects his material and constructs his treatises accordingly. He thus leaves to theory only so much room as is required to found and stimulate the individual ethos or social order. Nothing beyond this is of any use. He considers it neither constructive nor applicable, since in this case reason and ethics are not complementary.[81]

It goes without saying that Grotius thereby rules out or declares immaterial a great part of metaphysics and Christian dogma. I shall not go further into this now, but it is obvious that these are the very points on which his theological opponents advanced their criticisms. They found it unacceptable that Grotius, in the wake of the later Stoa, should declare ethics to be the centre, indeed the essence, of philosophy. They felt that the uniqueness and the individuality of Christian revelation were thus stifled. They saw the truth about God, His freedom and grace, threatened by this compelling reduction and restriction to what is rational and ethical. Indeed it was because of this reduction that Grotius — in spite of himself, for he carried on a heated polemic with Socinus (*De Satisfactione*, 1617) — was accused time and again of Socinianism whenever he appeared with new fruits of his theological production.[82]

Let us return to the *Meletius*. It will now be clear what motivated Grotius when he came to describe the Christian concept of religion, to separate theory and practice, and to effect a division between dogmatic principles on the one hand and ethical precepts on the other. The term 'dogmatic' in this connection should not lead to misunderstanding. The term is used in a general philosophical sense and not in a specifically Christian one. The same applies to the term *decreta* which is in no way connected with the term as used in Calvinistic theology. In this Grotius closely follows

---

[80] It is striking that Grotius, when talking about physics, in particular recommends the study of just those parts of that science which are important to ethics, *ibidem* 385: "...in physicis nihil est praestantius et ad moralem sapientiam conducibilius ea parte quae animae nostrae naturam functionesque persequitur."

[81] Cf. the utterance from his later years, *Votum pro pace* (1640) (IV 676a 3-4): "Hostis non sum, nisi eorum dogmatum quae credo noxia *aut pietati aut societati humanae* (italics PM)."

[82] See C. W. Roldanus, *Hugo de Groot's Bewijs van den waren godsdienst*, Arnhem 1944, 80 ff.; A. H. Haentjens, *Hugo de Groot als godsdienstig denker*, Amsterdam 1946, 90 ff., and the as small as fundamental art. by Renée Voeltzel, 'La méthode théologique de Hugo Grotius', in *RHPR* 32 (1952), 126-33 (130 n. 27).

the vocabulary of Cicero and Seneca, and uses the term *decretum* in the sense of 'theoretical foundation' or 'doctrine'.

In chapter III, the theoretical principles and suppositions of the Christian religion are further defined. There are four groups dealing with the following themes:
1. *decreta* about God in relation to Himself — God's being and qualities.
2. *decreta* about God in His relationship to His creation.
3. *decreta* about man as God created him.
4. *decreta* about man as he appears from experience — the nature of evil.

Needless to say these themes are again debated in a running discussion with the Ancients. The precise structure and articulation of this chapter is discussed in the next paragraph of this introduction. I shall now dwell for a moment on the debate on anthropology.

On this point there is a marked tension, as is already evident from the above survey of the themes. On the one hand Grotius states that man has been created a good being, the image of God,[83] while on the other experience teaches that man is ungrateful to God and inclined to hate his neighbour.[84] This paradox obliges Grotius to elaborate further on this point. First he talks about the nature of evil to which the tension is due, and then he describes the course of return, how man, having strayed away from God and estranged himself from his neighbour, is granted forgiveness and healing. The transition to this momentous part of the treatise runs as follows:

> "Since, therefore, man, because of his failings, is prone to viciousness and liable to punishment, it follows that any religion has become obsolete which does not show the way to remission and reparation of sins. For he who deserves punishment cannot hope for a reward, and he who is sunk in vice cannot by himself rise up. But that religion has not been abolished can be deduced from the very fact that God both furthers the human race and for it prolongs the use of this world; and to what other end than that he be worshipped by man? There is, therefore, indeed a remission of sins as well as a restoration of fallen man..."[85]

In the same vein there follows an exposition on remission and mediation. Grotius argues that the pagans had tentatively sought reconciliation and had developed ideas about a mediator.[86] All this was fulfilled by Christ, whose true mediation is borne out by his deeds as well as by the fact that everything concerning him has come true as predicted. The fruit of his

---

[83] *Mel.* 30-33. Cf. § 6, Analysis of the contents.
[84] *Mel.* 34-39. Cf. § 6, Analysis of the contents.
[85] *Mel.* 43.254-261.
[86] *Mel.* 44 sq.

work is universal: with the condition of penance and belief, it benefits humanity in its entirety.

Grotius concludes this chapter with a discussion on the restitution of the relationship between God and man — in other words of religion as such — and inserts a passage on the reliability of the Bible.[87] The reparation is achieved in three ways: first, by Christ's removing ignorance about matters divine, then by the example he set, and lastly by the arcane power of the Holy Ghost.[88]

The picture of Christ as Grotius draws it shows unmistakable Erasmian features. It is the gentle, humble, compassionate and suffering Christ who emerges.[89] No less characteristic is what he has to say about the work of the Holy Ghost, the effect of which is that man is not only summoned to live a good life but also receives the strength to do so. The Ancients, he remarks, may have had an inkling of the impossibility of virtuousness existing without God, but they failed to emphasize it adequately. How different is the Christian religion which renders well-founded homage to God as the One who really restores man and makes him good.[90]

Grotius elaborates the consequences of this doctrine in two directions, and the letters he wrote at the time show that he had the Counter-Remonstrants and the Remonstrants in mind.[91] Upon the former, convinced as they are of human impotence, he impresses the urgent invitation by the Spirit to be active and to have absolute faith in God; the latter, who rely too much on their own power, are called upon to realize that man is powerless without assistance from heaven and that true virtue is a gift from God.

Elaborating on the theoretical principles of the Christian religion as he had set them down in chapter III, Grotius unfolds their ethical implications in chapter IV. The beginning of this chapter is apologetic and presents a number of positive judgements from non-Christian authors on Christian ethics.[92]

As to its design the chapter is the counterpart of chapter III. While in the third chapter the argumentation is determined by the various *decreta*,

---

[87] *Mel.* 52-55.
[88] *Mel.* 51, 56, 58.
[89] *Mel.* 56. Cf. the image of Christ as it is represented in Grotius' tragedy *Christus Patiens* (1608) (*Dichtwerken* I 2a/b 5).
[90] *Mel.* 57.466-467: "... christiana religio saluberrima moderatione Deo solidam laudem tribuit hominis reparati..."
[91] *Mel.* 57. Cf. *App.* II no. 4.52 sq.
[92] *Mel.* 59.

here the discussion is based on the various groups of *praecepta*. Grotius only uses this term sporadically though; he prefers *officia* (duties), which makes for more clarity as regards his real intention. For what this chapter in fact does is to develop a theory of Christian ethics. In other words, Grotius drafts a system of rules which man, in accordance with the Christian religion, should observe in the various circumstances of life.

He divides these duties into four categories, to which he adds a number of more general ethical rules.
1. *officia* towards God.
2. *officia* towards mankind.
3. *officia* towards society.
4. *officia* towards oneself.
5. other rules.

This chapter does not require much explanation. As regards the first group of duties, I have already briefly mentioned the fact that Grotius censures the Ancients for totally failing to bring to light that man's foremost and highest duty is to honour God.[93] In their ethical treatises, he says, they either ignore it or they regard this duty as no more than part of the obedience due to the authorities. This had led Varro, for instance, to the insolent pronouncement that religions, even though they be false, must be preserved out of respect for the law. "What else can this be," he exclaims, "but invalidating religion by making it into an institution?" How different is the Christian religion, impressing upon people that they must honour, love, and worship God everywhere and at all times. "This is its constant aim; this is what it is all about." (*Hoc semper agit; huc refert omnia*).[94]

Having thus indicated the keystone of the structure of the Christian doctrine of duties, Grotius further specifies the duties of man to God. Some of them relate to inner life — faith and prayer —, others refer rather to external activity. The latter are regulated by prohibitions on the one hand and by commandments on the other. The prohibitions are to be divided into those which concern words and those which concern deeds. The former can be instanced by the vain invocation of God's name, the latter by the worship of God in images or an excessively ostentatious display of ritual.[95]

As regards the commandments concerning God, participating in the weekly public worship is mentioned as the first, and recommended as eminently pleasing to God.

---

[93] See above n. 65.
[94] *Mel.* 60.28-29.
[95] Cf. § 6, Analysis of the contents.

"Indeed if concord between people and the worship due to Himself are so dear to God, He must be even more pleased with concord between people in their worship of Him."[96]

With a digression on the sacraments of baptism and communion, in which heathen parallels are again brought to the fore, and with the remark that Christians place the observance of ritual rules second to active proofs of love, Grotius concludes his survey of man's duties to God. He then continues his argumentation with a disquisition on man's duties to mankind (*humanum*), distinguishing between duties to mankind as such, to society and, finally, to man himself. We have a foretaste of *De iure belli ac pacis* when Grotius, speaking about the duties to mankind, says that for Christians an act of violence or robbery is not legitimated by the fact of its being called war.[97] A Christian excludes nobody from his love. Unlike Aristotle, for instance, he makes no distinction between Greeks and barbarians, and does not regard the latter as a different species. On the contrary: he is convinced that they too are human beings. For the same reason hatred and vengeance should be unconditionally rejected, for all people are created equally in the image of God. Everyone should do unto his neighbour as he himself wishes God to do unto him, that is to behave with mercy and compassion. It is particularly this latter virtue, Grotius points out, which is extremely rare in the ethical treatises of the Ancients.[98]

The duties to society partly concern the family, partly the *res publica*. Sternly repudiating the concept, developed above all by Plato, that women are common property, he stresses the sanctity of monogamous matrimony and unequivocally rejects divorce.[99]

With regard to society he posits that Christian laws both serve the individual ethos and further civic spirit. Christianity upholds respect for the authorities at all levels. The citizen prays for the magistrate, submits to the burdens imposed by him, and follows the prescribed rules, unless they contravene God's commandments.[100]

With regard to the individual, the first duty Grotius mentions is the preservation of, and the care for, himself. Suicide, thought to be admissible by several classical thinkers, is rejected on the grounds that man was not placed in this world by chance but by divine decree, and is thus not free to desert his post without being summoned. And never should the Christian consider death a greater evil than the sin of which he is guilty.

---

[96] *Mel.* 65.79-81.
[97] *Mel.* 69.149-151.
[98] *Mel.* 70.174-176.
[99] *Mel.* 71.
[100] *Mel.* 72-73.

He must bear his cross and not recoil from the flames, for the Christian, unlike the philosophers, has a true consolation against death.[101]

Next, Grotius deals more elaborately with the question of how Christians should behave in particular circumstances, what they should do with honour, wealth, and pleasure. He concludes his catalogue of duties with the formulation of a number of ethical rules of a more general nature, all relating to the same extent to the various aspects of life. He says, for instance, that in those cases in which neither prohibitions nor commandments prevail the Christian should invariably keep in mind the interest of his neighbour; that promises must be kept, even those made to enemies; that trespassers are bound by the commandment of penance, and so on and so forth.[102]

He rounds off this chapter with an apologetic eulogy of the civilizing influence on the world exercized by the Christian religion, ending with the words:

> "And if Christian life would answer to its name all over the world, we would live in a truly Golden Age, without wars, without quarrels, without poverty, in the greatest peace and harmony, an age of plenty for every single one of us."[103]

We have already seen how the patriarch Meletius again comes onto the stage in the Epilogue. Grotius wholeheartedly agrees with Meletius' conviction that, by and large, people prefer to fight over dogmas rather than to live according to God's intentions, and he supports this conviction with an urgent appeal for toleration, peace and concord. He points out that a great number of dogmatic quarrels are merely concerned with words and relate to questions of no ethical importance. Conversely, the ethical rules are clearly established and consequently everybody knows what he should do. The number of necessary doctrinal points ought therefore to be limited to the most obvious ones, and anything going beyond that should be relegated to the judgement of experts, who should investigate them, inspired by the sacred Scriptures and revering brotherly love. And if it so happens that there are people who err on central issues they should not be judged too harshly, for it is quite possible that they err unwittingly, and their ignorance could well be remedied by a benevolent approach.[104]

---

[101] *Mel.* 75-76.
[102] *Mel.* 77-87.
[103] *Mel.* 88.363-366.
[104] *Mel.* 89-91.

6. *Analysis of the contents*

INTRODUCTION

1. A sense of kinship and solidarity is disappearing in our country. 2. This also applies to religion. Christians are hostile to one another. 3. But Christ teaches that we should love concord. We should therefore reflect on what we have in common. 4. Grotius recalls discussions he had on this subject with the widely-travelled Johannes Boreel. 5. Boreel had told him that the patriarch Meletius always emphasized the common denominator among Christians. Grotius announces his intention of expressing this common denominator in his own manner.

I. PROOF OF RELIGION

6. In agreement with other religions Christianity confesses that God exists and that He rewards those who love Him. Proof of God's existence.

7-11. God as remunerator.
7. God is a *natura intelligens*, possessed of a perfect free will.
8. God attends to heavenly and human matters. He is omnipotent and good.
9. Man is gifted with reason and freedom of will.
10. God is a Legislator.
11. God is just.
12. Christianity shares all these views with other religions.

II. PURPOSE OF RELIGION: THE HIGHEST GOOD

13. The purpose of religion is beatitude: absorption in God.
14. Beatitude goes together with freedom from suffering and with immortality.
15. The highest good is not to be found in this life or in virtue.
16. Beatitude is a state in which the body is assimilated with the soul.
17. The values considered by others as the highest good are all contained in the Christian doctrine.
18. Christianity teaches that the body will be resurrected and that the soul will live for ever.

III. CONTENT OF RELIGION: ITS THEORETICAL TEACHING

19. In religion a distinction must be made between doctrines and ethical precepts.

20-25. God in relation to Himself.
20. God is One.
21. God is unqualified, eternal, the highest Being.
22. God is Being, Logos, and Spirit.
23. In this triple manifestation He is One.
24. God is omniscient and good. He knows evil but does not create it.
25. The effects of God's Omniscience and Goodness in relation to man.

26-29. God in relation to the Creation.
26. God is the Creator.
27. Creation refers to visible and invisible things.
28. Everything is subordinate to man, but man is subordinate to God.
29. God is the Ruler of everything. Evil originates from man's will.

30-33. God's intention in creating man.
30. Man has been created a good being after the image of God.
31. Man has been created with affects.
32. Man has been created to worship God.
33. What is the worship of God?

34-40. Man as he really is. The nature of evil.
34. Man is evil and ungrateful to God.
35. He hates his neighbour instead of loving him.
36. The entire human species is beset with evil.
37. Not all sins are alike.
38. Each sin is an insult to God and therefore punishable.
39. Punishability is maintained, because it is proper to evil, which, once committed, is irrevocable.
40. Evil persists because God withdraws His support from whomever turns away from Him. It augments as a result of wrong education and the bad examples we provide by doing it.

41-43. What is taught by Christianity.
41. Christianity preaches the goodness of God and teaches man to have a poor opinion of himself.
42. Repudiation of false views on this score held by the Stoics and Pharisees.
43. The necessity of remission and reparation.

44-50. Absolution and mediation.
44. Man owes his faith in absolution to God's revelation.
45. Even the heathens have tentatively sought reconciliation with God, and
46. developed thoughts about a mediator.
47. Christianity teaches that mankind has been given a mediator who effects reconciliation.
48. Acting as a substitute, Christ delivered man from his just punishment.

49. Both the deeds of Christ and the fact that everything concerning him happened as had been prophesied, testify to God's activity in and through him.
50. Forgiveness is granted to mankind in its entirety on the condition of penance and faith.

51-56. Reparation of the relationship between God and man.

51. The reparation of the relationship between God and man is effected in the first place by Christ, God's Word, removing the ignorance about matters divine.
52. The reliability of the divine writings appears from the lofty fashion in which God is spoken about, from the quality of the ethics recommended and from the consensus among the Biblical authors.
53. In addition to this there is the antiquity of the divine writings, as well as
54. the simplicity with which the Highest is spoken about.
55. A consequence of this simplicity is that the truth is easily accessible to everybody.
56. The relationship between God and man is furthermore repaired by the example Christ set, as well as
57. by the mysterious power of the Holy Ghost.
58. The external circumstances of life are of no significance with regard to the supreme good.

IV. CONTENT OF RELIGION: WHAT IT PRESCRIBES FROM A PRACTICAL VIEWPOINT

59. Non-Christian writers give a favourable judgement about Christian ethics.

60-67. Duties to God.

60. The Christian religion gives priority to the worship of God and the love of Him.
61. The Christian religion demands that we believe in God, and
62. that we invoke Him in prayer.
63. Some acts are forbidden, some commanded by God. It is forbidden to take God's name in vain; to make any graven image of Him; or
64. to worship Him with a superabundance of rites and ceremonies.
65. He prescribed assemblies in order to be honoured.
66. Furthermore, He gave the signs of baptism and communion.
67. For Christians, factual tokens of love take precedence over the observance of ritual rules.

68-70. Duties to mankind.

68. The duty of Christian charity.

69. Charity implies: refusal of the term 'barbarian'; love for the enemy; rejection of the notion of vengeance;
70. forgiveness; compassion.

71-74. Duties to society.
71. The family.
72. Matrimony.
73. Rejection of divorce.
74. The commonwealth.

75-81. Duties to oneself.
75. Rejection of suicide.
76. The Christian outlook on death.
77. The Christian attitude to honour;
78. to wealth and poverty;
79. to food and lust.
80. The value of fasting.
81. No extra-marital sexuality.

82-87. Other rules.
82. When performing acts which are neither forbidden nor commanded the Christian should bear in mind the interest of his neighbour.
83. As regards the use of language the rule prevails that the Christian should never swerve from the truth.
84. Promises must be kept, even those made to enemies.
85. Thoughts and inner life are to be submitted to God.
86. In thoughts, words, and deeds the Christian seeks to obey God.
87. For trespassers of the rules the commandment of penance comes into force.
88. What the world owes to the Christian religion. A golden age would dawn if all people were to live a truly Christian life.

EPILOGUE

89. Patriarch Meletius believed that discord among Christians was due to the fact that people quarrel about doctrine rather than live according to the commandments.
90. Quarrels about doctrine concern side issues, not life; rules pertaining to the way of life are eternal and unambiguous.
91. The number of necessary doctrinal points should be limited as much as possible and only to those that are absolutely unequivocal.

7. Reception

It sounds paradoxical to talk about the reception of a work that has never been published and had already passed into oblivion in the author's lifetime. Nevertheless the use of the term is justified in the case of the *Meletius*. Indeed we already saw that Grotius sent his manuscript for perusal to four intimate friends, who mainly expressed their reactions in letters which have been handed down to us.[105] Scarce though this evidence may be, we are not left completely in the dark about the reception the treatise encountered.

The intimates in question were Johannes Boreel, Petrus Cunaeus, Apollonius Schotte, and Antonius Walaeus. One can be dropped immediately, and it is a great pity that this should be the very man who had played such an important part in the conception of the work, the man who had given Grotius such a vivid description of his meeting with the venerable patriarch Meletius, and to whose judgement Grotius looked forward so much. I refer, of course, to Johannes Boreel. This scholar, about whom we know regrettably little and who certainly deserves closer investigation, has left us no written statement concerning the *Meletius*, nor do we have any other means of knowing what he thought of it. This does not necessarily mean, of course, that Grotius himself was unacquainted with Boreel's opinion.

What is equally obscure is the actual procedure of sending the manuscript to the Zealand friends. Did they redirect the *Meletius* to one another, in the meanwhile communicating their comments to Grotius, or did the successive readers send it back to Grotius, for him to send it on each time from The Hague? The latter possibility seems the most plausible, and presumably Walaeus was the first in line. Being a theologian, he was the obvious person for Grotius to apply to for a first criticism of his maiden theological work. It is not clear who followed after Walaeus, but so much is certain: Grotius incorporated Walaeus' remarks before sending the manuscript to Boreel.[106] A few months later, the manuscript appears to have been in the hands of Cunaeus, who had received it from Schotte. This is all we know about the circulation of the *Meletius*.

The written reactions from Cunaeus and Schotte are very limited and considerably less revealing than those from Walaeus. The latter went into the *Meletius* deeply — he did so twice[107] —, and expressed his opinion in three elaborate epistles to which Grotius replied with two letters. The value of these letters is greatly enhanced by the fact that in this case we have both sides of the argument at our disposal. They bring us into contact with the susceptibilities and tensions of the time, give us a better

---

[105] See above, 15.
[106] Cf. Grotius to Walaeus, *App.* II no. 4.4-6.
[107] Walaeus to Grotius, *App.* II no. 8.11-13: "...ignosces ut spero audaciae meae, si de pauculis, quae *aditerata lectione* (italics PM) scripti tui adnotavi, te rursum commonefaciam."

insight into Grotius' intentions, and allow us a glimpse over his shoulder while he was putting the finishing touch to the work. For all these reasons I shall go more deeply into this correspondence, but not before glancing at the biography of Walaeus and his dealings with Grotius.

Antonius Walaeus (1573-1639) was first educated at the Latin school in Middelburg and then read Divinity at the young University of Leiden, where Trelcatius, Junius, and Gomarus were his teachers.[108] Immediately after the termination of his studies the father of his friend Apollonius Schotte enabled him to make an *iter academicum* by way of France, where he stayed for one year and was offered a professorship at Vienne, to Geneva. There for close on a year he lodged with the enigmatic Charles Perrot,[109] with whom he struck up a friendship. He attended the lectures at the Academy, got to know the patriarch of the Calvinists Théodore de Bèze, became more proficient in French, and soon received permission to give Divinity classes. After a short stay in Basel, where he was likewise given teaching duties, he returned to the Netherlands in the autumn of 1601. In 1602 he was called as minister to Koudekerke, a position he was to hold for three years, after which he changed it for one in Middelburg. Here he worked for many years, and soon also assumed the extra duty of teaching Greek language and philosophy at the local Latin school. After the death of Arminius (1609) there were some, including Grotius, who tried to procure for Walaeus a position at the University of Leiden.[110] This effort failed at first when the controversial Conrad Vorstius was decided upon, but ten years later the desired appointment was effected. After the close of the Synod of Dort, which Walaeus had attended as delegate of the States of Zealand, he was conferred the honour of being appointed professor at the 'purged' faculty of Divinity at Leiden. He held this office until his death in 1639. The choice had been a fortunate one, for he was competent and lucid and, like his colleague Johannes Polyander, combined a Calvinistic conviction with a gentle nature.

---

[108] See G. P. van Itterson, s.v. 'Walaeus, Antonius', in *BLGNP* 2, 452-54; to the literature there mentioned may be added Meertens' article cited n. 36. For his survey of the relationship between Grotius and Walaeus Meertens did not make use of Grotius' relevant remarks in his *Memorie van mijne intentien*, resp. *Memorie van mijn bejegening*, (= Fruin, *Verhooren*, passim).

[109] See the present author's 'Charles Perrot (1541-1608). Een onbekend advies van zijn hand over een geschrift van Georgius Cassander', in *Kerkhistorische Studiën*. Feestbundel uitgegeven ter gelegenheid van het 85-jarig bestaan van het Kerkhistorisch Gezelschap S.S.S., (ed.) Hans van der Meij (e.a.), Leiden 1987, 63-88.

[110] J. D. de Lind van Wijngaarden, *Antonius Walaeus* (thesis Leiden), Leiden 1891, 29.

8. Portrait of Antonius Walaeus

How and when Walaeus and Grotius made each other's acquaintance is not easy to ascertain. It is possible that their common friend Apollonius Schotte was a party to it,[111] or perhaps the professor Franciscus Junius

---

[111] So Meertens in his (n. 36 above) mentioned article, 77.

(† 1602) with whom Grotius lodged for some time, and for whom both felt a deep respect. However this may be, a close friendship developed between Grotius and Walaeus which, up to a certain degree, even survived the escalation of the Truce quarrels when it became increasingly clear that the two men held different views. Walaeus felt great respect for Grotius, for his knowledge and his position, and he was convinced of his integrity.[112] Grotius, in his turn, considered Walaeus a cultured and educated theologian, a Calvinist willing to listen to reason, and one who, even though he belonged to the churchmen, was as committed to peace in the Republic as he was himself.[113]

The first palpable evidence of their friendship — evidence suggestive of a confidential relationship of longer standing — dates back to 1611, when Grotius sent the *Meletius* to his Middelburg friends to be commented on.[114] A few years later (1615) he also presented the manuscript of *De satisfactione* to Walaeus.[115] In both cases it was accompanied by the request to criticize candidly, as a friend, and in both cases Walaeus answered promptly and satisfactorily. When Walaeus in his turn published *Het ampt der kerckendienaren*[116] in 1615, a work primarily directed against Wtenbogaert but implicitly also against Grotius' *Pietas*,[117] he did not fail to send his friend a copy of it. He added a personal letter which displayed the remarkable and all but naive expectation that Grotius might be made to change his mind with regard to the relationship between Church and State.[118] No answer in writing ever came, as far as we know.

When the Truce quarrels had reached their dramatic climax and the trials had been conducted, it was Walaeus who was approached by Jacob Schotte, deputy of Zeeland to the Generality and father of Apollonius, to inform Oldenbarnevelt, Hogerbeets, and Grotius of the verdict. It was then still the death penalty for all three of them, and Walaeus was supposed to give them pastoral comfort. In the case of his friend Grotius

---

[112] De Lind van Wijngaarden, *o.c.*, 42 n. 2.

[113] The beginning and the close of the letters exchanged reveal something of their mutual feelings although allowances must be made for courtesy.

[114] See above n. 24 and n. 27.

[115] *BW* I no. 410, 396-97.

[116] Knuttel, *Pamfletten* no. 2294. One finds a copy of Walaeus' work in Grotius' library, see Molhuysen, 'Bibliotheek', 56 no. 143.

[117] Cunaeus to Grotius, *BW* I no. 416, 504: "Dum hic sum intelligo in lucem brevi exituras Antonii Walaei commentationes adversus Utenbogardii librum, in quo ille rerum ecclesiasticarum potestatem dominatumque principibus et magistratibus adscripserat. *Eadem opera confutavit quoque cuncta argumenta, quae pro opinione ista extant in Pietate tua...* (italics PM)".

[118] *BW* I no. 436, 428-29. The letter also contains a reply to a lost letter of Grotius, as Meertens, *o.c.*, 77 rightly remarks.

Walaeus refused categorically, for "how could he comfort him where he himself was in need of comfort?". In the cases of Oldenbarnevelt and Hogerbeets he declared himself ready, on the condition that someone else would announce the verdict to them and that he would be excused from witnessing the execution. He was granted this request. Meanwhile, the death sentences of Grotius and Hogerbeets had been commuted to life imprisonment. So Walaeus had only to assist the Grand Pensionary in his last hours, a pastoral task he performed to perfection.[119]

In the letters he wrote from prison to Caspar van Vosbergen and Prince Maurice, Grotius reminded them of his association with Walaeus with a view to convoking a National Synod in order to settle the differences which had arisen. From a later letter to Maurice, written after his escape from Loevestein, it appears that the Prince through Walaeus' intermediary had made certain pledges to Maria van Reigersberch, Grotius' wife. In Grotius' correspondence from the years that followed, the name of Walaeus is occasionally mentioned, but there is no evidence whatever pointing to any personal or written contact between both men after the sentence.[120] So this friendship, too, fell victim to the religious quarrels.

In the first letter Walaeus wrote to Grotius on receiving the *Meletius* he manifested his great enthusiasm for this latest work. He called the treatise admirable in many respects, said that it showed that the author was a true scholar and sincere Christian, and praised the method used, which he qualified as absolutely 'novel'.

> "Since the way you treat this subject is entirely novel I have no doubt that the work, if published, will be of the utmost importance for Christianity as a whole; in the first place for those who must be gradually led to the Christian belief, or those who, put off by the quarrels between certain theologians, have developed an aversion to reading sacred Scripture."[121]

This very laudatory comment is accompanied by an admonition to be prudent, reminding us once more of how tenuous relations were only two

---

[119] De Lind van Wijngaarden, *o.c.*, 47 ff. Den Tex, *o.c.*, III 726 ff.

[120] See Meertens, *o.c.*, 78.

[121] *App.* II no. 1.35-39. The very positive opinion of the Counter-Remonstrant Walaeus on Grotius' definitely non-Calvinistic treatise may be explained, not only by his admiration for Grotius' genius but also by his personal preference for the Aristotelian philosophy on the one hand, and his interest in ethical problems on the other. Proof of both is to be found in the larger work Walaeus composed during his Middelburg years entitled: *Compendium ethicae aristotelicae ad normam veritatis christianae revocatum* (*Opera Omnia* II, 261-292). See De Lind van Wijngaarden, *o.c.*, 171-88. — For Grotius' attitude towards Calvinism, see the present author's 'Hugo Grotius as an Irenicist', in *Grotius, Proceedings*, 55-6.

years after the Truce. Walaeus, conscious of Grotius' superiority, modestly conceded that he could not dictate anything to him, but he nevertheless cautioned him against certain pronouncements which, should the work come to be published, might very well be misinterpreted by some to the detriment of the salutary influence the treatise might have. In order to prevent this from happening he pointed out three points which, in his opinion, ought to be reconsidered and corrected. In decreasing order of importance, these points were 1. the irenical programme in general, the attitude to Rome and heretics; 2. the doctrine of the H. Trinity; 3. the relationship between grace and free will.[122]

Grotius replied to Walaeus' remarks with a longer letter, to be followed by a rejoinder from Walaeus. But this was by no means the end of the exchange of views, for Walaeus' comments mattered to him. He occasionally adopted his suggestions for correction and submitted the altered passages to him. This gave Walaeus another chance to pore over the entire text and to come up with a new list of comments.[123] Since Grotius did not react to this, I shall pass them over and only refer to the commentary in which they have been incorporated. For easy reference I have grouped together similar points from various letters in my account of the correspondence.

Walaeus' warning to be particularly cautious about certain people's susceptibilities did not go unheeded. In his reply, Grotius told him that, after having sent his manuscript to Zealand, he himself read it through once more and had noticed roughly the same points to be sensitive and liable to misunderstanding. Readers with sympathy for his intentions would not have any difficulty in adapting to the text. It would of course be still better to exclude any possibility of offence, but this would not be easy

> "for either one or another party would consider me as uncompromising. It is for this very reason that I started considering whether it would not be better to suppress the birth of this brainchild completely, or at least to postpone its publication till more peaceful times."[124]

What he said at this point, a few months after the completion of his *Meletius*, would indeed ultimately lead to his decision to forgo publication, but for the time being, at the end of 1611, it had not yet come to this. He continued working on his text and gave careful thought to the three points Walaeus had put before him.

---

[122] A fourth point is mentioned in the correspondence: Holy Scripture, but here the two friends did not disagree. See *App.* II no. 1.39-49; no. 2.77-83.
[123] See above n. 107.
[124] *App.* II no. 2.11-17.

INTRODUCTION

1. In conformity with his irenical nature and intention Grotius had asserted that Christians, instead of keeping in mind the essential tenets they had in common, again and again emphasized the confessional differences which generally concerned details and were uncertain or not strictly necessary to know.

When Walaeus protested against this idea he did not belie his Calvinistic conviction. He conceded that some differences were unimportant, but by no means all of them. In particular certain dogmas of the 'papists' constituted a direct threat to the 'stronghold of the true faith', and this equally applied to the doctrine of the Antitrinitarians, who distorted Christendom into some sort of Turkish religion. He had no doubt whatever that Grotius entirely agreed with him, and opined that a few slight touches would easily remove any offence the text in its present form might have given.[125]

This remark, which touched on a very central point in Grotius' irenical programme, sparked off an elaborate discussion, extending over several letters. Grotius admitted that the papists' teachings were a very serious threat to the 'stronghold of the faith', but that, in his opinion, did not alter the fact that the foundations of the stronghold were also present in the Church of Rome. And this, he said, was much more important than that that Church entertained a number of objectionable 'particular opinions'. He approvingly quoted Franciscus Junius, who used to say: "With regard to the foundations (of faith) the papists err only in so far as they do not drift away from these foundations." Grotius thought that with the concept of religion as he had developed it, the particular opinions held by Rome could be undermined and nullified. In this respect he expected much from unspecified Roman Catholic theologians of repute — presumably referring to Georgius Cassander and other Erasmian minds with similar leanings within the Church of Rome —,[126] who

---

[125] *App.* II no. 1.22-23: "Quae tamen verba... facili flexu ita a te emolliri poterunt, ut iusta offensionum occasio plane adimatur." See also *App.* II no. 3.10 sq.

[126] See *App.* II no. 2.24 sq.: "...quia profecto spero etiam cordatos in ipsa romana ecclesia viros non posse illam impietatem approbare." Maybe he also had in mind a man like Jeannin, of whom he says in the *Memorie van mijn intentiën* (ed. Fruin, *Verhooren,* 48): "Ick wierd ook gevraecht off ick met Jeannyn propoost hadde gehadt om de Papistische religie met de onse te accorderen: welcke vrage quam uyt de leste woorden van mijn prefatie voor 'Christum patientem' (= *BW* I no. 114, 98-100 and *Dichtwerken* I 2, pars. 5a and b, 39-57), die my oock ten quaedste waren naegeduydt...Ick seyde hyerop, dat Jeannyn veel erreuren van de Roomsche Kerck erkende ende hopen gaf dat de Coning, dye smaeck hadde gehouden van de religie, door sijne authoriteyt in Vranckrijck reformatie soude willen te wege brengen; dat ick hem hyertoe hadde geänimeert, verthoonende, soo lange de afgoderije, tyrannije ende andere grove erreuren bleven in het Pausdom, gheen apparentie te zijn van de gescheurde Christenheyt te verheelen; dat ick gedenckende het voornemen, dat in Vranckrijck was geweest ten tijde van het concilie van Trente, gelijck sulcx can blijcken uit de gedruckte acten, ende daerby overleggende

had openly declared that everything true and believed by Protestants was also acknowledged by Roman Catholics, but that the latter had occasionally added falsehoods of such a nature that they could not go together with the acknowledged truth. This led him to conclude that if religion were restricted to those truths on which the Christian churches of all times agreed, Papism would necessarily collapse, being based on individual opinions.[127]

He hit out considerably more fiercely when tackling Antitrinitarians and similar groups. He denied them the right to call themselves Christians, and even refused to call them heretics. Their assertions, he said, were contrary not only to the Christian belief but to all belief in general, and this to such an extent that they could best be considered a kind of Muslims. It is clear that both friends wholly agreed on this point, in accordance with the prevailing opinions of their time. Grotius informed Walaeus that, because of the utterly reprehensible character of Socinian and similar doctrines, he had refrained from including notions of this sort in his idea of *consensus*, on which he had based his concept of religion. For the same reason he had not gone into dogmatic questions such as the perpetuity of the Word, the doctrine of satisfaction, *praescientia* and *immensitas dei*, each of which points had been doubted by these apostates.[128]

Pleased as Walaeus must have been with this repudiation of Antitrinitarianism, he took just as much exception to Grotius' opinion of the 'papists'. This led him to give a more elaborate statement of his view of the Church of Rome.[129] He was prepared to adopt the formulation that this Church, too, was based on the true foundation of the faith, but his standpoint was that the foundation was in this case robbed of its exclusivity and thereby of its power. The Church of Rome, he said, gives with the one hand what it takes away with the other. It acknowledges the one foundation but places it next to other foundations, with disastrous

---

hoe de Reformatie in Engelant met trappen was voortgegaen, altijdt hadde verhoopt dat door de Coning Hyndrick de Vierde de suyveringe in Vranckrijck soude beginnen; dat oock veele wijze luyden achten sulcx de oorsaeck geweest te zijn van syn doodt.''

[127] *App.* II no. 2.37-39. This view of the matter had its direct effect on his ideas about international Church politics. His expectation in these years was that if the protestants, i.e. the churches which had in fact undertaken the necessary cleansing of the temple, would join together in a close alliance, Rome would be forced to follow. The yeast of the *religio repurgata* would then penetrate that church as well, and expel the tyranny under which she now languished. For more details, see the present author's 'Hugo Grotius as an Irenicist', *Grotius, Proceedings*, 58-9.

[128] *App.* II no. 2.40sq.: ''Samosatenianos autem et si qui sunt similes, non modo Christianorum sed nec haereticorum nomine dignor... hos a Mahumetistis non longe separo''. For his opinion on Antitrinitarians, see also *Pietas* (IV 99a 41-b8).

[129] *App.* II no. 3.25-80, slightly paraphrased.

results. On the one hand reconciliation by Christ is taught, whereas on the other hand it is obliterated by the system of merits. Rome proclaims Christ as the unique Mediator, but at the same time advances the intercession of the saints, and so on. Thus a monstrous alliance of truth and untruth had come into existence, which was depicted as much too innocuous if one applied to it the categories of essential and accidental, and if one made it seem as if the particularities of this church only concerned matters of minor importance. The situation was far more serious: truth and untruth had been mingled in a fatal way, with the result that the message of salvation was endangered. It was the Antichrist who was active here, and he was the one who led souls to their doom. Instead of belittling the differences between the Christians, as Grotius did, it should be stated uncompromisingly that the differences were anything but trifling. At the same time, however, one should show that parties agreed in many respects and on very essential points, and it should be impressed on people that if they held to these points they might be assured of their salvation on the strength of the promise given by the Gospel.[130]

Grotius was not willing to alter his text along these lines, and, oddly enough, he believed there was no need to do so since they were essentially of the same mind! "As regards the papists", he said, "there is no disagreement whatsoever between us, even though we may not use the same words, as is bound to happen frequently."[131] He then once more repeated his previously formulated point of view, in so far adjusting himself to Walaeus' criticism that he now called the 'peculiarities' (*peculiaria*) of the Church of Rome '*Antichristiana*', but for the rest he stuck to his idea that the points of agreement between Christians were infinitely more important than their differences. He accentuated this even more by saying that in his *Meletius* he had deliberately glossed over the differences, the better to enforce his exhortations to love one another.[132] He refused to budge, so we cannot but reach the conclusion that on this important issue of irenicism and the relations with the Church of Rome Walaeus' critical comments went all but unheeded.

2. In the first version of his *Meletius* Grotius had been reticent about the H. Trinity. Walaeus regretted this, and found it advisable for Grotius to express more clearly that in this case it was not a matter of natural powers (δυνάμεις) in God but of 'hypostases'. He pointed out that even though

---

[130] *App.* II no. 3.70-76.
[131] *App.* II no. 4.9-11: "...de papistis nulla inter nos dissensio est etsi verbis forte alius aliis, ut fieri solet".
[132] See above n. 52. In his contemporary letters to Casaubon he develops the same program. See for instance *BW* I no. 224 (7 Febr. 1612), 197 and hereabove n. 52 and n. 127.

the doctrine of the H. Trinity had always been left out of the controversies, this central dogma ought nonetheless to be strongly defended because it was assailed by the heretics.[133]

Grotius replied that he found this difficult. While he had intended to write an introduction for people who had to be converted to the Christian faith, and had therefore tried to use clear and simple terms, he could not but concede that on this matter he had failed. The hallowed term 'hypostasis' was of no use, for it required too much explanation and was beyond the comprehension of catechumens. In an attempt to clarify in a concrete manner how one should think about the H. Trinity he had therefore resorted to an analogy, the analogy of the human mind, as Augustine, Duplessis-Mornay, and Junius had done before him. But he had come to recognize that in order to repudiate the heretics the concept of 'hypostasis' was indispensable, it being the only means of bringing out clearly the difference between the 'person' and 'qualities' of God.[134] Bearing in mind the introductory character of his treatise, he asked Walaeus to give some thought to which formulation was preferable.

Walaeus complied immediately, but said that in all fairness he, too, was hard put to it to find intelligible terms to cover this concept. The safest way to proceed was to stick to the language of the Scriptures, "for no one but God Himself can bear witness to the depth of His being." Even the Church Fathers, who had gone exhaustively into this question, had been unable to find any better analogies than that of the human mind and of light, whereby they too had followed the Scriptures. He did indeed suggest comparing the nature of the human mind, but he recommended working out the analogy slightly differently from what Grotius had done initially. He also suggested elucidating the mystery of the perpetual generation of the Son by the Father by comparing it with the human mind, which turns inwards upon itself, produces a perfect image of itself, etc.[135]

Where the H. Trinity was the central principle of religion, Grotius said in his reply, he had heeded Walaeus' advice and inserted the term 'hypostasis' in his text in the second instance. Admittedly this was a departure from his quest for comprehensibility, but this disadvantage was outweighed by the possibility that the difference with heretical views might be insufficiently clear. He added bitterly that had he not lived in

---

[133] *App.* II no. 1.15-22; no. 3.82-86.
[134] *App.* II no. 2.53-59. "Itaque tentabam an possem qui modus de Deo loquendi tutissimus dicitur ἀποφαντικῶς innuere id quod res est, addita insuper similitudine humanae mentis, quam inter veteres Augustino aliisque, et inter nostros Plessaeo, etiam Iunio, prae caeteris placuisse memineram..."
[135] *App.* II no. 3.81 sq.

a time "as unsettled as it was pregnant with distorted errors" he might very well have acted differently.[136]

He did not, however, want to adopt Walaeus' elaboration of the analogy of the human mind in order to clarify the doctrine because the terms employed about the Holy Ghost in this argumentation had no parallel in the Scriptures. He had therefore preferred to refer to the Holy Ghost as *virtus Dei atque efficacia*, in agreement with Calvin and both the French and the Dutch confessions. But in order to emphasize that it was not incompatible with reason to observe distinctions in God, he had referred to Aristotle and also used the notions *intellectus* and *voluntas*, lest it might seem that he was averse to Platonisms.[137]

All in all we can safely say that in this case Walaeus' critical remarks did not fail to have an effect on the final textual form of the *Meletius*. In particular the insertion of the notion 'hypostasis' in the passage on the H. Trinity, intended to repudiate Antitrinitarian aberrations, is to be traced back to his suggestion.

3. As regards the highly controversial issue of the freedom of the human will in its relationship to grace, Grotius had expressed himself in more general terms, which gave Walaeus cause to remark:

> "Your arguments about the freedom of human will after the Fall will be favourably interpreted by those who are not involved in the recent controversies, but the others, weak though their grounds may be, will rashly reproach you with being someone who prefers to proclaim his own novel opinion. I for one would rather you did not give them grounds for such a triumph."[138]

This heartfelt entreaty implies criticism as well as concern. Walaeus wanted Grotius to speak out more unambiguously, so as to avoid being accused of 'modernism'.

Grotius replied that he was very pleased with what Walaeus had observed, and then pointed out that where the problem of the free will was concerned, he had attempted to make the best use of formulations from the *patres* "not unacceptable even to our theologians". He objected to elaborating the text and to entering into further detail, for not only

---

[136] *App.* II no. 4.30-36. Complaints of this sort were a very common phenomenon in the world Grotius lived in. For more details, see Wilhelm Kühlmann, *Gelehrtenrepublik und Fürstenstaat. Entwicklung und Kritik des deutschen Späthumanismus in der Literatur des Barockzeitalters*, Tübingen 1982, 31 ff. ("Bedrängnis der 'litterae': Zur Tradition und Funktion humanistischer Zeitklage im Schatten christlicher Geschichtstheologie").

[137] *App.* II no. 4.42-49. Cf. note to Mel. 22. For Calvin, see Werner Krusche, *Das Wirken des Heiligen Geistes nach Calvin*, Berlin [1957], 8 ff.

[138] *App.* II no. 1.28-33.

would this run counter to the intention of his treatise, which after all was to emphasize the 'common factor', but it would also bring him into conflict with the Greek Fathers, if not with Augustine. He then continued:

> "as to those in this country who have recently started to dispute about these and other questions, I would not dare to condemn their opinions, since I am not sufficiently knowledgeable about them, but I openly reject the course they want to follow. For if there was something obscure then it ought to have been investigated by a council of wise and pious men instead of being proclaimed before the ignorant people or even before the magistrates in such an embittered way."[139]

Contrary to what one would expect from a Counter-Remonstrant Walaeus did not insist but even said that he considered the question of free will less important than the two other ones. He was of the opinion that the main point in this matter was that two obstacles be avoided. In the first place Pelagianism, which ascribed to the human will what can only be given by God and in the second place the Stoic doctrine of fate, which again and again exculpated man's transgressions even to the point of making God co-responsible. If these boundaries were observed, in other words if both Pelagianism and Stoicism were avoided, Walaeus believed that peaceful disputations about the free will should be permitted, as had always been the case in the past. Of late, however, people tended to lose sight of this balance. Some had accentuated God's offer of grace to such an extent that they had detracted from His justice. Others had been guilty of doing just the opposite. According to Walaeus, the church would now experience a more peaceful time if Arminius had respected these limits and submitted his opinions to wise men. He concluded:

> "But I trust that in this matter you will act as prudently as you did — to quote your own words — with regard to the views on grace held by the Greek Fathers. For just as you restrained your pen in that matter, so as to avoid any semblance of being in conflict with these Fathers and Augustine, I hope that in this matter also you will try not to prejudice the agreement of the Reformed Churches."[140]

Grotius countered this somewhat more trenchant enunciation of Walaeus with the remark that the purpose of his book did not allow him to deviate on the point of free will from the Fathers' judgement, but that he did not want to outrage 'our churches' either. So if Walaeus could make some suggestions as to how to represent the view of the churches more clearly without running the risk of diverging from the language and the meaning

---

[139] *App.* II no. 2.68-74.
[140] *App.* II no. 3.133-136.

of the Ancients, he would be very grateful to him. "For I do not expect to be able to satisfy other severe people if I fail to prove my pronouncements to an utterly fair judge such as you are."[141] Wherever feasible within the limited scope of his treatise he had dissociated himself from Pelagianism. As to the other matter he could not help saying that if in his text he had made a stand against Stoics[142] and Manichaeans, the adherents of the strict doctrine of predestination should not immediately take this as directed against themselves. As Walaeus had very correctly pointed out to him, the matter ultimately hinged on not declaring God to be the cause of sin and rejection, and not making man the cause of salvation.

The intensive correspondence on the *Meletius* between the two friends ended in Grotius' deciding not to publish his book. The decisive issue was the question of free will, the very point that Walaeus considered the least important. Grotius could not comply with his friend's wish that he be more explicit on this score, in other words that he toe the line of the churchmen, because this would be at the expense of "what people have in common", i.e. the idea of *consensus*. Any infringement of this was inadmissible because this was the very foundation of the appeal for toleration and reciprocal love for the sake of which the book was written in the first place. If, therefore, it could reasonably be assumed that this intention would not be realized, or, worse, that the work would only give rise to irritation and rage in some people, it was better to forego publication altogether. Hence the decision: "*Praematur hoc foetus, neque certa damna subeamus, in spem fructus incertam*".[143]

Walaeus could agree with this decision, albeit with difficulty:

> "It is only reluctantly that I write down my opinion on the question whether you should publish your booklet, as learned as it is pious. I am quite convinced that if it is read with the care it deserves, the Church of Christ will reap its not inconsiderable fruits but at the same time I fear that

---

[141] *App.* II no. 4.57-58: "Neque enim spero me aliis duris hominibus satisfacere posse si tibi aequissimo iudici probare φράσεις non potero."

[142] When in the *Adamus Exul* Grotius describes how Satan tries to seduce Eve, he puts a Stoic argumentation in his mouth. (*AE*, 41 = *Dichtwerken* I 1a, 113.1071-76): "Ne crede pomi unius ob dispendium/Debere certam protinus mortem sequi./ Petire poterunt, perpeti vitae Deus/ Quod destinavit? Fata res omnes agunt:/ Praevisa tantum facimus, & ab alto venit/ Quodcumque patimur."

[143] *App.* II no. 4.69-73: "Sed, ut alteris literis scribebam (= *App.* II no. 2.11-17), non est tanti qualecumque hoc opusculum, ut propterea quisquam, praecipue autem eae ecclesiae, quas ego omnium purissimas profiteor, offendi debeant, quare, si aliter vitari non potest, prematur hoc foetus, neque certa damna subeamus in spem fructus incertam."

9. Facsimile of the minute of Grotius' letter to [Apollonius Schotte], [3. April 1612]

    the temper of our age and of the church will hardly be able to tolerate this healing hand."[144]

The bitter pronouncements by the other friends are indeed in contrast to the sympathetic resignation manifested by this judgement. When Grotius had taken his final decision not to publish he wanted to retrieve the copy of the *Meletius* that was still in circulation. On 3 April 1612 he talked about it with Schotte, who on the same day wrote the following letter to the Leiden professor Cunaeus:

---

[144] *App.* II no. 8.4-9 (cited as motto of this Introduction). In an earlier letter Walaeus had remarked, *App.* II no. 3.19-24: "Editionem operis tui si premas offensa quidem fateor vitabitur, sed et fructus tam pulchri laboris peribit..."

"Grotius addressed me on the subject of his treatise, which you received from me. And since, he said, he had been warned by friends that some theologians — how touchy these people are nowadays! — pass a judgement on this work as though he had talked about the Christian religion in too general terms, he asked me to write to you with the request to return it immediately. Not so much because he should distrust your fairness and prudence, but rather because he thinks that an attack from gadflies of this sort can best be warded off by keeping silent for some time, and thus removing the cause of their irritation."[145]

Cunaeus sent the manuscript of the *Meletius* back to Schotte by return, adding a letter in which he, too, vented his vexation about the theologians:[146]

"I am surprised that our ossified theologians have found anything to find fault with in the *Meletius*. Indeed Grotius treated the whole matter in such an erudite and elegant way that, even if they combined their efforts, all those illustrious high-priests together could not produce anything remotely resembling it I should think, however great their pains and care. (And the irony of it is) that it is these very men who, when they render inviolable their laws and decrees, extend the limits of Theology far beyond what is permissible by its nature."[147]

Such was the way in which three friends of Grotius received his *Meletius*, the first theological treatise from his hand. All three were impressed by the fruit of his labours. It is striking that it was particularly the Counter-Remonstrant Walaeus who was convinced of the salutary influence it might have. In 1611/1612 however, the religious tensions had mounted to such an extent that a plea for *consensus*, toleration, and peace, like the one under discussion, would fall on deaf ears, or, worse still, might fan the flames. This consideration forced Grotius to retain the *Meletius* in manuscript and to put off its publication until more peaceful times might dawn.[148] Tragically enough, this hope was never fulfilled during his

---

[145] See below *App.* II. no. 6.
[146] The aversion to the '*rabies theologorum*' (Melanchthon) is a stereotype in Christian humanist circles. For some other examples, see the present author's 'Jean Hotman's Syllabus of eirenical literature', in *Reform and Reformation: England and the Continent c 1500-c1750*, Oxford 1979, 179-'80. Petrus Cunaeus appeared in 1612 with his *Sardi Venales, Satyra Menippea in huius seculi homines plerosque inepte eruditos* (Ahsmann/Feenstra, *Bibliografie*, no. 125 sq.), in which theologians were not forgotten. Brandt, *Historie* II, 203-'06 gives some fragments of the *Sardi Venales* in Dutch translation. The work was dedicated to Apollonius Schotte, as were Cunaeus' theological theses *exercitii causa* defended under J. Arminius (Ahsmann/Feenstra, *Bibliografie*, no. 121). See also C. van der Woude, *Sybrandus Lubbertus. Leven en werken, in het bijzonder naar zijn correspondentie*, (thesis Kampen), Kampen 1963, 240.
[147] See below *App.* II. no. 7.
[148] *App.* II no. 2.16-17: "...deliberare coepi an non rectius premerem foetum, aut certe editionem in pacatiora tempora differrem."

10. Portrait of Petrus Cunaeus

lifetime, but it is doubtful whether this is the very reason why the Meletius was never published by him. It can rather be assumed that, once he had produced his *De veritate*, he considered the *Meletius* to be superannuated and that it was never published for that reason.

8. *Commentary: justification and explanation*

In the following commentary I wish above all to elucidate Grotius' argumentation with examples from his own works. To let him be *sui ipsius interpres* was the obvious thing to do for a number of reasons. In the first place there is a clearly discernible constant element in his thought and outlook. Hesitantly compromising with modern psychological categories we could denote this constant element as 'authoritarian', just as from a cultural point of view we would call it 'classicist'. Once he had decided that something was right, rational, and essential — and in the case of this prodigy this occurred in his early years —, he stuck to it till the end of his life.

The discovery and elaboration of what he saw as right, rational, and essential came about through his encounter with Antiquity, both classical and early Christian, which to the typically Christian humanist[149] and professional classicist that he was represented an almost mythical greatness, about which he possessed an extraordinarily extensive and thorough knowledge.

The notion of *consensus*, developed particularly by the Stoics, is an instance of the perception Grotius had already acquired in his youth as a result of his encounter with Antiquity, and which would remain essential to him for the rest of his life. In the *Meletius*, *consensus* is the cornerstone of Grotius' concept of religion, and it recurs over and over again in the works he wrote subsequently. Another example of a leading principle to which he remained faithful all his life — and in this, too, he concurred with the Stoics — is the idea of the primacy of ethics, to which I have already referred.[150] At this point I merely wish to emphasize that he acquired this view equally early in his life, and that it remained essential until the end.

In addition to his constancy, Grotius shows a second noticeable quality: his memory. This was well-nigh inexhaustible. As a consequence everything he absorbed in his industrious life was always at his disposal. And this not only because he put it down in writing for his own use, but above all — and this, it would seem, is typical of the man — because he immediately fitted it into the categories of his frame of reference. I shall clarify this with an example.

---

[149] The term 'Christian humanist' is used here as defined by P.O. Kristeller in his *Renaissance Thought. The Classic, Scholastic and Humanist Strains*. A revised and enlarged edition of "The Classics and Renaissance Thought", New York/Evanston/London [1961], 86: "...it is probably preferable to limit [the term Christian humanist] to those scholars with a humanist classical and rhetorical training who explicitly discussed religious or theological problems in all or some of their writings."

[150] See above 29 ff.

When we encounter the hundreds of hitherto virtually unstudied excerpts he has taken from works by others,[151] we are struck by the fact that, rather than summarizing in a few words the proposition of the author in question, he wanted to derive from it the arguments he could use himself. In other words, he worked like a typical barrister, like someone who views what he finds in others exclusively in function of its usefulness for his specific purpose and construction.[152] This — his frame of reference — had, as I said before, been established since his early years, with the result that the fruits of his wide reading had a quantitative rather than a qualitative function. His frame of reference was unquestionably enriched and enhanced by what he found in others, but it was barely, if at all, altered by them, since its foundations had been conclusively laid from the start. This can be seen in texts like *De satisfactione*, *De veritate* and *De iure*, at which he kept on working after their publication. The number of references increased considerably but the argument as such practically always remained untouched. He obviously had no sense of doubt about his own scheme of reference, but rather appropriated the phrase: *Noli perturbare circulos meos*.

It is, therefore, hardly surprising that the same concepts, the same arguments, and the same references should recur again and again. I availed myself of this circumstance and elucidated the *Meletius* primarily by consulting Grotius' other writings, thus letting the author explain his treatise himself. To this purpose I made use of a large number of his works, both theological and non-theological. While doing so, I strongly felt the unity of his work, and regretted the fact that research into it should be so compartmentalized. Jurists tend to concentrate exclusively on his juridical works, classicists on his *Poëmata* and tragedies, theologians on his *Annotationes* to the Old and New Testament, philosophers on *De veritate*, and so on. Consequently his estate has been split up at the expense of the internal connections and of the coherence so characteristic of his oeuvre in which everything is always interrelated.

That Grotius regarded this coherence as self-evident emerges from his numerous 'autocitations', which repeatedly defy our classifications of disciplines. In his *Annotationes* he refers to *De iure*,[153] in *De veritate* to the

---

[151] See above n. 13, Eyffinger's work.
[152] Cf. P. Haggenmacher's excellent remarks in a recension, *Grotiana* NS 6 (1985) 49: "...la démarche grotienne est avant tout celle d'un avocat... Avocat, il le reste en vérité jusque dans ses exposés en apparence les plus théoriques, les plus détachés des questions concrètes: toujours il défend une cause, même si c'est celle du genre humain; toujours il plaide... Toutes ses oeuvres spéculatives, qu'elles soient du droit ou de la théologie, présentent une forte dimension pratique, apologétique."
[153] For instance *Annot. in NT* ad Mt 5: 43 (II 71a53) with reference to *Iur.* II 15 9, 3 (396), or ad Hebr. 11: 6 (III 1053a 23-25) where he writes: "Vide plura, si vacat, in

same work,[154] in the *Annotationes* to *De veritate*,[155] and so on. A striking instance is also his tragedy *Adamus Exul*, which he brought out at the age of eighteen, and to which he added a list of theological and philosophical terms and subjects[156] as though he wanted to confirm that what he had written in the foreword was by no means an exaggeration:

> "... eisdem horis et pietatem exercui, et divinae humanaeque Sapientiae studium et poësin".[157]

Another example of the cohesion of his activities is that, when asked about his views on the doctrine of the H. Trinity, he refers to his sacred poetry.[158]

Because of the kindred subject matter *De veritate* was the first text to qualify for comparison with the *Meletius*. Roughly speaking, the two works are related like the first blueprint to a finished design: the outlines are established but the details and articulation have yet to be worked out. This comparison immediately proved fruitful because most of the quotations from the *Meletius* showed up in the later work. This made identification all the easier, for at a later stage Grotius added a wealth of notes to *De veritate*, accurately giving the source of all his references.[159]

A comparison with this work also proved useful where the context was concerned, since in it Grotius again defended the same views and the same message, but in a much broader and more detailed form. Numerous statements in the *Meletius* could thus be clarified by juxtaposing them to passages from *De veritate*. The differences between the two

---

libro nostro secundo de Iure Belli ac Pacis XX 46 (= *Iur*. II 20, 46 (518-20))." Cf. also *Annot. in VT*, 'Lectori' (I, xxxxx 2): "Si quis vero haec nostra utiliter legere volet, is necesse est sibi comparet quae de Veritate Religionis Christianae scripsimus cum annotatis, item de Iure Belli ac Pacis cum annotatis, et quae ad Evangelia annotavimus; saepe enim lectorem ad ista reiicimus."

[154] For instance *Ver*. I 16 annot. 22 (IV 16b 11) refers to *Iur*. II 20, 45 (516), and annot. 32 (IV 17a 11) to *Iur*. II 2, 2 (186). In fact *Iur* II 20, 45-46 (516-20) is to be considered as a summary of *Ver*. I.

[155] In *Annot. in VT* ad Gn. 1: 3 & 5 (I 1a 41-2 & 52-3) he refers to *Ver*. I 16 annot. 45 (IV 26b 26-39). See note to *Mel*. 54.

[156] Grotius, *Sacra in quibus Adamus exul tragoedia*, Hagae 1601, 77-80 (= *Dichtwerken* I 1a, 184-87): "Index quo praecipua quaeque aut Theologiam, aut Philosophiam aut alias scientias spectantia... monstrantur."

[157] *Ibidem* [aiij]. Cf. Cic. *Off*. I 53: "sapientia... *rerum divinarum et humanarum scientia*, in qua continetur deorum et hominum communitas et societas inter ipsos." Grotius, *Par*. III 33: "Quod si philosophia est, ut certe fatemur omnes, *rerum divinarum humanarumque scientia* primam eius esse partem theologiam negare non possumus."

[158] In a post-script to a letter to G. J. Vossius from 1 Jan. 1639 (*BW* X no. 3917, 14) he writes: "...si quis meam de summa Trinitate sententiam scire cupiat, reperturum quod satis sit in poematis... 'Cf. also note to *Mel*. 23.40.

[159] *TMD* no. 944.

texts should not be underestimated, however. Even though they display the same basic idea, the defence of the Christian religion is still highly elementary in the *Meletius*; the proof of its truth is not very detailed, the polemic with Judaism and Islam practically absent, and explicit references to Christian authors are conspicuously few. One gets the impression that Grotius only acquired a profound knowledge of the (early) Christian writers after 1611. At the time of the composition of the *Meletius* his knowledge was presumably mainly limited to the Apologists of that time.

I can be brief about the other writings mentioned in the commentary. The *Pietas Ordinum* (1613), which he brought out two years after the *Meletius*, is only adduced for comparison once.[160] It did not have much to offer for our purpose, because the nature of this ecclesiastical political apology is different from that of the *Meletius*. The polemical treatise *De satisfactione*, directed against Socinus and published in 1617, is also referred to rarely.[161] This is because, as we have seen, Grotius deliberately refrained from polemicizing with Antritrinitarians in his *Meletius*.[162] I have already discussed what is chronologically the next work, the *Bewijs*, or *De veritate*.

When he started working on his *Bewijs*, he also began composing what was later to become the famous *Annotationes in Vetus et Novum Testamentum*. This work, originating in the wish to write a commentary on the Sermon on the Mount (Mt. 5-7), developed over the years into a complete commentary on the Bible. The time Grotius spent on this matter can be divided into two periods: 1619 to 1621, and the period after 1638.[163] When he escaped from Loevestein (March 1621) he had completed his commentary on the synoptic Gospels.[164] Because the *Annotationes* to the

---

[160] *TMD* no. 817.
[161] *TMD* no. 922.
[162] See above n. 128.
[163] For the origin and development of the *Annotationes in Novum Testamentum*, see W. C. van Unnik, 'Hugo Grotius als uitlegger van het Nieuwe Testament', *NAKG* NS 25 (1932), 1-48 (reprinted in W. C. van Unnik, *Woorden gaan leven*, Kampen 1979, 172-214). Furthermore *TMD*, 555-'57, 560, 561, and H. J. de Jonge, 'Hugo Grotius: exégète du Nouveau Testament', in *Grotius, Proceedings*, 97-116. In these studies no use has been made of Grotius' *Memorie van mijn bejegening* (Fruin, *Verhooren*, 70), where he makes revealing remarks about the works which were behind his *Annotationes*: "Mijne occupatiën geduyrende den voorn. tijd waren het lesen van Godts woordt, insonderheyt van het Nieuwe Testament, daer ick by heb gelesen Paraphrasin ende Annotationes Erasmi, Annotationes Bezae, Drusii en Casauboni, oock bij wijlen yet uyt Harmonia Calvini. Ick heb oock gelesen veel in Eusebii Historia ende Epiphanio adversus Hereses, Clementem Alexandrinum ende Tertullianus heel uyt; gelijck mede Scriptores Historiae Augustae. Ick heb oock bij wijlen wat gelesen in Plutarcho..."
[164] Cf. Grotius' letter to G. J. Vossius from 8. Oct. 1620 (*BW* II no. 606, 35) and Stobaeus, *Dicta poëtarum*, prol. ([aiiij^v] — 3): "Iamque ad Lucae finem perveneram, cum admirabili beneficio Dei e vinculis (sc. Lupisteni) exemtus sum."

Gospel of Matthew are by far the most specific, they are the ones most frequently referred to in the commentary.

Occasionally reference is also made to *De imperio summarum potestatum circa sacra*, a work likewise composed in this period but only published after Grotius' death (1647).[165] In a well-documented argumentation it describes the relationship between Church and State in the Erastian sense.

One of the first works by Grotius to be published in Paris is entitled *Dicta poëtarum quae apud Stobaeum extant* (1623).[166] To this Greek author (*c.* 500 AD) we owe numerous otherwise unknown fragments from poets and thinkers from Antiquity. In the Prolegomena to his edition — from which I have quoted above,[167] but which should be read in full in order to do justice to what Grotius aimed at and to the lines along which he thought —, he tells how he started working on his translation of Stobaeus' fragments while a prisoner in The Hague (1618) and continued to work on it at Loevestein.[168] He added two treatises by Plutarch and Basil, likewise with a Latin translation.[169] In these treatises the young are instructed how to deal with poetry, how pronouncements by poets should be compared with those by philosophers, etc. In all probability Grotius was already familiar with Stobaeus' work in 1611, for the *Meletius* contains quite a number of quotations from it. The same goes for Plutarch's *De audiendis poetis*, which Grotius used to enrich his edition. Certain passages in the *Meletius* have unmistakably been written under its influence even though the source is not named.[170] Generally speaking we can safely say that he had long been familiar with Stobaeus' text,[171] and that he made ample use of it in composing his *Meletius*.

---

[165] *TMD* no. 894.

[166] *TMD* no. 458. See also E. M. Meyers, 'Boeken uit de bibliotheek van De Groot in de universiteitsbibliotheek te Leiden', *MKNAW* NR 12 (1949) 251-79.

[167] See above 26ff.

[168] There is an ironic remark in the prolegomena of this work ([aiiij]). He tells us that when he was transferred from the prison in The Hague to Loevestein he had reached title 49. The theme of this is: *De vituperio regni*!

[169] It concerns Plutarch's *De audiendis poetis* (= *Mor.* 17D-37B), translated by Grotius under the titel: *Quomodo iuveni audienda sint poemata* and Basil's *Ad adolescentes de legendis libris gentilium*, translated by Grotius with the title: *Oratio ad iuvenes quomodo cum fructu legere possint Graecorum libros*.

[170] See below, note to *Mel.* 17. His edition was also intended to replace Canter's translation; see prol. ([aiiij]): "quos (sc. versus) autem verterat Canterus Graece Latineque doctissimus, ita verterat ut appareret in carminibus faciendis eum minus fuisse exercitatum." For Canter, see J. A. Gruys, *The Correspondence of Theodorus Canterus (Dirk Canter, 1545-1616). An Inventory*, Nieuwkoop 1978, (*Bibliotheca Bibliographica Neerlandica* 9).

[171] A pointer in this direction is what he communicates in his prol. (aiij^v): "Ego cum alia quae apud Stobaeum extant fragmenta *veneratus sum semper* (italics PM), tum pro meo in artem poeticam affectu singulariter dilexi quas ipsius beneficio servatas habemus

As a supplement to his edition of Stobaeus' *Dicta poëtarum* Grotius published a new collection of ancient texts in 1626, entitled *Excerpta ex tragoediis et comoediis Graecis*.[172] It contains some of the same material, but it is different in that this time it is not arranged by topic but by author.[173] Moreover, Grotius enlarged the material; that of the *comici* by also introducing earlier collections,[174] that of the *tragici* by himself collecting statements from a larger number of pagan and Christian authors, especially the Apologists.[175] In his preface he refers to what he had explained in greater detail in the prolegomena to his previous edition, and he once more emphasizes that material of this kind must be assessed in accordance with the standards laid down by the Prophets and Apostles.[176] Even though we are concerned in this case too with an edition completed much later than the *Meletius*, it stands to reason that he had long been familiar with the subject matter.

De iure belli ac pacis, the masterpiece Grotius published in 1625,[177] also shows clear connections with the *Meletius*. Of course these connections are primarily in the religious parts of *De iure*, but in other respects too the *Meletius* reminds us repeatedly of this work, just as *De iure* elucidates many passages in the *Meletius*.

The inevitable conclusion to be drawn from the comparison of the *Meletius* with Grotius' other works is that it fits in perfectly with the whole of his oeuvre, and that the seeds of many of his later ideas can already be found in it. The commentary will demonstrate this time and again.

---

poetarum reliquias.'' Grotius practised poetry particularly in his younger years, i.e. from 1598 to 1608. Cf. A. C. G. M. Eyffinger, *Grotius Poeta. Aspecten van Hugo Grotius' dichterschap*, (thesis Amsterdam), Den Haag 1981 (= Eyffinger, *Grotius poeta*) 164 ff.

[172] *TMD* no. 468.

[173] Cf. preface, (aij): ''Volo enim hanc nostram collectionem illius Stobaenae quasi supplementum esse; unde et ad Stobaeum illam editionem passim hic te paginis annotatis remittimus. Hoc interest, quod ibi versus in suos locos digesti sunt, hic vero ponuntur sub poëtarum ac fabularum titulis.''

[174] In this he followed Andreas Schottus S. J., who also drew his attention to Canter's textcollection, corrected by Scaliger and Schottus himself. See preface (e - [e^v]), and *BW* II no. 845, 300-04, and nr. 861, 320-21.

[175] Preface, (e): ''... tragicorum quoque nunquam editas antehac reliquias annotaveram, lectis in hoc Platone, Aristotele, et eorum explicatoribus, Philone praeterea, Plutarcho, Sexto Empirico, oratoribus Graecis et oratoriae artis magistris, historiarum scriptoribus, Aeliano, Athenaeo, et tragaediarum atque Aristophanis scholiastis; *Iustino quoque, Theophilo, Athenagora, Clemente aliisque scriptoribus Christianis* (italics PM).'' The last names are all of Christian Apologists.

[176] Preface ([aij^v]): ''quia multa sunt, praesertim de rebus divinis, quae sola rationis indagine ad liquidum perduci nequeunt, quod et Plato agnovit, constituendum de his secundum ea quae olim Hebraeis Prophetae obscurius, nobis autem apertissime Christus et Apostoli eius prodiderunt: a quibus etiam nunc solis petenda est regula vitae Deo placiturae.''

[177] *TMD* no. 565.

9. Sources

When discussing Grotius' edition of Stobaeus I already touched upon the problem of the sources of *Meletius*. In anticipation of what more competent scholars may say in the future I should like to make some general remarks in conclusion.

Particularly in his letter to Dumaurier we find some indication as to Grotius' preference with regard to the authors of Antiquity.[178] This indication is corroborated by the *Meletius*, in which the greater part of the authorities mentioned in this letter are cited. There is hardly any point in reiterating all those names, for they are of secondary importance as such. Of greater relevance is the question to which of these authors should be ascribed an essential role in the composition of the *Meletius*.

This question can be answered by referring primarily to Aristotle, Cicero, Seneca, and Plutarch. In my opinion it is their views which are most strongly incorporated in the work. At the same time we should bear in mind that Grotius was inclined to harmonize the views of his heroes. Boundaries thus tend to fade into one another, and sharp distinctions are made impossible. Setting aside possible subjective motivations — Grotius was deliberately eclectic —, this tendency to harmonize may be connected with the fact that in his religious thought he closely followed the early Christian Apologists who also effected such a harmonization. Very revealing indeed is what he confesses in the Prologue to his *De iure*:

> "For my part, both here and elsewhere I avail myself of the liberty of the early Christians, who had sworn allegiance to the sect of no one of the philosophers, not because they were in agreement with those who said that nothing can be known — than which nothing is more foolish — but because they thought that there was no philosophic sect whose vision had encompassed all truth, and none which had not perceived some aspects of the truth. Thus they believed that to gather up into a whole the truth which was scattered among the different philosophers and dispersed among the sects, was in reality to establish a truly Christian body of teaching."[179]

For telling examples of harmonization from our work I refer to the summary argument for the existence of God, in which Grotius combined

---

[178] See above, 33ff.
[179] Cf. *Iur.* prol. 42 (21): "Ego et hic et alibi veterum Christianorum sequor libertatem, qui in nullius philosophorum sectam iuraverant, non quod eis assentirentur qui nihil percipi posse dicebant, quo nihil est stultius, sed quod nullam esse sectam putarent quae omne verum vidisset, et nullam quae non aliquid ex vero. Itaque veritatem sparsam per singulos, per sectasque diffusam, in corpus colligere, id vero existimabant, nihil esse aliud quam vere christianam tradere disciplinam." From "veritatem sparsam" onwards this is an adapted citation of the 'Christian Cicero', Lactantius (*Inst.* VII 7, 4). For this qualification of Lact., see Charles B. Schmitt, *Cicero Scepticus. A Study of the Influence of the Academia* in the Renaissance, The Hague 1972, 25 n. 20.

Aristotelic and Stoic concepts[180], and to his views of the Creation and the H. Trinity, in which he combined ideas of Aristotle and Plato.[181]

Of Aristotle, whom he quotes more than once not only verbally but also in spirit, Grotius had the profounder knowledge. We see this from the theses he defended in his Leiden years under Pierre Dumoulin, and which, as Sassen pointed out, represent a well-nigh literal translation of passages from Aristotle's *Physics*.[182] The *Meletius* contains evidence of his familiarity with Aristotle's *Metaphysics*, but far more striking is the influence Aristotle's ethical treatises exercised on the work in question, as we see in several places, particularly where Grotius speaks about the nature of evil.[183]

When I was discussing the structure of the *Meletius* and briefly went into the essential distinction Grotius makes between *decreta* and *praecepta (officia)*, I already mentioned Cicero and Seneca.[184] In my opinion the significance of their works for the nature and the content of the *Meletius* can hardly be overestimated. Ever since his youth Grotius was familiar with Seneca. This emerges in his tragedies *Adamus Exul* (1599) and *Christus Patiens* (1608), both modelled on his revered example.[185] The same goes for Cicero, of whose works Grotius had a very thorough knowledge, as is even proved by his choice of words.[186] Certain passages from the *Meletius* are almost unintelligible unless read in conjunction with Cicero. That, for example, is the case with the passage on the supreme good, the intention of which only becomes clear by comparing it with Cicero's *De finibus*.[187] It certainly looks as if Grotius had this work next to him when he was writing the passage, but he does not mention it.

Plutarch has so far been mentioned briefly. The emphasis he lays on ethical and practical activity, his aversion to speculative thinking, and the particular attention he pays to religion, greatly appealed to Grotius, and led him to consult this popular philosopher with pleasure. In the *Meletius* Plutarch's *De audiendis poetis* is referred to more than once. Grotius also got to know some of Plutarch's views through Eusebius.[188]

Besides Plutarch Maximus Tyrius (120-185) should be mentioned as providing a philosophical body of ideas. Some forty popular

---

[180] *Mel.* 6.
[181] *Mel.* 22-23.
[182] F. Sassen, 'Grotius philosophe Aristotélicien', *Grotiana* IX, Amsterdam (1941-'42), 38-53. See also n. 77.
[183] *Mel.* 39.
[184] See above, 35ff.
[185] See Eyffinger, *Grotius poeta*, 8-15, and, by the same author, the introduction to *Dichtwerken* II p. 5a & b, 31 ff.
[186] See, for instance, note to *Mel.* 2.32; *Mel.* 17; *Mel.* 18; *Mel.* 29; *Mel.* 52.
[187] See note to *Mel.* 17.
[188] Cf. *Ver.* I 22, annot. 10 (IV 31a 51-4).

philosophical and ethical essays (*Dissertationes*) from the hand of this itinerant philosopher, who lectured in Athens and Rome under the Emperor Commodus, have been handed down to us. Grotius greatly valued him, quoting him repeatedly and approvingly not only in the *Meletius* but also in *De veritate* and *De iure*.[189] His appreciation is also apparent from the fact that Grotius himself was later to translate one of Maximus' essays into Latin. He grew acquainted with Maximus through the edition Daniel Heinsius had made of this work in 1607, a copy of which is to be found in his library.[190]

As for the Christian authors I have said before that, apart from the works of the Apologists — Justin Martyr, Lactantius[191], Eusebius of Caesarea and Augustine (*De Civitate*)—, the *Meletius* gives no evidence of Grotius having been thoroughly familiar with the writings of the (early) Christian authors at that stage. In any case there are conspicuously few references to Christian writers, in contrast to everything he wrote after the *Meletius*, and in particular to *De veritate*. This raises the question of what actually was the extent of his theological knowledge at the time of the composition of the *Meletius*, and when he acquired it. I shall mention three 'sources'.

In the first place, it should be borne in mind that much of what is nowadays contained within the boundaries of theological specialism was at the time part of culture in general. Grotius, being the eminent participant in this culture that he was, was thoroughly conversant with a number of *theologoumena* as a matter of course.

In the second place, we have the irenical Calvinist Franciscus Junius. In his Leiden years Grotius lived for some time in his house, and this cannot but have greatly influenced his theological development. All his subsequent letters and writings testify to his indebtedness to Junius in this respect.[192]

---

[189] E.g. *Ver.* I 16 (IV 16a 5) and annot. 44 (IV 18a 38-9) and *Iur.* I 2, 8, 16 (79); II 20, 5, 2 (469); II 20, 8, 4 annot. (476); II 20, 10, 6 (484); II 24, 10, 1 (589); III 1, 14, 2 (629).

[190] See Molhuysen, 'Bibliotheek', 55 no. 32. For the different editions of this work, see Paul R. Sellin, *Daniel Heinsius and Stuart England*, with a short-title checklist of the works of Daniel Heinsius, Leiden/London 1968, 232-'33, nos. 260-271. Grotius translated Maximus' *Diss.* 19, under the title: *An data divinatione aliquid sit in nostra potestate*. This piece is part of a larger collection of translated texts, entitled: *Philosophorum sententiae de fato et de eo quod in nostra est potestate*. Cf. *TMD* no. 523sq. J. H. Waszink in his article entitled 'Classical Philology', incorporated in *Leiden University in the Seventeenth Century. An Exchange of Learning*, ed. Th. H. Lunsingh Scheurleer & G. H. M. Posthumus Meyjes, Leiden 1975, 171, qualified Heinsius' edition as 'fairly superficial'.

[191] Works of both authors were in Grotius' possession, see Molhuysen, 'Bibliotheek', nos. 289 and 330.

[192] For a survey of the relationship Junius/Grotius, see Chr. de Jonge, *De irenische ecclesiologie van Franciscus Junius (1545-1602)*, (thesis Leiden), Nieuwkoop 1980, 166-69, and Henk J. M. Nellen, *Hugo de Groot. Erflater*, Weesp [1985], 100 n. 18.

As a third 'source' there is the Frenchman Duplessis-Mornay. In 1581 this well-known Huguenot leader published a voluminous work, *De la vérité de la religion chrestienne*, which was soon translated into several languages and widely circulated.[193] At the beginning of his *De veritate* Grotius mentions it as one of the works he used when preparing his own apologetic treatise of the same title.[194] The correspondence with Walaeus shows that he knew and consulted Duplessis' work when he was composing the *Meletius*.[195] It may be mentioned in passing that when he was writing his *De veritate* Grotius also consulted Raymundus' of Sabund work, the *Liber Creaturarum* — better known as *Theologia naturalis* —, as well as Ludovicus Vives' *De veritate fidei christianae*.[196] I am not able to prove that the former writing (which was praised by Grotius' teacher Scaliger[197]) had any influence on the *Meletius*. As for Vives I am still less certain. His work might have been used by Grotius at the time; for that reason I have referred to it a couple of times in the commentary.

These three 'sources' — besides the apologetic literature, which was in fact Grotius' introduction to Christian theology — may suffice to explain the provenance of the Christian material in the *Meletius*, and at the same time delineate the boundaries of Grotius' theological erudition at this stage in his life.

---

[193] For more details about this work, see Laplanche, *o.c.*, 16 ff.

[194] Cf. *Ver.* I 1 (IV 3a 9-22): "Non enim ignoras (sc. J. Bignon)...quantum excolerint istam materiam philosophica subtilitate Raemundus Sebundus, dialogorum varietate Ludovicus Vives, maxima autem tum eruditione tum facundia vestras Mornaeus...te quidem...facile spero me posse absolvi, si dicam, me lectis non illis tantum, sed et Iudaeorum pro Iudaica vetere, et Christianorum pro Christiana religione scriptis, uti voluisse..."

[195] See above n. 134.

[196] See above n. 133.

[197] Cf. Scaliger to Casaubon (30. Aug. 1603) (in Scaliger, *Opuscula varia antehac non edita*, Paris. 1610, 498-99): "Addebas de quibusdam in Petri Galathini disputationibus. Scito illos libros esse compendium duorum ingentium voluminum, quibus titulum Pugionem fidei fecit auctor Raimundus Sebon, monachus Dominicanus, eximius philosophus, sed nimis allegoriis et anagogis indulgens, ut non solum ille *Pugio fidei* ostendit, sed et liber *De theologia naturali*. Ii igitur libri adhuc extant in collegio Fuxensi Tolosano, ex quibus omnia hausit Petrus Galathinus Franciscanus, qui nomen auctoris tacuit, vel ut sibi opus vindicaret, vel quia acerrimum semper intercessit inter Dominicanam familiam et Franciscanam odium..." Scaliger confuses here Raimundus Martini O.P. († 1284), author of the widely disseminated and very influential *Pugio fidei adversus Mauros et Iudaeos*, with Raimund of Sabund, author of the by no means less known *Liber creaturarum* (= *Theologia naturalis*). Otherwise he is right in stating that Petrus Galatinus O. F. M. († 1540), when preparing his *De arcanis catholicae veritatis* (Ortona 1518), never admitted having plundered Raimundus' Martini *Pugio*. See A. Kleinhans, s.v. Raimundus Martini in *LThK* VIII 363. A fine edition of Raimund of Sabund, *Theologia naturalis seu liber creaturarum*, is that of Friedrich Stegmüller, Stuttgart — Bad Cannstatt 1966.

10. *Explanatory remarks on textual form and translation*

In § 2 above the most relevant facts about the manuscript and text of the *Meletius* and the design of the present edition have been indicated. They can be summed up as follows:

— The editor is responsible for the arrangement into chapters and paragraphs.

— Marginal Latin translations of Greek quotations and terms in the text are printed in italics and inserted into the text between round brackets.

— Whenever Greek quotations were absent in the text, they have been traced by means of the Latin translations in the margin and inserted in the text between square brackets.

— Other marginal notes have been put in a separate list.

— The underlinings, probably applied by Grotius himself, have also been listed separately.

— Spelling and punctuation have been modernized.

— The use of capitals has been reduced and made uniform.

— Where Grotius gave a Latin translation of a Greek quotation it was obviously superfluous to give this quotation twice in English. In those cases the English translation is based on the Latin translation by Grotius, even if it is not always entirely correct or complete.

— In translating the quotations from classical authors use has occasionally been made of the relevant volumes of *Loeb's Classical Library*.

TEXT AND TRANSLATION

MELETIUS

SIVE

DE IIS QUAE INTER CHRISTIANOS CONVENIUNT EPISTOLA

[INTRODUCTIO]

1 Saepenumero ego ex te, amicorum clarissime, cum alia utilia permulta, tum illud longe iucundissimum audire me memini, cum in ultimis Asiae locis degeres, quo alios quidem lucri, te vero discendi cupido detulerat, ibi si quis tibi occurreret ex his nostrae Europae partibus, non aliter a te exceptum quam populares, imo quam consanguinei solent. Scilicet tibi illud naturae bonitas et humanitatis studia suadebant. Sed alioqui etiam aliis id evenire credibile est, quia coniunctionem illam, quae in turba perire solet atque consumi, infrequentia et raritas, et externa circum omnia commendant. Itaque nos qui hic vivimus non modo peregrinos arbitramur Europaeos caeteros, sed Germani in supernates atque infernates distinguimur. Infernates primum belli vixdum sopiti memoria dividit, mox alii Geldri, Frisii alii, quin Hollandos Zelandosque coniunctissimas semper nationes utinam nomina tantum, non etiam affectus discernerent. Taceo nunc urbes plus quam aemulas, et in urbibus vicorum factiones, domuumque magnarum certamina, quae cum inspicimus, non est dubium, quin alieniores et vicini et propinqui inter se videantur, quam tibi in Syria degenti, aut Itali, aut ipsi denique Hispani.

2 Idem video in religione accidisse. Ex quo enim christianum nomen se latissime diffudit, et fracta inimicorum vi inter se opinionibus primum, mox animis dissentire vacuum fuit, varia et nomina et studia nasci coepere, quae Christianis Christianos tam alienos facerent, quam non Christiani Christianis fuerant. Coepit iam olim ille morbus, sed patrum nostraque aetate eo excrevit, ut amplius quo procedat non habeat. Non enim frigus animorum nec simultates modo, sed odia iraeque implacabiles et, quod vix ante auditum, bella haud alio magis obtentu sumta, quam religionis eius, cuius propositum pax est. At si aut Indos illos, ad quos felicissime navigamus, aut quibus cum tu vixisti Turcas, aut qui nunc se nobis inserunt Iudaeos respicere liberet, deberemus vel illorum comparatione in animum revocare oblitam prope necessitudinem. Quomodo enim nos non coniungit, quod nos omnes ab illis aut omnibus aut singulis separat?/

3 Si christianam appellationem sibi quisque seclusis aliis vindicat, saltem aliud quaeratur nomen quod nos pariter ab illorum quos dixi profanitate secludat. Sed aliud profecto non invenietur quam illud ipsum a Magistro

inditum, cui tum quoque, cum per ignorantiam non paremus, parere   35
tamen nos omnes profitemur. Nihil esse tam magnum ad discordiam
potest, quin hoc ipsum ad concordiam maius sit, doctorem unum sequi,
et quidem eum, qui discipulos non agnoscat, nisi colentes concordiam.
Itaque ego adversus nova quotidie dissidia et alios in fluctibus fluctus
consolari me et recreare soleo eorum cogitatione, quae Christianis hacte-   40
nus Dei beneficio integra manserunt, quae cum sint et maxima et certissima et utilissima, facile apud me tantum valent ut, dum illa considero,
minora alia et incertiora nec aeque utilia interim seponam. Saltem illa
nos, ut ita dicam, privilegia cives unius esse civitatis evincant.

4   Qua de re utinam tecum ut olim saepe cum una essemus, ita nunc   45
quoque disserere liceret. Quicum enim libentius hac de re loquar, quam
cum eo qui raro exemplo ostenderis veram iurisprudentiam non humanarum tantum, sed et divinarum rerum notitiam complecti, quique et
hostes christianitatis optime noris veteres novosque, Graecis et Hebraeis
literis abunde instructus, et ipsas Christianorum sectas penitus inspexe-   50
ris, non has modo in quas nos scindimur, sed Graecos, Armenios, Maro-
nitas, quos inter tu cum viveres, etsi in plerisque rectius quam ipsi senti-
res, non tamen continuo aut tu illis non Christianus aut illi tibi non
videba<n>tur.

5   Nunc cum et locorum intervalla et munerum necessitas nos una esse   55
non patiantur, conscribam illa quae tibi saepe Patriarcham Meletium
exponere solitum aiebas, sed ea lege, ut tu qui rectius nosti, mutes et cor-
rigas; neque enim dubito quin et tibi suave futurum sit ista in memoriam
revocare et mihi fructuosum eadem perfectius ex te discere. Ille igitur
Patriarcha quidem Alexandrinus, sed et Constantinopolitanam ecclesiam   60
regens, vir venerandae sanctitatis et in omni eruditionis genere versatis-
simus—nam et Latine, quod Graecis hominibus insolitum, loquebatur,
et clarissimos eius linguae scriptores cunctos evolverat—, tum vero
amantissimus pacis christianae, non sine lachrymis detestari nostra dissidia solebat, et orare ut aliquando oculos mutuo aspectu efferatos ad Tur-   65
2ʳ cas et Barbaro-/rum gentium colluviem verteremus. Urgebat autem
praecipue τὰ τοῖς χριστιανοῖς ὁμολογούμενα (*ea de queis inter Christianos consentitur*), quae et plura esse dicebat et maioris multo momenti quam vulgo
putarentur, una opera ostendens esse in iis quaecunque in ulla philosophorum schola aut populorum institutis optima haberentur, et praeter   70
haec propria multa coeteris omnibus incognita, quae ille quidem singu-
lari facundia ornabat, nos autem qua possumus diligentia persequemur.

66   *Barbarorum*] ms. Barbari-/2ʳ/orum

I

6 Habet igitur hoc primum in se christianitas, quod religione utitur communi quidem cum multis, non tamen cum omnibus. Impii enim et quos ἀθέους dicimus hoc limite arcentur. Religio autem nulla sine duobus illis quae ad Hebraeos apostolus commemorat, ut credatur esse Deus, deinde remunerari eos, qui ipsi placere studeant. Esse Deum non modo consensus hominum latissime patens, sed et ordo ex se dependentium causarum rerumque gradus clarissime testantur. Quare huius rei veritas tam manifesta est, ut tot saeculis paucissimi fuerint, qui aliud dixerint, magis forte quod mallent rem se non ita habere quam quod ita sentirent.

7 Ut autem remunerator sit Deus, quaedam necesse est ante statui. Requiritur enim primo ut sit Deus intelligens natura, quod hoc ipso satis evincitur, quia non potest res facta suo factore esse nobilior. Non igitur aut mundus aut quae vulgo natura rerum dicitur Deus est, sed celsius et augustius quiddam. Nec intellectum tantum, sed et voluntatem, et quam vocant προαίρεσιν habere debet Deus. Sunt enim quae haec habent non habentibus perfectiora. Et ea ipsa voluntas debet esse libera nec impedita, quia et hoc ad perfectionem pertinet et per naturam fieri non potest ut suprema causa aliqua alia sit superior; quae ratio Stoicos refellit stultissima peruasione Deum sub fati necessitate ponentes. Unde ille impius versus:

Quod fore paratum est, id summum exsuperat Iovem.

Diversus ab hoc minus insanus magorum veterum error eadem opera refellitur, qui conceptis quibusdam verbis aliisve rebus cogi Deum posse dicebant, quae omnia Deum voce ponunt, re tollunt.

8 Statuendum praeterea Deum curare res a se factas nec tantum coelestes, ut quidam voluere, verum etiam humanas, qua sententia Epicureos excludimus, qui si hoc dixissent, inspicere Deum ac regere omnia sine ulla molestia, nihil errassent. Nunc foedissime/lapsi sunt, putantes usum intellectus ac voluntatis molestum esse, quo tamen nihil est suavius, praesertim si omnipotentiam addideris. Nam quae sunt in regendo difficultates, eas regentium imbecillitas facit. Crudeles sunt patres qui liberos genuisse contenti exponunt. Deus autem nisi bonus est, Deus non est. Adde quod ordo universi admirabilis non conditorem modo, sed et rectorem Deum loquitur. Nihil autem minus regium quam viliora regni curare, partes autem nobilissimas extra curam ponere.

9 Ut autem remunerationi locus sit illud quoque tenendum est, esse hominem ζῶον λόγικον καὶ προαιρετικόν. Quod si est, ut ipsa docet experientia, hinc etiam fatum illud Stoicorum tollatur necesse est. Si enim omnia futura ex causis penderent necessariis, frustra condita esset vis deliberativa in homine et voluntas in utrunque versatilis. Frustra autem

esse quicquam statuere in rerum natura, maximeque in homine, hoc est imperitiae arguere naturae auctorem.

10   Sequitur porro ut Deum esse legislatorem fateamur. Nam si προαίρεσιν (*praeelectionem*) habet Deus, habet et homo. Deus autem superior est, homo inferior. Et superiora agunt in inferiora, prout superiora agere et inferiora pati nata sunt. Consequens est Deum κατὰ προαίρεσιν (*secundum praeelectionem*) agere in hominem. Haec autem actio προαιρετικοῦ (*praeelectivi*) superioris in προαιρετικόν (*praeelectivum*) inferius, qua tale est, utcumque nihil aliud est quam lex sive imperium. Verum autem hoc esse sensus conscientiae omnibus argumentis validius convincit.

11   His positis id quod de remuneratione dictum est facillime conficitur. Iustum enim est legem servanti praemium, violanti poenam tribuere. Deus autem iustus est et iuste agit. Ad hoc legislator omnis servari expetit suas leges. Adhibet igitur ea omnia quae hoc efficere possunt, quae quidem in ipsius sunt facultate. Nihil autem est efficacius quam obsequium praemio invitare. Et potest Deus praemia tribuere, quod legislatores humani saepe non possunt. Tribuit igitur.

12   Haec illa sunt principia quae communia habet christiana religio et cum falsis omnibus, et cum veris quidem, sed minus perfectis, qualis est primum naturalis religio, inde mosaïca. Haec qui tollit, is vere dici potest religionem tollere, rem in mundo maximam. Quid enim utilius meliusve quam honesta rectaque omnia ab hominibus non fieri modo, verum etiam cogitari? Leges autem humanae id praestare non possunt, ut quas

3ʳ   non cogitationes modo, sed et facta pleraque effugiant. Religio autem / potest, et quidem sola.

Expedit esse deos et, ut expedit, esse putemus,

ait poeta. Nos verius: expedit esse religionem, est igitur religio. Non omisit enim sapientissimus rector instituere ea quae maxime expediunt.

II

13   Veniamus ad propiora et, ut omnibus quae fiunt κατὰ προαίρεσιν, necesse est finem primo investigemus. Finis rei optimae optimus, at est religio res omnium optima. Finis igitur eius simpliciter optimus sive summum bonum. Quod autem sit summum bonum sive beatitudo hominis, inter philosophos diu summis contentionibus certatum. Christiana religio idem quod recta ratio monstrat, summum hominis bonum esse quam perfectissime frui eo qui per se est summum bonum, id autem est Deus.

14   Ut enim unam esse causam effectricem infiniti progressus impatiens natura nos docet, ita per eandem monemur propter unum uniusque causa esse omnia. Frui autem Deo non possumus nisi eo quod ad Deum

proxime accedit, mente scilicet. Sed cum beatitudo non partis sed totius sit hominis, sequitur caeteras animi partes ipsumque corpus menti perfectissime inserviendo participes fieri istius beatitudinis. Posito autem bono plenissimo necesse est removeri mala omnia; erit igitur coniuncta cum hac summa felicitate et indolentia et immortalitas.

15   Hinc apparet falli eos omnes qui in hac fragili vita summum hominis bonum quaesivere. Est quidem quod summum huius vitae bonum dici potest: inchoata nimirum Dei fruitio, cum certa spe vitae alterius. Sed simpliciter summum id bonum dici non potest, cui adsit et mortis expectatio et dolorum perpessio. Errarunt igitur philosophi omnes, etiam qui, quod omnium maxime est plausibile, in virtute huius tamen vitae bonum quaesiverunt. Nec mirum igitur, si paucos viros bonos imo nullos vere bonos fecere, cum persuasionibus falsis uterentur. Falsum enim est illud quo solo nituntur, expetendam propter se virtutem, quod certissima ratio refellit. Versatur enim virtus circa molesta maxime. At molestias nemo suscipit nisi propter aliud; unde rectius alii hoc ipso certissime probari dixere, vitam post hanc esse alteram, quia in hac vita plerumque bonis male, malis bene est.

> *Eurystheus facili regnet in otio;*
> *Alcmena genitus bella per omnia*
> *monstris exagitet coeliferam manum.*/

16   Sequitur etiam hinc falli et eos, qui vitam quidem statuunt alteram, sed summam beatitudinem collocant aut in victu potuque, ut Iudaei thalmudici, aut in veneris usu, ut Mahumetistae, cum Christiani et hoc et illud e vita beata eximant, ut indigentiae signa; τὸ δὲ εὐδαῖμον ἀνενδεές. Pecudum ista forte bona sunt, hominis neutiquam, in quo cum sit animus corpore praestantior, ut vera contingat felicitas, corpus animo assimilari, non animus corpori debet, et fieri σῶμα πνευματικόν (*corpus spirituale*), non πνεῦμα σωματικόν (*spiritus corporalis*). Vidit hoc partim Aristoteles, qui in Eudemicis: [ἥτις οὖν αἵρεσις], inquit, [καὶ κτῆσις τῶν φύσει ἀγαθῶν ποιήσει μάλιστα τὴν τοῦ θεοῦ θεωρίαν, ἢ σώματος ἢ χρημάτων ἢ φίλων ἢ τῶν ἄλλων ἀγαθῶν, αὕτη ἀρίστη, καὶ οὗτος ὁ ὅρος κάλλιστος· ἥτις δ' ἢ δι' ἔνδειαν ἢ δι' ὑπερβολὴν κωλύει τὸν θεὸν θεραπεύειν καὶ θεωρεῖν, αὕτη δὲ φαύλη. ἔχει δὲ τοῦτο τῇ ψυχῇ, καὶ οὗτος τῆς ψυχῆς ὅρος ἄριστος, τὸ ἥκιστα αἰσθάνεσθαι τοῦ ἀλόγου μέρους τῆς ψυχῆς, ᾗ τοιοῦτον.] (*Quae igitur possessio electioque eorum quae naturaliter bona sunt magis id efficit ut consuleretur Deus, quam aut corpus aut pecuniae aut amici aut bona coetera: haec sane optima est isque terminus pulcherrimus. Quod si qua talis est quae per copiam impediat Deum colere atque considerare; haec vero mala est. Id vero ad animam pertinet, isque animae praestantissimus finis: quam minimum sentire alteram illam atque inferiorem animae partem, qua talis est*).

17   Illud quoque animadversione non indignum, quae alii singula singuli

summum esse bonum voluerunt, ea in summo Christianorum bono cuncta reperiri. Nam sive voluptatem quaeras, aut eam quae in statu est et indolentia vocatur, cum Hieronymo philosopho, aut cum Cyrenaicis, eam quae in motu est, utrunque hic est et doloris omnis vacuitas, et suavissimus, non corporum — id enim animum impedit — sed animorum motus gaudiumque et laetitia; seu cum Stoicis virtus placet, et hic vera est, addita insuper ea, quam virtuti Aristoteles coniungit perfectae vitae prosperitate.

18   Ex hac summi boni ad totum hominem pertinentis perfectissima natura Epicureos simul et partem Iudaeorum Sadducaeos refellimus. Sequitur enim ex ante positis corpus humanum aut nunquam interire aut revicturum, animum quoque aut revicturum aut interire nunquam. At corpora interire monstrat experientia; reviviscent igitur. Animum vero non interire cum philosophis plerisque — nam Epicurei, ut veterum quidam dicebat, non aliter philosophi dicuntur quam homo pictus homo dicitur — sentit christiana religio, adstipulante non modo vetustissima / omnium prope gentium fide, sed ipsa etiam ratione qua discimus in animo mentem esse, Dei imaginem, perpessionis expertem. Reperto fine religionis, quibus in rebus ea consistat, videamus.

III

19   Religio igitur, cum in actione versetur ea quae est κατὰ προαίρεσιν, omnes autem voluntatis actiones intellectus praecedat, necessario duas habet partes: θεωρητικήν unam, πρακτικήν alteram; illam constituunt δόγματα, hanc παραινέσεις. Latine decreta et praecepta vertit post Ciceronem Seneca, in quibus duobus omnem de moribus deque officiis doctrinam sitam esse demonstrant. Decreta interdum et placita et scita et sententiae vocantur. Decreta in omni scientia activa nec extra rem esse debent nec supervacua, sed quae aut ad agendum incitent aut quid agendum sit et quomodo, aliquatenus praemonstrent. Quare, cum religio inter hominem Deumque intercedat, decreta religionis ad Deum et divina, hominem et humana pertinent, non qua in se sunt modo, sed qua se mutuo respiciunt.

20   Inter haec decreta primum merito locum obtinet Deum esse unum, quod ex iisdem argumentis convincitur, quibus Deum esse credimus. Omnia enim ab uno et propter unum; tum perfectissima Dei natura et beatitudo rerumque omnium regimen idem requirunt. At quantam

60   *perfectae*] ms. perfecta
3   θεωρητικήν] ms. θεωρικήν
13   *obtinet*] ms. obtinent

humani generis partem inexcusabilis ille πολυθεότητος error obsedit olim, atque etiamnum obsidet!

21 Praeterea quicquid praestantissimum omnino aut dici aut cogitari potest, id christiana religio Deo tribuit, caetera removens. Asserit igitur Deum esse simplicissimum, infinitum, optimum; contra corporeum, compositum, mutabilem, terminatum aut loco aut tempore destricte negat. Ita Plutarchus Iudaeos ait credere θεὸν ἄφθαρτον, ἀγέννητον, εὐποιητικόν; Tacitus *unum numen, summum et aeternum neque mutabile neque interiturum.*

22 In hac igitur una et simplici natura primum id ipsum quod est esse intelligitur; secundo ratio divina; tertio virtus, quae duo et Aristoteles in Deo notasse videtur, appellans νοῦν καὶ ἐνέργειαν. Nisi enim haec haberet, esset rebus a se factis imperfectior. Ratio illa λόγος et σοφία vocatur quidem et a Platonicis, sed et res ipsa et nomina a Christianis clarius explicantur. Rursum ipsa Dei virtus apud Christianos et hoc nomine vocatur

4v / et Spiritus, quae vox non modo τὸ ἀσώματον, sed vero et τὸ ἐνεργετικόν designat. Sunt autem haec in Deo non ut partes nec ut qualitates, sed alio quodam modo ineffabili ita inter se distincta, ut τρεῖς ὑποστάσεις unus sint Deus, ὥστε ταὐτὸν, inquit Aristoteles, νοῦς καὶ νοητόν (*ita ut idem sit mens et quod mente intelligitur*).

23 Haec ita se in Deo habere, quanquam humana ratio reperire quidem per se non potuit, ubi tamen audit assentit facile. Videt enim congruere hoc omne divinae maiestati, nec terrere eam ab assensu debet, quod modum quo ista tria sint unumque non capiat, cum et in animo nostro, qui tanto est inferior, et ipsam animi naturam et intellectum et voluntatem agnoscamus, et tamen animum unum quam maxime fateamur et impartibilem. Sunt et in sole; novimus et sidus ipsum et lucem et vim igneam, nec tamen dividimus in plures, qui ideo quod solus est nomen accepit.

24 Cum vero intellectus sit perfectio scire quam plurima, voluntatis autem virtus optima velle atque operari, sequitur Deum sapientia esse omniscium, virtute optimum, ac proinde quae mala sunt scire quidem, non tamen aut velle proprie aut facere, quod maximum pietatis fundamentum est. Abeant igitur poetae, soli olim theologiae magistri, quos Plato, Varro aliique summo iure reprehenderunt, quod ea quae hominibus quoque foeda essent, de diis suis narrarent, pugnas, adulteria aliaque facinora. Abeant et impiae voces:

αἰαῖ [, τοδ' ἤδη θεῖον ἀνθρώποις κακόν
ὅταν τις εἰδῇ τ'ἀγαθόν, χρῆται δὲ μή.]
(*ah, ah, et illud in Deo verum est malum,
ubi quis videt meliora, non sequitur tamen.*)

Item:
> [θεὸς μὲν αἰτίαν φύει βροτοῖς,
> ὅταν κακῶσαι δῶμα παμπήδην θέλῃ.]
> (*proserit culpam Deus*
> *saevire quotiens in domos tutas libet.*)

Cui par illud:
> *Crimen erit superis et me fecisse nocentem.*

Item:
> *Hoc placet, o superi, vobis cum vertere cuncta*
> *propositum, nostris erroribus addere crimen?*

Tollit religionem ista opinio. Quomodo enim et Deum amare potest, et malum odisse, qui Deum mali credit auctorem? Illud ergo verius:
> εἰ θεοί τι δρῶσιν αἰσχρόν, οὐκ εἰσὶν θεοί./

Et Cleanthis:
> [Οὐδέ τι γίγνεται ἔργον ἐπὶ χθονὶ σοῦ δίχα, δαῖμον,
> οὔτε κατ' αἰθέριον θεῖον πόλον, οὔτ' ἐνὶ πόντῳ,
> πλὴν ὁπόσα ῥέζουσιν κακοὶ σφετέραισιν ἀνοίαις.]
> (*Ni per te, deus alme, nihil fit per sola terrae.*
> *Perque sali fluctus, perque altitonantia regna,*
> *praeter sponte malis sua quae vecordia saevit*).

25 Et tamen haec ipsa mala, quae a Deo non fiunt, ab ipso tamen et curari et dirigi tum recta ratio, tum christiana religio docet. Summi autem usus sunt in religione credita Dei omniscientia et perfectissima bonitas. Omniscientia enim hoc efficit ut in omnibus secretissimis, non factis modo, verum et cogitatis, Deum revereamur praesentem; bonitas autem, ut et ipsi boni esse nitamur, iuxta illud Pythagoricum ἕπου θεῷ et Christi illud: *Estote perfecti sicut Pater vester perfectus est*. Omnia autem quae de Deo dicta sunt in unum collecta hoc efficiunt, ut ipsum ob naturam perfectissimam admirari, ob mentem sapientissimam honorare, ob bonitatem denique eximiam amare ante omnia debeamus.

26 Iam vero si Deum non modo qualis in se est consideres, sed ἐν σχέσει quam habet ad res alias, duo de Deo haec eadem religio perhibet: factorem esse rerum omnium et rectorem. Factorem esse iisdem liquet argumentis quibus Deus esse convincitur, causarum nimirum serie, quae nisi in una prima quiescere non potest; cui accedit, quod hoc ipsum et Deo est honorificentius, et ad pietatem conducibilius. Cum igitur Plato genitum vult mundum, Aristoteles aeternum, errant sane, at ipsorum argumenta hoc ipsum probant, quod Christiani credimus. Nam et Plato recte colligit coepisse aliquando mundum, nec minus recte Aristoteles non esse genitum; sequitur ergo ut factus sit.

27 Et cum mundum dicimus, non tantum ea quae videntur comprehendimus et inter haec hominem, sed et ἀόρατα, mentes nimirum sive naturas

Deo inferiores, superiores homine, intelligentes atque operantes, quas deos et δαίμονας multi vocavere. Δαίμονας quidem ob intellectus praestantiam, deos autem improprie. Nam si πολυθεότης certis rationibus explosa est, sequitur hos non proprie deos dici, sed propter quandam participationem divinae maiestatis; qua in parte Christianorum magistri ut e<or>um errorem radicitus exciderent, qui ut appellationis, ita honoris similitudine opera haec opifici aequaverant, verbo quoque abstinere et angelos dicere maluerunt, ut ipsius Dei non socii, sed ministri intelligerentur.

28   Fecisse autem docetur Deus omnia sui causa, nam, ut modo dicebamus, non modo effectrix causa, sed et finis omnium rerum ultimus unus idemque / esse debet, certo tamen ordine. Atque adeo, ut rectissime Stoici dixere, coetera omnia hominis causa, hominem simpliciter sui causa fecit Deus. Quod esse verissimum hinc intelligitur, quia non potest dominus esse rerum aliarum, nisi qui ipse actionum suarum sit dominus, hoc est, qui προαίρεσιν habeat. Hanc autem non habent res factae aliae praeter hominem et illas quas diximus mentes. Harum autem mentium ea est natura ut rerum aliarum usum non desiderent. Restat igitur ut hominis causa facta sit et terra et mare et aër et ignis et bestiae et quae ex terra nascuntur, coelum denique ipsum et sidera.

29   Rectorem autem Deum cum dicimus, non tantum Epicureorum tollimus fortuitos concursus, sed et Stoicorum vim fatalem, ex aequo nocentia pietati dogmata. Regendo enim servat Deus, non corrumpit institutam a se naturam rerum ac praesertim tributam mentibus προαίρεσιν. Unde illa solvitur quae diutissime philosophos exercuit quaestio τοῦ θεοῦ τὰ ἀγαθὰ διδόντος, πόθεν τὰ κακά; Nimirum ἐκ τῆς προαιρέσεως, quae ipsa cum a Deo data sit bona certe est, sed potest sua sponte ad malum prolabi, Deo quidem et vetante et dissuadente, non tamen per vim impediente, ne semel recte datam libertatem auferat, sine qua nec praemium potest consistere. Malum igitur sive peccatum ex liberrima et mentium illarum simpliciorum et hominum voluntate processit, a lege opificis sui sponte desciscentium; qua in parte Manichaeis eorumque similibus occurritur, qui aut materiam aut aliud quoddam necessarium mali statuunt principium, et quosdam a natura ita esse factos, ut boni aut esse aut fieri nullo modo possint. Istae enim persuasiones et in Deum contumeliosae sunt et hominibus verum super peccatis dolorem et studium resipiscendi auferunt.

30   Veniamus ad ea quae de homine sunt decreta, quorum quaedam iam ante attigimus: constare eum corpore et mente; habere vim προαιρετικήν; nobilissimum esse atque dignissimum omnium quae videntur rerum, imo et rerum aliarum dominum. Addamus factum esse a Deo procul dubio bonum, neque enim potest is qui optimus est malum facere; imo,

ut et philosophorum quidam christianae doctrinae congruenter dixerunt, effigiem quandam Dei esse hominem, conditum scilicet ad ipsum Dei exemplar, et quidem cum facultate, ut ad ipsum id exemplar connitendo propius propiusque posset accedere. Iam vero ab initio non plures, sed unum factum esse hominem, inde genitos coeteros ideo verius est, quia melius et ad mutuam charitatem atque amicitiam efficacius, quippe cum et iurisconsulti *nefas esse insidiari hominem homini* hoc ipso validissime probent, quod *cognationem inter nos / quandam natura constituerit.*

31   Πάθη quoque homini esse a Deo indita contra Stoicos solos cum philosophis aliis Christiani rectissime sentiunt, ipsa sane hominis natura hoc ipsum demonstrante, in qua certa membra, qui fontes sint atque sedes τῶν παθῶν, etiam medicis enumerantur. Haec quoque sententia non parum ad pietatem facit; contraria enim doctrina, nisi de verbis pertinaciter cum usu litigat, facit ἀστόργους καὶ ἀνελεήμονας.

32   Σχέσις autem hominis ad Deum haec est, quam et ante attigimus, quod in hoc factus sit, ut Deum colat. Quod ipsum et philosophis omnibus diximus placuisse, nec male nonnulli ex ipsa humani corporis constitutione idem colligunt, quae et recta est et coelum respicit. Unde antiquissimi Phoenicum theologi hominem [Ζοφασημίν] hoc est οὐρανόσκοπον dixere.

33   Quomodo enim non ob hoc potissimum factus esset homo, ut faceret quod et poterat et maxime debebat? Poterat autem Deum colere, nam ideo mentis usum acceperat, et debebat, non modo ob praestantissimam Dei naturam, sed insuper ob beneficia ab ipso accepta, quod scilicet per eum homo esse coeperat, quod erat rebus aliis nobilior, quod denique res tantae ipsius commodis inservire iussae erant. Colere autem Deum haec omnia complectitur: ipsum amare, admirari, vereri, cupere ipsi placere, timere ne displiceas, odisse quae ipsius legi sunt contraria; quae omnia, cum παθῶν sint nomina, hoc ipsum quod ante dictum est probant, non debere ea ex homine evelli. Neque enim sufficit opus praeceptum praestare, nisi hoc ipsum facias pronissima animi totius omniumque partium contentione. Qualis homo esse debeat in summa dictum est.

34   Nunc ad ea decreta veniamus, quae id quod est, experientia adstipulante, definiunt. Statuitur ergo longe aliter se habere hominem quam habere debeat: esse enim ingratum adversus Deum et vere malum. Cum enim ante omnia amare et colere Deum debeat omni animi nisu, illum rebus omnibus praeferre, illius immensa beneficia grate aestimare, contra tamen fieri conscientia sua cuique testis est.

35   Adde quod Deus secundum semetipsum nullam rem esse homini commendatiorem voluerit atque hominem alterum, quippe ut cognatum hominis et imaginem suam. Utrunque enim ratio docet, et communis originis atque sanguinis summam esse coniunctionem atque necessitudinem, et, si, grati esse velimus, non eum modo amandum qui nos summis

affecerit beneficiis, sed et eos qui ipsum proximitate aliqua contingant. Contra autem videmus fervere odiis atque dissensionibus omnia. Quin plurimae actiones,/ etiam quae bonae nobis videntur, vitiosae sunt, quia vitiosum est quod parte aliqua suae rectitudinis destituitur, bonum autem nihil est, nisi quod integre bonum: καλὸν μὲν γὰρ ἁπλῶς, παντοδαπῶς δὲ κακόν (*simplex est bonitas, at mala multis modis*). Ubi igitur non est animus purus atque integer et firmissimum propositum Deo inserviendi, ibi κατόρθωμα (*perfectum officium*) sive recta esse actio non potest.

36   Neque vero mirum adeo videri debet hominem ad deteriora prolapsum, cum innumera malefacta vim huius inferioris naturae excedentia, quorum testes sunt omnium gentium historiae, manifeste evincant, etiam ex mentibus illis nobilioribus quasdam ad prava se vertisse, quas deinde consequens est omnibus modis allaborasse, ut et hominem in consortium suae malitiae perducerent; effectumque id eo facilius, quia sensus qui sunt in homine quot virtutis sunt materiae, totidem ad peccandum praebent illecebras. Sparsam autem per omne genus humanum hanc pravitatem, si non singulis sua dictaret conscientia, ipsa communis hominum miseria et natura facta ipsi pro matre noverca ostenderent. Neque enim φιλάνθρωπος Deus tam obnoxiam aerumnis hominum vitam pateretur, nisi culpae omnes inveniret obnoxios.

37   Interim Stoicorum alius error merito a Christianis reiicitur, peccata omnia esse aequalia, quod falsum esse conscientia ipsa clamat, quae pro delictorum magnitudine magis minusve nos reos agit. Quippe et leges ipsae inter se inaequales sunt pro materiae diversitate, alia superior, inferior alia. Et ab eadem lege aliud factum alio longius abit, sicut et in obliquis lineis, non quia omnes a recta recedunt, iccirco par etiam omnium est obliquitas. Neque tamen non gravis per se censenda est culpa, etiam si qua cum aliis collecta levissima est.

38   Habet enim hoc omne peccatum, quod eo Rex summus, Pater optimus, benefactor liberalissimus offenditur, et quidem ab homine quem ille rebus omnibus praetulit et tot eximiis donis ornavit. Cum ergo homines omnes extra legem Dei exorbitent, sequitur hinc primum omnes mancipia esse vitiorum, deinde obstrictos poenae, quae quidem poena κατὰ τὸ ἔννομον tanta esse debuit, quantum manebat praemium legis observatores.

39   Prius illud decretum hinc fluit, quod omne vitium in praeceps ducat. Τὸ ἀγνοεῖν, inquit Aristoteles, ὅτι ἐκ τοῦ ἐνεργεῖν περὶ ἕκαστα αἱ ἕξεις γίγνονται κομιδῇ ἀναισθήτου (*sensu plane carentis est ignorare circa res singulas ex operationibus fieri habitus*), quod ille duobus exemplis explicat: lapidis nimirum iacti, quem qui iecit antequam iaceret, in manu sua habuit et non iacere potuit, postea vero iactum revocare non licet;/ ac praeterea

hominis ex intemperantia et neglectu medicorum aegrotantis, in cuius potestate fuit non aegrotare, nunc autem non est amplius. Deinde addit egregie: [οὕτω δὲ καὶ τῷ ἀδίκῳ καὶ τῷ ἀκολάστῳ ἐξ ἀρχῆς μὲν ἐξῆν τοιούτοις μὴ γενέσθαι, διὸ ἑκόντες εἰσίν γενομένοις δ'οὐκέτι ἔξεστι μὴ εἶναι.] (*sic et iniusto et intemperanti ab initio licuit non fieri talibus, unde et sponte sunt tales, postquam autem facti sunt tales, non licet illis amplius talibus non esse*). Seneca quoque non ineleganter: *inter coetera mortalitatis incommoda et haec est caligo mentium nec tantum necessitas errandi sed errorum amor.*

40   Adde quod Deus auxilium suum, quod homini maxime necessarium est ad recte secundum Deum vivendum, merito subtrahit his qui perfide a se desciverunt. Praeter haec, quae et in principibus fuerunt humani generis, accedunt in posteris prava genitura, prava educatio, prava exempla undique.

41   Haec doctrina longe saluberrima est, nam et Dei bonitatem illustrat, quod amare homines perseveraverit, etiam pessime meritos, et in homine id efficit quod tutissimum est, ut submisse de se sentiat, quod ipsum in omnibus fere philosophis desideres. Nemo enim illorum homines ita reos agit, et ad ταπεινοφροσύνην adducit atque religio christiana. Est et hic usus, quod facilius aliis ignoscit, qui se quoque meminit non innocentem. Seneca: *Si volumus aequi rerum omnium iudices esse, hoc primum nobis suadeamus, neminem nostrum esse sine culpa.*

42   Damnamus igitur Stoicorum θεομαχίαν, e quorum numero Sextius *Iovem plus posse* negabat *quam bonum virum*; Deum *non* vincere *sapientem felicitate etiam si vincat aetate.* Quin eousque processit insaniae, ut Deum antecedi diceret a viro sapiente, quod Deus extra patientiam esset malorum, sapiens supra patientiam. Eadem opera damnantur et Pharisaeorum καυχήματα et omnium eorum qui se suapte ope putant aut poenam effugere posse aut praemium consequi.

43   Quandoquidem igitur homo propter vitia et vitiositati et poenae iacet obnoxius, sequitur religionem omnem intercidisse, nisi et remissionis et reparationis inveniatur via. Nam qui poenam debet, is praemium non potest sperare et qui immersus est vitiis, surgere per se non potest. Atqui non esse eversam religionem hoc ipso colligi potest, quod Deus et humanum genus propagat et mundi huius usum ipsi prorogat: quo, nisi ut colatur ipse ab homine? Est ergo et remissio quaedam peccatorum et lapsi hominis reparatio nec remissionem peccatorum tantum esse quandam necesse est, sed hominum quoque fidem eius fieri, ut veniae certus
7v   / placere Deo studeat. Et haec fiducia proprium quoddam munus est christianae religionis, de qua loquens Zosimus, auctor non christianus, ait hanc esse ipsius ἐπαγγελίαν παντὸς ἁμαρτήματος καὶ πάσης ἀσεβείας

250   *diceret*] ms. dicerent

ἀπαλλαγήν (*pollicitationem ab omni peccato omnique impietate liberationem*). Et alibi hanc religionem vocat: δόξαν πάσης ἁμαρτάδος ἀναιρετικὴν καὶ τοῦτο ἔχουσαν ἐπάγγελμα τὸ τοὺς ἀσεβεῖς μεταλαμβάνοντας αὐτῆς πάσης ἁμαρτίας ἔξω παραχρῆμα καθίστασθαι (*persuasionem quae peccatum omne tollat et quae hoc promissi afferat, participes sui factos confestim extra omne peccatum collocare*). 270

44 Sed multum refert cui rei haec fiducia nitatur, nam quam periculose circa hanc rem erretur Plato monstrat, cum gravissime exagitat ut morum corruptrices eas religiones, quae per τελετάς facilem ac parabilem promitterent peccatorum veniam. Videntes igitur hoc periculum qui Platonem secuti sunt, et inter eos Porphyrius, negarunt certam aliquam et 275 universalem rationem purgandorum animorum, quam ipsi θεουργίαν vocant, posse inveniri. Attamen nisi hac inventa nulla erit religio. Fatendum igitur, nisi Deus prodidisset, nihil certi potuisse homines assequi in quo fiduciam hanc veniae collocarent. Attamen operae pretium est videre quomodo velut in tenebris palpitantes alii aliis propius ad verum 280 accesserint.

45 Primum igitur gentes ferme omnes in hoc consenserunt, χωρὶς αἱματεκχυσίας οὐ γίνεσθαι ἄφεσιν, quia scilicet culpa in Deum commissa minore quam mortis supplicio expiari non posset. Sed et illud scire debuerunt minus vilem esse bestiarum conditionem quam ut possent esse 285 hostia homini succidanea. Quidam igitur populi homines immolarunt, in quo primum homicidae erant, neque enim eius rei praeceptum exstabat ullum eius qui praecipere posset. Deinde in eo iterum fallebantur, quod eum, qui reus et ipse pro suo capite poenam deberet, putarent piaculum pro aliis posse fieri, cum ut hominem reperissent innocentem — qui nus- 290 quam erat — tamen unus par non erat aut humano generi aut genti alicui expiandae.

46 Rursum in hoc et gentibus et philosophis plerisque convenit, quod homini, praesertim quem sua culpa a Deo alienatum quodammodo agnoscerent, quaerendum crederent interventorem, qui se inter Deum 295 hominemque velut interponeret. Unde ad daemonum cultus se contule-
8r runt, quod eorum naturam inter divinam et / humanam mediam esse arbitrarentur. At Porphyrius vitium τῆς ἀγνοίας (*inscientiae*) negabat repurgari posse alia ratione quam διὰ τὸν νοῦν τὸν πατρικόν (*mentem illam paternam*). Est autem hominum depravatio cum ignorantia summa atque 300 caecitate coniuncta.

47 Haec omnia ita in unum colligit veritas christiana, ut doceat datum esse homini μεσίτην, non talem qui nec homo sit nec Deus, sed qui esset utrunque, illum ipsum nimirum λόγον πατρικόν, qui divina virtute verus homo factus sit, ut posset homines expiare δι' αἱματεκχυσίας (*per fusionem* 305 *sanguinis*). Nam et ut mori posset hominem esse oportebat, et vivificare alios nisi Deus ipse non poterat. Huius capitis prae caeteris omnibus

fructus est praecipuus. Primum enim impedit, ne homines peccata sua parvi pendant, ut illi faciunt qui se levi aliqua victima aut donariolo liberari posse existimant. Non potest enim non esse pergrave cuius κάθαρμα factus sit ipse verus Dei filius. Deinde altera a parte desperationi hominum occurrit, quorum conscientia in aliis purgationibus acquiescere non potest. In hac sola potest, cum videat dignum culpis suis pretium. Postremo amorem Dei erga homines nulla res efficacius testari potest et nos proinde excitare ut tam benignum parentem amemus mutuo.

48 Nobilis est Zaleuci historia, qui statuta a se lege ut oculi eruerentur adultero, filium suum eius criminis manifestum ita a caecitate liberavit, ut sibi unum, alterum filio oculum erueret. *Ita*, inquit Valerius Maximus, *debitum supplicii modum legi reddidit, aequitatis admirabili temperamento se inter misericordem patrem et iustum legislatorem partitus.* Plus Christus fecit qui, ut nos totos a poena liberaret, semet ipse substituit. Hoc autem ipsum, ut modo in re simili dicebamus, non ideo minus credibile est, quia modum quo Deus unus idemque cum homine fuerit, non intelligimus. Nam ne animi quidem nostri cum corpore quod foedus sit, quod vinculum, comprehendimus et tamen utrunque hoc unum esse hominem non dubitamus.

49 Accedit quod philosophi plerique statuunt Deum interdum in humanis mentibus habitare, quo sensu Amelius Platonicus citabat illum Iohannis Evangelistae locum, ἐν ἀρχῇ ἦν ὁ λόγος et quae sequuntur, καὶ ὁ λόγος σὰρξ ἐγένετο, perperam quidem ille ea verba interpretatus de eo inhabitandi modo, qui in omnibus viris sanctis / est Deus, qui modus ab illo eximio atque ineffabili, qui vocatur καθ' ἕνωσιν ὑποστατικήν, immensum differt, sed potest tamen et iste ad illum esse credendi via. Sed tarditatem assensionis humanae expugnant omni telo validius admiranda Christi opera, quae adeo vim omnem humanam et creatarum mentium excedunt, ut bene rebus expensis multo sit difficilius non credere Deum fuisse ista qui fecerit quam credere; praesertim cum et illa ipsa opera et natale Christi tempus et maiores et patria et vita omnis et mors aliquot ante saeculis vatum concentu praedicta fuerint.

50 Venia autem haec de qua diximus, cui pateat videndum nunc est. Eam christiana religio docet patere toti humano generi, contra quam statuit Iudaeorum invidentia, qui omnes praeter se gentes ab ea spe exclusas volunt. Non tamen omnes eam reipsa consequuntur, offertur enim haec venia sub lege poenitendi et credendi, quorum prius ad omnem veniam requiri solet. Nemo enim sapiens gratiam criminis cuiquam facit, quem sciat eius criminis non poenitere; alioqui impunitate accenderetur peccantium malitia.

Veterem ferendo iniuriam, invites novam.

Alterum autem et veracitas Dei requirit, cuius promissis diffidere contumeliosissimum est, et ideo quoque id necessarium est, quia alia ratione id quod universim offertur, singulatim accipi non potest, nisi per fidem. Et, ut ante diximus, nemo ad Deum amandum atque colendum potest assurgere, nisi qui ante certam de prioribus culpis veniae fiduciam conceperit. Haec sanae rationi quam maxime consentiunt. Ἡ μεταμέλεια, ait quidam, [σώτειρα δαίμων;] [τὰς μὲν γὰρ ἄλλας ἀναιρεῖ λύπας ὁ λογος, τὴν δὲ μετάνοιαν αὐτὸς ἐργάζεται δακνομένης σὺν αἰσχύνῃ τῆς ψυχῆς καὶ κολαζομένης ὑφ'αὑτῆς] (*poenitentia sancta omnino diva, et eorum qui peccarunt, sospitatrix. coeteros dolores tollit ratio, solam poenitentiam ipsa efficit, quae pudore mordetur, et punitur in semet ipsa*). Et ut haec poenitentia homini corrigendo utilissima est, ita fiducia in Deum ad Dei ipsius gloriam plurimum pertinet. Ita fit ut haec venia vere talis sit qualem esse [συγγνώμην] (*gratiam*) volunt philosophi, [οὐδὲ κατὰ νόμον, οὐδὲ κατὰ νόμον, ἀλλὰ ὑπὲρ νόμον καὶ ὑπὲρ νόμου] (*nec iuxta legem nec contra legem, sed supra legem et pro lege*).

51 Quod ut rectius intelligatur, ad reparationem hominis veniamus / quae remissionem ordine subsequitur. Ad eam necessaria sunt remedia, e quibus primum est quo purgatur ignorantia, qua non sublata necesse est durare vitia. Est autem haec in homine summa, nam ut bene Aristoteles, [ὥσπερ γὰρ καὶ τὰ τῶν νυκτερίδων ὄμματα πρὸς τὸ φέγγος ἔχει τὸ μεθ' ἡμέραν, οὕτω καὶ τῆς ἡμετέρας ψυχῆς ὁ νοῦς πρὸς τὰ τῇ φύσει φανερώτατα πάντων] (*ut vespertilionum se oculi ad lucem habent diurnam, ita mens animaque nostra ad ea quae per se sunt manifestissima*). Nec id tantum quod res divinae per se longe humanum captum superent, sed praecipue quia peccatis mens obruta et rebus sensibilibus mancipata ad illas recte considerandas semet erigere non potest. Remedium autem huic rei aliud esse non potest quam divinae veritatis a Deo facta patefactio. Apud gentes Christi ignaras dii ferme de rebus humanis loquebantur, de diis autem tantum homines, cum tamen multo dignius sit Deo suam naturam, sua beneficia hominibus exponere quam consultum super belli exitu aut re aliqua simili responsa reddere. Iterumque summa sit in homine impudentia audacter aliquid affirmare de rebus tantis nullo auctore. Habet hoc ergo privilegium christiana religio quod sola quicquid de Deo rebusque divinis tradit, id se a Deo ipso accepisse profitetur, cuius vox per sanctissimos vates ac postremo per ipsum θέου λόγον enuntiata, quo certior ad nos perveniret, scriptis quoque comprehensa est.

52 Eorum scriptorum veritatem imprimis evincat quod tam in historia quam in praeceptis nihil non Deo dignum, nihil non ad optimos mores perducens doceat, cum contra et poetae et philosophi et quicunque se doctores aliorum professi sunt, multa Deo indigna, multa absurda, imo a bonis moribus dissona doceant, historiae autem omnes circa alia occupatae eum usum qui praecipuus esse debebat ferme negligant. Accedit quod in hominum libris, etiam qui sectae sunt unius, nusquam tanta

consensio. At sacra Christianorum scripta non modo sibi cohaerent, sed multis in partibus narrationis suae testes etiam inimicos possunt adducere.

53 Iam vero et antiquitas veritati addit dignitatem. Antecedit autem eorum librorum qui partem istius voluminis faciunt antiquitas omnes humanos libros et argumento et scriptione. Varro ex veterum auctoritate tempus omne dividebat in ἄδηλόν, μυθικόν et ἱστορικόν (*incognitum, fabulosum, historicum*). Primum enim tempus / esse dicebat, quod ante diluvium fuisset, cuius nihil sciretur. Secundum a diluvio ad tempora Iliaca, in quo regnarent fabulae. Tertio iam lucem historiae apparere. At sacra illa veraque historia et tempus quod Varro fabulosum vocat, et id quod ignotum fatetur, una narrationis serie connectit. Scriptorum in hoc volumine primus Moses, Diodoro vetustissimus legislatorum, ante cuius aetatem scripta nulla possunt proferri; nec mirum, cum Graeci, unde omnis literatura in alias gentes emanavit, literas ipsas a Phoenicibus se accepisse fateantur, quae quidem Phoenicum literae eaedem sunt quae Hebraeorum, unde et nomina literarum apud Graecos Phoenicia sive Hebraica./

54 Adde iam simplicitatem summam dictionis cum maiestate coniunctam. Dionysius Longinus rhetor qui περὶ ὕψους (*de sublimi dictione*) scripsit, ait id ὕψος, id est, quod rebus divinis convenit, optime observatum a Iudaeorum legislatore, quem vocat ἄνδρα οὐ τὸν τυχόντα, ἐπειδὴ, inquit, τὴν τοῦ θεοῦ δύναμιν κατὰ τὴν ἀξίαν ἐχώρησε κἀξέφηνεν, εὐθὺς ἐν τῇ εἰσβολῇ γράψας τῶν νόμων, "εἶπεν ὁ θεός", φησι, τί; "γενέσθω φῶς, καὶ ἐγένετο, γενέσθω γῆ, καὶ ἐγένετο" (*Virum non e vulgo, divinam enim virtutem ex dignitate comprehendit explicuitque, cum in ipso legum scripsit initio, "Dixit", inquit, "Deus, fiat lux et facta est. Fiat terra et facta est"*).

55 Simplicitas autem praeterquam quod pars magna est maiestatis etiam huc pertinet, ut omnes, etiam indocti, ibi sine circuitu inveniant id quod saluti pariendae sufficiat. Non hic per φυσιολογίαν, non per harmoniae modos, non per mathematicas lineas numerosque ut apud Pythagoram, Platonem atque alios, ad Dei cognitionem aerumnosis ambagibus homo circumducitur, sed planis verbis primoque intentu patefecit quicquid didicisse est necessarium, ita ut nec tarditas ingenii nec quaerendo victu occupata paupertas nec sexus aut aetas, dummodo rationis capax, quemquam secludat a veritate tam obvia. Quod et ipsum insigne est argumentum non esse illas alias veras ad Deum cognoscendum vias, quia non in commune omnibus patent. Deus autem, qui communis omnium Deus est et omnibus idem, sine dubio talem instituit ad se veniendi rationem, quae aeque aperta sit et facilis. Haec autem doctrina, extare certam religionis regulam a Deo traditam, et Dei bonitati convenit et plurimum ad parandas regendasque mentes pertinet, ne homines inter tot diversas philosophorum sententias / et populorum instituta incerti fluctuent aut hoc obtentu ab omni religione abstineant.

56   Alterum quod hominem restaurat est perfectissimum Christi exemplar. Philosophi Stoici praesertim dicunt non minus hominem exemplis iuvari quam verbis, imo magis saepe. Epictetus deliberantes nos, quid in re quaque facere oporteat, vult ad Socratem respicere, Seneca ad Catonem, alii ad Herculem, alii ad Ulyssem; quorum omnium facile esset multa prave facta commemorare, mendacia, dolos, libidines, contumaciam, ita ut qui eorum vitam pro norma sequi velit, errare saepenumero debeat. Tum qui eos videat in quibusdam peccasse, dubitare potest an in caeteris recte fecerint. At Christiani eum sibi proponunt imitandum, cuius nulla culpa argui potest; cuius tota vita plena est non violentiae et armorum, ut Mahumetis et sperati Iudaeis Messiae, sed pietatis, charitatis, mansuetudinis, patientiae. Et ne nos terreant molestiae quae plerumque subeundae sunt virtutem sequentibus, idem ille ut molestiarum et virtutis, ita rursus summi praemii et foelicitatis exemplum praebet post atrocissimas contumelias, cruciatus, mortem denique patienter toleratam, palam revocatus ad vitam, inde in coelum evectus et ex ipso coelo vi admirandorum operum testatus regem se factum et dominum rerum omnium, ut tantae gloriae participes se fore considerent quicumque ipsius insisterent vestigiis. Quae quidem ratio movendi animos quam sit efficax, facile quivis intelligit. At hanc praeter christianam religionem nulla habet.

57
11ʳ   Tertium maximumque remedium est arcana Dei virtus sive Spiritus animum hominis ad recte vivendum excitans, impellens, / regens atque confirmans. Quaesitum est inter philosophos, εἰ γένοιτό τις θείᾳ μοίρᾳ ἀγαθός (*num quis bonus fiat divina sorte?*) Et sentiunt quidem plerique fieri divino beneficio viros bonos, manifestis rationibus, quia Deo dignum est id dare quod est optimum, et homini sponte sua prolapso in vitia ad capessendam virtutem auxilio opus est. Ita Seneca: *Deus ad homines venit, immo quod propius est, in homines venit. Nulla sine Deo mens bona.* Sed minus tamen illi hoc solent urgere quam oportet. Unde factum est, ut homines minus serio a Deo expeterent id quod ipsis maxime erat necessarium, at christiana religio saluberrima moderatione Deo solidam laudem tribuit hominis reparati, ita tamen ut non sentiat invitum quemquam bonum fieri, sed volentem. Ita duo evitantur pericula: hinc desperatio ob imbecillitatem, cui succurrit fiducia Dei adiutoris, ita ut iam vere cessantibus dici possit cum Seneca: *Nolle in causa est, non posse praetenditur*, inde fastus et confidentia, quae refraenantur hoc ipso quod homini sua ostenditur inopia, cum docetur virtutem, sine qua ipse nullus est, a se non habere, sed a Deo donatam accipere, contra illam superbissimam Stoico-

462 *capessendam*] *ms.* capessandam

rum vocem: *Mentem bonam stultum est optare, cum possis a te impetrare.* Haec sunt de homine ipso decreta.

58 De rebus humanis hoc unum satis est: praeter veram virtutem, hoc est religionem, caetera esse ad summum hominis finem ἀδιάφορα. Non litigant Christiani de verbis nec intercedunt, ut Stoici, quo minus vita, sanitas, eruditio, honos, divitiae, bona dicantur; mors, morbi, ἀπαιδευσία (*eruditionis penuria*), ignominia, paupertas, mala. / Imo putant utile esse, ut ista verba, ut usu recepta sunt, ita maneant, quo magis homo et pro illis gratias se Deo sciat debere et haec contra norit aut peccatorum esse poenas aut patientiae experimenta. Id enim ut serio sentiatur, necesse est et illis gaudere hominem, ut naturae congruentibus, et his indolere ut contrariis. Hoc interim tenendum est neutra istorum boni supremi atque ultimi aut dandi aut auferendi ius habere, sed posse fieri aut virtutum aut vitiorum materiam, prout utrisque aut recte aut secus utimur. Et decreta quidem hactenus.

IV

59 Ad praecepta venturos operae pretium est inspicere, quid in summa de his ipsis senserint etiam illi qui aliam religionem profitebantur. Strabo Iudaeos illos veteres, quorum traduces et ὁμόδοξοι (*doctrinae socii*) Christiani, vocat ἄνδρας τιμῶντας τὸ θεῖον καὶ εὐγνώμονας (*viros numinis reverentes et probos*) et de Mosis successoribus loquitur hunc in modum: οἱ δὲ διαδεξάμενοι χρόνους μέν τινας ἐν τοῖς αὐτοῖς ἔμειναν δικαιοπραγοῦντες καὶ εὐσεβεῖς, ὡς ἀληθῶς, ὄντες (*et successores per aliquot tempora institutis iisdem inhaerere, vere pii vereque iusti*). Et de eisdem agens Trogus Pompeius, aut qui eum concidit Iustinus, ait eorum *iustitiam* fuisse *religione permixtam*. Plinius de Christianis: *solitos se sacramento non in scelus aliquod obstringere, sed ne furta, ne latrocinia, ne adulteria committerent, ne fidem fallerent, ne depositum appellati abnegarent.* At Ammianus Marcellinus: *Christiana professio nihil docet nisi iustum et bene.* Sed propius haec praecepta per partes suas considerentur.

60 Sunt ergo officia erga Deum alia, alia circa homines, alia circa humana. Officiorum quae Deo debentur prima esse debet ratio, ut est apud Christianos. / Qua in parte non possunt satis culpari veteres prope omnes qui de officiis aut moribus scripsere, apud quos haec pars aut silentio tota praeterita, cum tamen sit potissima, aut certe non aliter praecipitur quam qua pars est obedientiae civilibus institutis debitae, adeo quidem ut Varronem aliosque non puduerit scribere retinendas esse religiones, quamvis falsas et falsorum deorum, legum reverentia. Quin senatus romanus ius sibi arrogavit deos faciendi quos vellet. Quod quid est aliud quam religionem statuendo tollere? Ipsi philosophi aliter

sentiebant quam loquebantur, cum tamen nullius rei sanctior esse debeat veritas. Christiana igitur disciplina hoc ipso statim philosophos omnes et legislatores vincit, quod omnibus locis, omni tempore Dei cultum, amorem, venerationem, hominibus commendat. Hoc semper agit; huc refert omnia.

61 Quae de Deo praecipiuntur partim interna, partim externa sunt. Interna sunt quae animo peraguntur, in quibus excellunt duo illa: credere Deo et Deum invocare. Et credere quidem Deo difficile sane est aliis quid Deus dicat nescientibus; Christianis ipsam Dei vocem asservantibus id facile est; qua de re ante egimus.

62 Invocare etiam Deum rem periculosissimam ait Plato, fassus se quid orare deberet nescire. Et poetae ostendunt multa infelicissima eventura hominibus, si preces eorum exaudirentur. At Christiani docentur primum orare, contra quorundam nomine magis quam re philosophorum impietatem, qui Deum orandum negant. Deinde contra communem ignorantiam / docentur, quid orare debeant, scilicet ea quae ad Dei gloriam atque honorem pertinent, ut ipse colatur, ipsi obediatur per omnia; deinde quae ad ipsos, et ad hanc quidem vitam, nihil ultra naturae necessaria, ad alterius autem vitae subsidia culparum veniam et a culpis custodiam.

63 Externarum actionum Deum spectantium vetantur quaedam, iubentur aliae. Vetitarum aliae versantur in vocibus, aliae in factis. Circa voces vetamur Deum aut profane aut temere et sine reverentia nominare, quod profecto multo plus quam quod alii vetant duntaxat peierare. At quantum hinc olim magna pars hominum abiit, cum videamus libros auctorum plenos acerbissimis in Deos convitiis? Ad facta quod attinet, primum inter vetita illud apud cunctas fere gentes olim receptum, Deum per imaginem exprimere. Disputarunt haec Platonici, εἰ ἀγάλματα θεοῖς ἱδρυτέον (*sintne ponenda diis simulachra*)? Pythagoras inter philosophos, inter legislatores Numa imagines poni vetuere. Damnat easdem et Euripides et Seneca. Adrianus quoque imperator templa instituit sine simulachris. Rationem in iudaicis institutis recte Tacitus expressit: *Egyptii pleraque animalia effigiesque compositas venerantur, Iudaei mente sola unumque numen intelligunt: profanos, qui deum imagines mortalibus materiis in species hominum effingunt; summum illud et aeternum neque* mutabile *neque interiturum. Igitur nulla simulachra urbibus suis, nedum templis sunt.* Nimirum et Deo incomparabili indecorum cum re ulla comparari et homini de Deo cogitanti non oculi modo et sensus, / sed animus quoque ab omni materia ac re sensili quantum fieri potest avocandus est, ut intelligatur simplicissima illa et supra omnem naturam natura.

48 *quam*] ms. quum

64   Rursus et hoc cavet christiana religio, ne Deus operose et per innumeros ritus colatur, qua parte non veterum modo gentium religiones antecellit, quae multos ritus comminiscebantur Deo iniussos ideoque ingratos, sed ipsam quoque iudaicam, plenam et ipsam sumtuosis et molestis caeremoniis. Hoc autem praeter quod pars magna est libertatis et insigne Dei beneficium, etiam monet nos, praecipuum Dei cultum in mente consistere.

65   Inter externa quae praecipiuntur ad cultum Dei pertinentia, hoc maximum est, frequentare eos coetus qui Dei colendi causa instituuntur, ubi Dei oracula exponuntur, homines ad religionem excitantur et publicae subeuntur preces. Nam si Cicero ex philosophorum sententia recte dixit, *nihil* esse *principi Deo, qui omnem* hunc *mundum regit, quod quidem in terris fiat, acceptius quam concilia coetusque hominum iure sociatos*, quid de iis coetibus existimandum qui in hoc habentur, ut multi religiosi homines Deum pari studio et communi affectu colant? Si enim concordia hominum Deo tam grata est gratusque est ipsi suus cultus, quam grata ipsi esse debet in ipsius cultu hominum concordia? Et hoc ipsum ut facilius observaretur certa pars temporis cultui divino et coetibus habendis seponitur, dies nimirum septima quaeque, prudentissima moderatione inter crebras ab humanis actibus avocationes et longa religionis oblivia. Quod si / intellexisset Seneca atque alii, numquam Iudaeorum sabbata ignaviae assignassent, cum nulli tempori sua magis constet ratio quam quod temporis auctori impenditur. Hic et illud sane notandum est, quod apud gentes Christi ignaras conventus sacrorum causa, sine ulla populi institutione, solo spectaculo et externo quodam apparatu peragebantur, neque praecepta de rebus divinis ac ratione vivendi antistites sacrorum, sed philosophi tradebant. Unde apparet illorum religionem vanam fuisse atque inutilem. At apud Christianos praecipuum in quod convenitur est, ut Dei voluntas velut per interpretem audiatur.

66   Tum deinde adduntur signa, pauca quidem nec operosa, sed ad movendos animos efficacissima. Ita enim decuit Deum omni ex parte nostrae imbecillitati succurrere, quando plerumque
Segnius irritant animos demissa per aurem,
quam quae sunt oculis commissa fidelibus.
Primum aqua omnes fere gentes usae sunt ad lustrationes.
Tu, genitor, cape sacra manu, patriosque penates.
me bello e tanto digressum et caede recenti,
attrectare nefas, donec me flumine vivo
abluero.

---

101   *caede*] ms. corde

Ita et Christiani aqua lustrantur, et ut constet non inanem esse caeremoniam, paucissimis vocibus totius religionis summa comprehenditur invocato Patre datore naturae, veniae Filio, sanctitatis Spiritu. In Mithrae sacris legimus panem et vinum usurpata et in Graecorum mysteriis praecipua Cereri ac Libero sacra sunt in panis vinique memoriam. Nimirum sunt haec duo praestantissima Dei munera / in usum huius vitae. Sed sicut religio docet hanc vitam alterius venturae ducem esse, ita Christiani istis muneribus longe maiorum munerum memoriam repraesentant. Cum enim ὁ θεοῦ λόγος nostri causa humanum corpus sanguinemque induerit, ut victima pro nobis fieret nosque sibi coagmentaret, sane illud corpus ac sanguis non minus sint oportet pastus animorum quam panis et vinum pastus sunt corporis et sanguinis. Quantum haec distant a priscarum gentium mysteriis in quibus multa obscaena, pleraque ludicra, omnia vero eiusmodi, quorum rationem ipsi antistites idoneam non possent reddere?

67   Hic autem retinendus quoque non est error quidam latissime patens, sola caeremoniarum observatione vitae alterius faelicitatem parari, quo nihil est ad evertendos bonos mores validius. Tale illud Sophoclis:

ὦ τρισόλβιοι
κεῖνοι βροτῶν, οἳ ταῦτα δερχθέντες τέλη
μόλωσ' ἐς Ἅδου. τοῖς δὲ γὰρ μόνοις ἐκεῖ
ζῆν ἐστι, τοῖς δ' ἄλλοισιν πάντ' ἐκεῖ κακά.

(*felices nimis, quicumque visis hiis prius mysteriis migrant ad orcum. Vivere hiis solis datum a morte, reliquis nil nisi immensum malum*). Quibus ille versibus multa hominum non initiatorum millia dicitur implesse desperatione. At Diogenes cuidam similem sententiam defendenti Pataecionem suorum temporum furem obiecit rogavitque an credibile esset in vita altera ei melius fore quam Epaminondae optime de patria et civibus merito, quod Pataecion esset μεμυημένος (*initiatus mysteriis*), Epaminondas non esset. Longe aliter Christiani, qui leges rituales non modo non credunt solas sufficere, sed etiam dignitate posteriores esse non dubitant iis quibus charitatis officia praescribuntur. Ad quas nunc veniamus.

68   Inter humana officia sunt quae homo aliis, sunt quae sibimet ipse debet. / Quae aliis debet, aut humanitati debet aut ordini in rebus humanis constituto. Humanitati uno verbo amicitia debetur ob cognationem naturae Deique imaginem. Qua in parte aut plus requirit christiana pietas aut sane clarius praecipit quam sectae caeterae. Plerique enim tantum actiones externas respiciunt, non in animum descendunt. In qua quidem externa innocentia simulque exacta rituum observatione Pharisaei fiduciam salutis superstitiose non minus quam improbe ponebant. At Christiani charitatem et ab animo et ab effectibus poscunt. Vita, libertas, honor, opes alterius iuxta sua cuique chara esse debent. Haec qui laedit

non facto modo, sed dicto, imo vel cogitatione sola coram Deo homicidii furtique peragitur reus, quo illa pertinet brevis et clara et imperatori Adriano laudata adeo regula: *quod tibi non vis fieri alteri ne feceris.*

69   Neque ergo Christianus, ut gentes totae, hoc excusatiora putat latrocinia, quod belli nomen induerunt, aut rapinas ideo, quod sub foeneris appellatione grassantur. Non ex vocibus aut exemplorum frequentia, sed ex rebus res iudicat. Tum vero, quamquam agnoscit propriam quandam necessitudinem eorum qui pietatis eiusdem studium profitentur, in quos idcirco ob plura vincula maior quoque et propensior esse debeat dilectio, neminem tamen hominem a suo amore excludit nec cum Aristotele Barbaros a Grecis, velut aliud animantium genus, separat et iniuriis imo servituti obiicit. Sed naturae credit hos quoque esse homines, ac proinde habendos fratrum loco, in quo Iudaei quam pernitiose ut nunc labantur et lapsi sint olim, Iuvenalis versus facile / indicant

Non monstrare vias eadem nisi sacra colenti,
Quaesitum ad fontem solos deducere verpos.

Et Tacitus: *apud ipsos fides obstinata, misericordia in promptu, sed adversus omnes alios hostile odium.* Quod plus est, etiam eum a quo iniuriam accepit, hominem meminit Christianus. Aristoteles et Cicero, ut naturae congruum, laudant ulcisci. Melius Platonici et Stoici iussere μὴ ἀνταδικεῖν (*iniurias non reponere*). *Ultio* a contumelia, ut inquit Seneca, *non differt nisi ordine.* Maior quippe imaginis divinae naturaeque coniunctio est quam ut qualecunque hominis factum eam possit divellere.

70   Adde quod erga hominem talis esse homo debet, qualem sibi Deum esse postulet. Hunc autem vult clementem et promptum ignoscere. Quare

det ille veniam facile cui venia est opus.

Iam vero ex huius religionis instituto parum est non laedere, nisi prosis qua possis, nisi alienis malis totus, nec minus sentiente, indoleas. Multa de beneficiis philosophi scripsere, sed praecipuam partem omisere, quae nobis homines quosdam hoc solo commendat quod miseri sunt. Nuditas, fames, sitis, morbus, carcer, exilium, tituli sunt quibus a natura debitum exigimur. Hinc illud philosophis quibusdam in tractandis officiis praeteritum silentio atque etiam culpatum; Deo interim atque humanitati gratissimum nomen ἐλεημοσύνη. Cuius haec quoque vel prima pars est, eos qui circa pietatem vel mores errant, comiter instituere. In diris Atheniensium erat εἴ τις μὴ φράσῃ τὴν ὀρθὴν ὁδόν (*si quis veram viam non monstrasset*). Haec bonitas ac charitas adversus homines omnes etiam sibi infestos, quam / multum distat a multarum gentium institutis, ut olim Spartiatarum, quorum omnis disciplina ad caedes ac praedas, non autem ad pacis studia comparata est.

71   Ordo quo constant res humanae duplex est: familia, deinde respublica.

In utroque quicquid optimum aut dici aut cogitari potest, id christianismus praecipit. Primum enim non vagos permittit concubitus, sed coniugiis eos devincit, ut suae cuique curae dominus, sui sint liberi, procul ab indignissima philosophi nomine Socratis et Platonis insania, qui communia ut omnia ita et uxores in optima republica statuunt. Quasi non natura doceat propria ac discreta rectius curari quam in commune confusa, atque ipse omnium gentium, extra paucas ab omni more humanitatis alienas, consensus satis ostendat quam res sacra sit matrimonium.

72 Nec cum quibusvis coniugium iustum esse Christiani sentiunt, ut Persae cum matribus, cum sororibus Asiatici reges et Athenienses. Sed ne vix divisus sanguis confestim in se redeat, ortus reverentiam et matrimoniorum licentiam certis finibus discriminant causasque amandi in plures spargunt. In hoc quoque cum Romanis naturam optime sequuntur, a qua pleraeque gentes olim et nunc Mahumetistae omnes desciverunt, ut viri unius uxor una sit. Itaque de illis haud iniuria dictum:

           num barbara nobis
est ignota Venus, quae ritu caeca ferarum
polluit innumeras leges et federa taedae
coniugibus, thalamique patent secreta nefandi
inter mille nurus./

16ʳ Naturam autem secutus Euripides:
           οὐδὲ γὰρ καλὸν
δυοῖν γυναικοῖν ἄνδρ' ἕν'ἡνίας ἔχειν,
ἀλλ' εἰς μίαν βλέποντες εὐναίαν κύπριν
στέργουσιν, ὅστις μὴ κακῶς οἰκεῖν θέλῃ.

Et de Germanis Tacitus: *nec ullam morum partem magis laudaveris. Nam prope soli barbarorum singulis uxoribus contenti sunt.* Nimirum amor, qui in coniugio debet esse maximus omnis affectus humani, diductus perit et rei familiaris custodia, quae naturaliter penes faeminam est, nisi uni non recte committitur.

73 Sic et individuas sine divortiis habere nuptias Christianorum lex est, contra quam pleraeque Orientis gentes ipsique Iudaei usurpavere, solis prope Romanis hac in parte laudandis quod sexcentos per annos infractam servaverint matrimoniorum fidem; scilicet et amicitiae summae, quanta inter coniuges esse debet, nihil tam contrarium quam posse abrumpi. Et commune onus a natura impositum, liberorum educatio, pariter quoque pertrahendum est. Et quid aliud sunt ista divortia quam adulteria colorata?

      toties quae nubit adultera lege est:
offendor moecha simpliciore minus.

Iam parentum ac liberorum et coniugum inter se officia, hinc imperandi lenitas, inde parendi constantia, par undique concordia iubetur astringere.

74 Ad rempublicam quod attinet, tales sunt Christianorum leges, ut appareat ipsorum maxime exemplo eosdem esse et viros bonos et cives optimos. / Non enim tribuni tantum plebis, sed omnes omnium magistratus sacrosancti Christianis, ut tradita a Deo potestate. Non hic asperis Stoicorum vocibus excitatur populus in regum regentiumque odia, non secessiones docentur, sed iubetur quisque ea quam accepit contentus republica rectores optimos votis exposcere, qualescunque tolerare, indicta onera subire, alacriter parere imperiis, etiam gravibus, dum Dei praecepta non violent — quae profecto doctrina ad continendas in statu suo civitates utilissima est, praesertim cum et rectores admonentur sedulo, ut meminerint summa Deoque proxima imperia sub Dei disquisitionem trahi.

75 Eorum quae sibi homo debet alia circa ipsum proprie versantur, alia circa ea quae sunt ipsius. Circa ipsum illud, ut vitam quisque suam, incolumitatem ac sanitatem omni studio conservet. Nec dubitat Christianus in illa diu agitata Platonis controversia, an semet interimere liceat, contra Catonem pronuntiare. Nam et naturale est omnibus se tueri et homo in hoc orbe non sorte collocatus est, sed divino iussu, velut in statione, quam deserere invocato non liceat. Feret igitur potius aerumnas, feret servitutem, quam impatientiam vivendi homicidio testetur.

Fortius ille facit qui miser esse potest.

Nec tamen gravate ubi se mors obtulerit, gratum quidem domicilium corpus, sed in spem magni praemii relinquet.

Ignavum rediturae parcere vitae.

76 Nunquam autem mortem tantum putabit malum, ut non peccatum quodvis maius esse credat, nec vitam paciscetur ille damno virtutis, / sed potius quam Deo vetitum quid admittat, in cruces ibit et flammas. Cuius verae fortitudinis exempla in Christianis saepe plura sub eius religionis hostibus unus annus tulit quam omnia mundi saecula in aliarum sectarum hominibus videre. Et merito, solus enim Christianus adversus mortem fida habet solatia, quae cum non habeant philosophi, fingunt falsa ideoque animum non penetrantia. Quid enim me iuvat, si dicas nihil esse post mortem, cum hoc ipsum ex aliquo in nihil redigi miserrimum et naturae adversissimum? Quid prodest, si naturae dicas esse mortem, non poenae, cum malum, quacunque ex causa veniat, malum esse non desinat?

77 Circa hominem sunt res, actiones, verba, cogitata; res, ut honores, divitiae, voluptas. Christianus honoris ac gloriae cupidinem suspectam habere iubetur, ut corruptricem virtutis, quae perit, si aliud potius quam Deum respicit. Si tamen obtingant ista, non praecipitur ut repudiet, sed ut omnem ipse honorem in bonorum datorem Deum reiiciat, semet ipse, ne pronus feratur, vitiorum imbecillitatis conscientia sufflaminet. Hoc

virtutum omnium decus ταπεινοφροσύνη (*animi submissio*) ante christianam disciplinam adeo plerisque fuit ignota, ut vix nomen eius usquam inter virtutes compareat.

78 Circa divitias, vetatur immoderata et immensum procurrens φιλοχρηματία (*habendi cupido*), cordis carnifex, tranquillitatis inimica. Iubetur contra quisque honesto artificio quaerere ea quae sibi familiaeque sunt necessaria. Siquid ultra obtulerit Deus, non insano quorundam philosophorum more in mare merget instrumenta vivendi, sed aliorum / inopiam sua copia sublevabit. Contra, si ignominia, si paupertas obtigerit, feret fortiter, non tantum quia corrigere non possit, id enim iners solatium non est, neque rursus ut ad se nihil pertinentia, quod contra naturae veritatem est, sed ut molestias sibi a Deo impositas, quarum sensu vitia corrigat, virtutem exerceat, ut aspera gustu, sed usu salubria medicamenta, ut dura certamina, sed per quae itur in praemium.

79 Voluptas maxime regnat in cibo, potu, venere, quibus addi possunt otium et somnus. Cibos potusque omnes a Deo humanis usibus donatos, Christianus grate interpretatur. Ideoque nec iudaicam in se servitutem accersit per ciborum discrimina nec cum Mahumetistis in vino vini damnat creatorem, sed moderate et sobrie his utendum discit, non quantum luxui aut cupiditati, sed quantum naturae satis est, praecipue temulentiam relegans ut prodigam bonae rei, tum vero rationi et valetudini inimicam. Cuius tamen vitii magisteria erant quae apud Graecos quondam sacrorum celeberrima orgia dicebantur.

80 Supra hanc quotidianam victus moderationem, alteram quoque novit indictitiam, cum, ut in preces surgat animus, in alia vergenti corpori pondus ac vires subtrahit ac proinde ieiunium usurpat, non ut rem per se Deo gratam, sed ut homini necessariam, quod philosophis intactum, in gentium sacris usurpatum quidem, sed more tradito, non ut ratio constaret.

81 Venus extra matrimonium interdicta. Qua in re miranda et philosophorum et legislatorum quotquot fuerunt caecitas.

Quidam notus homo, cum exiret fornice, macte
virtute esto, inquit sententia dia Catonis. /

Melius Epictetus περὶ ἀφροδίσια πρὶν γάμου καθαρευτέον (*ante nuptias abstinendum a venere*). Et Dion Chrisostomus in quadam oratione egregie demonstrat ex lupanaribus in alienos lectos gradum fieri. Nec difficile collectu erat, si naturam ducem sequerentur, venerem prolis causa institutam, prolem autem gigni non debere citra propositum rectae educationis, quae, cum utrique parentum incumbat, perpetuam etiam cohabitationem requirit. Otio somnoque tam frui quam uti fas habetur, eum ad modum, quem resolvendis corporibus animisque natura desiderat.

82 Circa actiones illa lex Christianis praecipitur, ut quicquid nec iussum

nec vetitum est id ita usurpetur omittaturve, prout aut factum aut infectum animos aliorum ad virtutem excitare aut offendere poterit. Quae cautio et ipsa propria est christianae φιλανθρωπίας (*animi erga homines affectus*) neque aliis aeque tradita.

83   Verbis quoque sua lex, a vero non deflectere. Cuius facilis defensio, vel contra Platonem quibusdam hominibus ius facientem mendacii. Non debet enim rei usus inverti. Datus est autem sermo homini a Deo, quo arctior inter homines societas esset, si ipsa etiam mentis concepta alter alteri communicarent. Et semel missa licentia in immensum abit tollitque illud utilissimum rebus humanis, ut homo homini credat.

84   Affine huic praecepto stare promissis. Quod christiana religio sanctius multo docet quam qui de officiis scripsere, ut Panaetius et, eum imitatus, Cicero. His enim auctoribus est quidem hosti publico servanda fides, at non est praedoni, non est tyranno, quod, inquiunt, cum illis / nulla sit humani iuris societas. Quae ratio falsissima est. Non potest enim homo esse quicum societas nulla est. Tum vero pactorum fides non homines, sed Deum respicit, qui adeo amat veritatem, ut velit et dici cogitata et dicta fieri. Omnibus igitur hominibus fides servanda est pactorum omnium, nisi quid forte promiseris Deo vetitum, quod et antequam promitteres tuae non erat potestatis.

85   Cogitationibus quoque lex praescribitur. Est enim non hominum lex, sed Dei, cui interna quoque et sine teste bonitas debetur. Lex autem est, quicquid fieri nefas sit, idem nec cogitari debere. Hoc est ipsum fontem malorum amoliri, radicem praecidere. Nam, ut et Seneca nobiscum fatetur: *Latro est etiam antequam manus inquinet. Exercetur et aperitur opere* malitia, *non incipit.*

86   Commune autem praeceptorum omnium hoc praeceptum est, non satis esse fieri quod iubetur, nisi fiat quia iubetur. Multi quaedam imperata faciunt, sed ut hominibus placeant, ut famae imponant, quos egregia voce ὑποκριτάς (*simulatores*), hoc est honestae vitae mimos, appellamus. Nec enim sunt viri boni, sed virum bonum agunt. At Christianus per omnes cogitationes, per dicta factaque diffundit sanctissimum propositum Deo obtemperandi, quod multo plus est quam id in quo philosophi plerique consentiunt ὁμολογουμένως τῇ φύσει ζῆν (*naturae convenienter vivere*).

87   Sed quia contra praecepta et vetantia et iubentia saepissime labitur nondum plane expugnatis vitiorum reliquiis infirma humanitas, unum est praeceptum quod vice omnium succedit, paenitentia moveri et veniam poscere. Cuius praecepti ratio in decretis pertractata est.

88   Absolutis / praeceptis operae pretium videtur inspicere, quantum orbis

338   *amoliri*] ms. amolire
348   *plerique*] ms. plerique omnes

christianae religioni debeat. Plerique populi antea barbari, feri, inculti, χειροδίκαι (*ius sibi dicentes manu*) hac demum disciplina mores et iura accepere. Quin gentes, quae humanissimae credebantur, ante hanc institutionem liberos suos exponebant palamque spectacula ludebant humano sanguine. Illud quoque per vim inventum in opprobrium naturae, hominum discrimen, ut liberi alii essent, alii servi, non impetu quidem, sed paulatim christiana aequitas e vita sustulit. Nec legibus poenisque opus est, quae matrimonia invitis ingerant, sed sublata libidinum licentia sponte homines ad nuptias ducit, prolemque civitatibus sufficit, non desultoriis ut ante coniugiis, sed firma atque indivulsa fide. Quod si ubique christiana vita nomini suo responderet, sine bellis, sine litibus, sine egestate, in summa pace atque concordia et rerum cuique sufficientium copia, aureum vere saeculum ageretur.

[EPILOGUS]

Hunc ferme in modum cum sanctissimus senex summam religionis christianae pertractasset, mirum deinde aiebat, quomodo qui tantis in rebus consentirent, tamen tam diversi atque discordes esse viderentur. Cuius mali causam inquirens, mihi, inquit, una haec videtur maxima, quod praeceptis posthabitis, maxima pars religionis circa decreta statuitur, perverse admodum, cum decreta ferme praeceptis inserviant et eo ducant. Adeo verum est quod Seneca inquit, disputare omnes malle quam vivere. Cum tamen praecepta plerumque clariora sint et minus implicita, itaque de praeceptis maxime consentitur. Sed ideo malumus in decretis ponere /, quia de decretis pugnamus cum aliis, de praeceptis nobiscum. Difficilius autem est sibi vim facere quam in alios litigare. Vellet homo quam minimo defungi, ideo religionem in controversias mutavit et quod scolarum fuerat, in vitam transtulit.

De praeceptis quoque si qua pugna est, ea ferme non ad mores pertinet — horum enim perpetuae et manifestae sunt regulae —, sed in his quae ordinis servandi causa sibi quisque constituit, in quibus brevis ad concordiam via est, suo quenque arbitrio permittere. Quid stultius quam quod Lacedemonii et Athenienses graecis civitatibus bellum intulerunt, hi ut ad plebis imperium, illi ut ad optimatum regimen cuncta transferrent. Similia apud Christianos multa. Quantae enim olim dissensiones hinc ortae, quod pascha alii alio die celebrarent? Irenaeus ad Victorem episcopum romanum prudenter scribit: Quid? non possumus concordes vivere, quamvis illi suis ritibus utantur, ut nos utimur nostris? Quadragesimam enim, alii biduum, alii quatriduum, alii decem, alii quindecim, alii viginti, alii quadraginta dies ieiunant et nihilominus concordia reti-

netur. In decretis autem multas controversias sola verba faciunt, quibus vitatis consensus apparet. Siqua est ulterior pugna, videamus, ne sit in rebus scitu non admodum necessariis. Et hic quidem error in primis est corrigendus, quod decreta a plerisque fiunt plura quam praeceptorum usus postulat. Fieri autem non potest, ut de omnibus quaestionibus omnes consentiant. Deinde, quod in his quisque, etiam perperam, semel didicit, id retinet mordicus. Nolunt quae iuvenes
> *didicere, senes perdenda fateri.*

20ʳ   Οὕτως ἄρα, ut Galenus inquit, δυσαπότριπτόν τι / κακόν ἐστιν ἡ περὶ τὰς αἱρέσεις φιλοτιμία καὶ δυσέκνιπτον ἐν τοῖς μάλιστα καὶ ψώρας ἁπάσης δυσιατότερον (*adeo excussu difficile est malum circa sectas ambitio et quod minime omnium elui potest, quin scabie quavis insanabilius*).

91   Huic ergo morbo remedium erit necessario credendorum numerum in pauca et maxime evidentia contrahere, de caeteris quae ad perfectum piae sapientiae pertinent semotis studiis, salva charitate, sacris libris ducibus inquirere. Postremo, siqui errent etiam in alicuius momenti rebus, superest non ut invidiosa criminatione impingamus illis quicquid error secum invitus trahit, sed ut benigna interpretatione sublevemus ignorantiae miseriam. Si enim peccatis ignoscere debemus quae contra praecepta cognita atque intellecta fiunt, quid ni et isti culpae quam nemo volens in se suscipit? Salviani memorabilis hanc in rem sententia est, ubi agit de odiosissimo sui temporis errore, cuius verbis optime hic sermo finietur. *Haeretici ergo sunt, sed non scientes. Denique apud nos sunt haeretici, apud se non sunt. Nam in tantum se catholicos esse iudicant, ut nos ipsos titulo haereticae appellationis infament. Quod ergo illi nobis sunt, et nos hoc illis.* [....] *Veritas apud nos est, sed illi apud se esse praesumunt. Honor Dei apud nos est, sed illi hoc arbitrantur honorem divinitatis esse quod credunt. Inofficiosi sunt, sed illis hoc est summum religionis officium. Impii sunt, sed hoc putant veram esse pietatem. Errant ergo, sed bono animo errant, non odio, sed affectu Dei, honorare se Dominum atque amare credentes. Quamvis non habeant rectam fidem, illi tamen hoc perfectam*
20ᵛ *Dei aestimant charitatem. Qualiter pro hoc ipso falsae opinionis errore* / *in die iudicii puniendi sint, nullus potest scire nisi iudex. Interim idcirco eis, ut reor, patientiam Deus commodat, quia videt eos, etsi non recte credere, affectu tamen piae opinionis errare.*

MELETIUS

OR

LETTER ON THE POINTS OF AGREEMENT BETWEEN CHRISTIANS

1 Time and again, my most illustrious friend, I remember — besides a great number of other instructive things — what you told me about that by far the most pleasant experience you had when you sojourned in the remotest regions of Asia; places where others went for profit, but you in order to satisfy your passion for learning; places where you received whomsoever crossed your path from our own European countries as fellow-countrymen, if not as relations by blood. No doubt you were prompted to this attitude by your innate kindness and your cultured humanity. But apart from this, this is likely to happen with others as well, since such a close relationship, which tends to be frustrated and lost in a crowd, is furthered when contacts are few and far between and also by all that is strange in the environment. Likewise we ourselves who live in these parts not only consider the other Europeans as foreigners, but even we as Germans are differentiated as High and Low Germans. Firstly, the Low Germans are kept divided by the recollection of a war which is hardly over; next, some are Guelders and others Frisians; and would that the peoples of Holland and Zealand, who always used to be so closely connected, differed only in name and not also in sympathy! Not to mention at this point the cities — rival centres rather —, the quarrels between city districts or the enmity between the great families. When we take all this into consideration, there is no doubt that neighbours and relatives seem more alien to one another than Italians or even Spaniards seemed to you when you stayed in Syria.

2 The same, I notice, has occurred in religion. For from the moment that the Christian name had become widespread and, once the strength of its antagonists had been broken, an opening had been created for them to differ first in opinion and then in conviction, different teachers and parties began to emerge alienating Christians from Christians in the same way as non-Christians had been strangers to Christians. That disease already started a long time ago. But in our age and in that of our fathers it has grown to such an extent that it cannot possibly go on any longer. For not only indifference or rivalry, but also implacable hatred and anger, indeed — something almost unprecedented — wars are

started under no other pretext than that of the very religion whose purpose is peace. Yet, if we were willing to consider the people of the Indies, to whom we send our ships so successfully, or the Turks among whom you (= J. Boreel) have lived, or the Jews who are now settling among us, we should be obliged to remember our almost forgotten kinship, even if only by comparing ourselves with them. For are we not strongly united by the very issue that separates us all from them, regardless of whether we consider them as a body or individually?

3   If everybody monopolizes for himself the name of 'Christian' to the exclusion of others, then at least another name should be sought which would likewise separate us from the profanity of those I mentioned just now. But surely no other name could be invented but the very name given us by our Lord, whom we all profess to obey, even though through ignorance we do not do so. No reason for discord can be so important that it would not be surpassed by that very reason for concord, to wit that we follow a single teacher, indeed him who acknowledges no disciples but those who devote themselves to concord. That is why, in the face of new conflicts every day and ever-regenerating disturbances, I usually find solace and new strength by reflecting on those things which God's goodness has kept intact for the Christians to this day; things which, by virtue of their being the greatest, the most certain and the most valuable, naturally mean so much to me that while I consider them, I put aside for the time being the other things which are of minor importance, less certain and less valuable. May these privileges, if I may call them that, at least prove to us that we are citizens of *one* community.

4   How I wish I could discuss this matter with you now, as when in the past we often sat together. Indeed with whom would I rather talk about it than with you, one of the very few who pointed out that true jurisprudence comprises not only knowledge of things human but also of things divine? You know so well who the enemies of Christianity are, both in antiquity and in modern times; you are so profoundly versed in the Greek and Hebrew literature, and have also made a thorough examination of the sects within Christianity, not only those which keep us divided, but also the Greeks, Armenians and Maronites, whom, when you lived among them, you did not as a matter of course consider to be non-Christians — even though in many matters you knew better than they — any more than they considered you as such.

5   But now that distance as well as professional duties do not allow us to meet, I shall write down what you told me the Patriarch Meletius often used to express to you; on condition, however, that you, who have the more accurate knowledge, will make the necessary emendations and corrections. I have no doubt but that you, too, will take delight in recalling

this, and that it will be profitable to me to learn about them more accurately from you. Now this Meletius was Patriarch of Alexandria and at the same time ruler of the church of Constantinople, a man of venerable sanctity and highly proficient in every kind of learning — for he even spoke Latin, which is unusual for Greeks, and he had read all the most famous authors in that language. He furthermore loved peace among Christians so much that he could not refrain from tears when execrating our dissensions, as he often did, and he used to beg us at long last to turn our eyes, made fierce by contemplating one another, on the Turks and the riff-raff society of uncivilised peoples. But above all he emphasized the points of consensus between the Christians. That, he used to say, was so much more universal and momentous than was commonly thought. At the same time his one concern was to point out that what was shared by all Christians contained everything that is held to be best in any philosophical school or among national institutions, and apart from this many specific points of its own unknown to all the others. All this he extolled in a remarkably eloquent way; we, for our part, can only try to expound it as meticulously as possible.

I

6   The first characteristic that Christianity has in common with many (movements) though not with all, is that it is a religion. The impious, therefore, and those we call atheists, fall outside this scope. But religion has no meaning without those two things of which the Apostle mentions in his letter to the Hebrews, namely that one should believe that God exists, and further that He rewards those who desire to please Him. That God exists is made abundantly clear not only by the very widespread consensus of mankind, but also by the order of mutually dependent causes and the hierarchy in the world. Indeed the truth of this is so evident that in so many centuries there have been only a very few who declared otherwise, more perhaps because they preferred that it should not be the case than because they felt that it were so.

7   As to God being remunerator, it is necessary to establish some points in advance. In the first place, it is prerequisite that God be an intelligent being, which is sufficiently proved by the fact that no product can be better than its maker. Therefore, God is neither the world nor what is commonly called nature, but He is something more noble and sacred. Nor is intelligence the only property God has, He must also possess a will, or what is called free choice, for those who have these things are more perfect than those who do not have them. And that will itself must be free and unimpeded, because this, too, pertains to perfection, and by the

nature of things it is impossible that some other cause should be superior to the supreme cause. This theory refutes the Stoics, who, in the stupidity of their persuasion, make God subordinate to the power of fate. Whence that ungodly verse:

What is fated to be, surpasses Jove the highest.

Likewise refuted is another, no less insane, error of the old magi, who alleged that God can be constrained by fixed formulas or other means, by all of which God is professed in words but in fact denied.

8   Furthermore, it should be stated that God attends to His creation; not only to the things celestial, as some would have it, but also to things human. With this axiom we exclude the Epicureans, who, had they said that God watches over and rules everything effortlessly, would have been in no error at all. As it is, they have fallen into gross error, thinking that it is an effort to apply intelligence and free will, whereas nothing could be easier, especially when you consider the role of omnipotence. For whatever difficulties arise in the act of ruling are due to the incompetence of the rulers. Those fathers are cruel who, content with having fathered children, expose them. God, however, is not God unless he is good. Add to this that the admirable order of the universe tells us that God is founder as well as ruler. Nothing, however, is more alien to the nature of rulers than to attend to the trivialities of ruling while neglecting the essentials.

9   For there to be a reason for reward, we must also accept that man is a rational being with free will. If this is correct, as experience teaches us it is, it follows from this, too, that the Stoic doctrine of fate should be rejected. For if everything that will happen in the future depended on necessary causes, man would have received his deliberative power and free choice between good and bad in vain. Now, to state that anything in creation, and above all in man, might be to no avail, is tantamount to charging the Creator with incompetence.

10   Furthermore, it follows logically that we acknowledge God as legislator. For if God has a free will, then so has man. But God is superior, man inferior. And the superior influences the inferior since the superior is destined to act and the inferior to be acted upon. Consequently, God acts upon man according to His free choice. This activity, then, of the superior free agent toward the inferior free choice as such is nothing but the law or authority. That this is true is proved by man's conscience more forcefully than by any other evidence.

11   From what has been said we may conveniently conclude our discussion about remuneration. For it is just that he who keeps the law should be rewarded and he who breaks it punished. Now God is just and acts justly. Moreover, every legislator wishes his laws to be respected. To this end

he employs everything that can effect this, in so far as it is within his means. Now nothing is more effective as an incentive to obedience than a reward. And God has the power to give rewards, which human legislators are often not in a position to do. Therefore, He does reward.

12 These are the principles which the Christian religion has in common with all religions, the false ones and the true but less perfect ones, such as, in the first place, natural religion, and, next, the Mosaic religion. He who abandons these principles can truly be said to be abandoning religion, the most important thing in the world. For what is more important and valuable than that man should not only consistently act but also think honestly and correctly? Positive laws cannot achieve this, since not only our thoughts but also most of our deeds evade them. Religion, however, and religion only, can achieve it.

It is profitable that there be gods, let us therefore assume that they exist, to quote the poet. But we are nearer to the truth, when we say: it is profitable that there be religion, therefore religion exists. For the ruler in his great wisdom did not fail to institute those things which profit us most.

II

13 Let us now turn to the subject proper. As is the case with everything that happens according to free choice, it is necessary first to inquire about ends. What is perfect aims at perfection, and religion surpasses everything in perfection. Therefore what religion aims at is simply the best, or the supreme good. But in what the supreme good, in other words human happiness consists, has long been most fiercely disputed among philosophers. Christianity agrees with right reason that the supreme good of man consists in enjoying to the fullest extent what is intrinsically the supreme good, and this is God.

14 For just as restless nature teaches us that there is only one effective cause of infinite progress, the same nature reminds us that everything exists because of One and for the sake of One. But we can only delight in God by means of that which is most like God, namely our mind. But since happiness concerns man as a whole and not merely part of him, it follows that it is by submitting as best we can the other parts of our soul and even the body itself to our mind that we can hope to participate in this happiness. Once goodness in all its fullness has been established, all evil must of necessity be removed; then, immortality and freedom from pain will be concomitant with this supreme happiness.

15 So it is clear that all who have sought man's highest good in this fragile life have failed. Now this can be said about the supreme good attainable in this earthly life: we can certainly begin to delight in God, with the firm

hope of afterlife. But we cannot call this the highest good without qualification, since it contains the prospect of death and the suffering of pain. All philosophers, therefore, are in error, even those who maintained most persuasively of all that this life's highest good is to be sought in virtue. It is, therefore, not surprising that they have succeeded in making few men good, indeed none truly so, for they employed false arguments. Indeed their one basic assumption is false, that virtue should be sought after for its own sake, a tenet that is unmistakably refuted by reason. For virtue is chiefly concerned with trouble. And no one will accept trouble unless for the sake of something else. Hence other philosophers declared, with better reason, that the certainty of afterlife is proved beyond possibility of doubt by the fact that in this life most often the good fare ill and the bad fare well.

> *May Eurystheus reign in undisturbed rest;*
> *May Alcmene's son in all the wars*
> *stir up the heavenly band with evil portents.*

16 From this it also follows that those too err who, even though they posit an afterlife, find their greatest happiness in food and drink, like the Talmudic Jews, or in sexual indulgence, like the Mohammedans, while Christians exclude both from a life of happiness as signs of an insatiable appetite; "for true happiness knows no needs". Food and sex may be good for cattle, for man they are certainly not, for, since in him the soul is superior to the body, he must, to achieve true happiness, assimilate body to soul, not soul to body, and become a spiritual body instead of a bodily spirit. Aristotle perceived something of this, since in the 'Eudemian Ethics' he states: "Therefore whatever mode of choosing and of acquiring things good by nature will promote the contemplation of God better than goods of body or wealth or friends or the other goods, that is the best mode, and that standard is the finest; and any mode of choice and acquisition that through excess hinders us from serving and from contemplating God — that is a bad one. This is how it is for the spirit, and this is the best spiritual standard — to be as far as possible unconscious of the other, inferior part of the spirit, as such."

17 There is another thing worth our attention, namely that those things that are separately considered to be the highest good by individual people, are collectively contained in the highest good of the Christians. For irrespective of whether you look for it in pleasure, either that which exists in passivity and is called freedom from pain, as does the philosopher Hieronymus, or, with the school of Aristippus, that which lies in activity, both are present in the Christian religion, absence of any suffering as well as the highly pleasurable experience by which the soul, not the body (since this only impedes the soul), is moved to joy and delight; or whether

you place the highest good in virtue, with the Stoics, this is also truly present here, in addition to the good fortune of a perfect life which Aristotle links with virtue.

18   On the ground of the perfect nature of this highest good that pertains to man as a whole, we reject the views held by the Epicureans and the Jewish sect of the Sadducees. For from the above it follows that the human body will either never perish or will be brought to life again, and likewise the soul will either live again or never perish. Now experience proves that bodies do perish; consequently they will be restored to life. That the soul does not perish is, in accordance with the majority of the philosophers (with the exception of the Epicureans, who, as somebody from antiquity said, are called philosophers in the same way that a portrait of a man is called a man), the view held by the Christian religion, agreeing not only with the age-old belief of nearly all peoples but also with that very reason which teaches us that our intellectual faculty lies in the soul, the image of God, free from suffering. Having thus established the purpose of religion, let us now consider its constituent elements.

III

19   Now religion, since it concerns actions based on free choice, while all voluntary actions are preceded by the understanding, necessarily consists of two parts: the one theoretical, the other practical. The former is made up of dogmas, the latter of ethical precepts. Seneca, following Cicero, renders these notions in Latin as *decreta* and *praecepta*, principles and rules, and they demonstrate that these two terms embrace all that is taught about customs and duties. Principles are sometimes also called tenets, decrees or opinions. In every practical science the principles should be neither irrelevant nor redundant, but should either incite to action or to some extent make clear what must be done and how it must be done. For this reason, since religion is intermediary between man and God, the principles of religion pertain both to God and things divine, and to man and things human, not only as they are in themselves but as they are in relation to one another.

20   That there is only one God deservedly holds pride of place amongst these principles. This is proved by the same arguments which convince us that God exists. For everything originates in One and exists because of One; moreover, the absolutely perfect nature and beatitude of God and his rule over the entire creation testify to this. But how great a part of the human species was once haunted by the inexcusable delusion of polytheism, and still is for that matter!

21 Moreover, the Christian religion, discarding all other things, attributes to God everything that is altogether the best that can be said or thought. It therefore affirms that God is most simple, infinite and best; while it categorically denies that God could be corporeal, composite, mutable, limited by space or time. Thus Plutarch says that the Jews believe that "God is immortal, ungenerated, and beneficent"; and according to Tacitus they believe in "one God, the highest and eternal, neither mutable nor perishable".

22 From this one and undivided nature we understand in the first place what 'existing' itself means; in the second place the divine reason; in the third place what power is. It appears that Aristotle too discerned the latter two in God, calling them 'mind' and 'energy'. Had God not possessed these, he would have been less perfect than his creation. Although the Platonists also called this reason 'word' and 'wisdom', yet the thing itself and the terms are explained more clearly by the Christians. Then again the power of God is so called by the Christians, or they call it Spirit, which expresses not only its immaterial but also its active nature. But these are in God not as parts or qualities, but mutually distinct in some other, ineffable way such that the 'three hypostases' are one God, so that, as Aristotle has it, "the mind and what is grasped by the mind are identical".

23 Even though human reason by itself has not been able to find out that God is like this, yet when it is told that this is so it finds it easy to agree. For it perceives that all this is consistent with the divine majesty, and it should not be deterred from agreeing by the fact that it could not possibly comprehend how these things are three and, at the same time, one, since we distinguish in the case of our own mind — which is so much inferior — the actual nature of the mind, the intellect and the will, and yet insist emphatically that the mind is one and indivisible. The same is the case with the sun: we know the celestial body as such, its light and its fiery power, yet we do not divide it into several parts; indeed it derived its name 'sol' from its being solitary.

24 Since the perfection of intelligence consists in knowing as much as possible, and the strength of free will in willing and doing what is best, it follows that God's wisdom is omniscient, his power supreme, and therefore, though knowing evil, He neither actually wills nor does it, thus providing the finest foundation of piety. So that should silence the poets, once the only masters of theology, who were most justly censured by Plato, Varro and others for telling deeds of their gods abominable even to man; such as violence, adultery and other crimes. It should also silence those godless words:

> *Alas! this too is truly evil in God,*
> *where one sees a better course yet does not pursue it.*

Or:
> *God generates guilt*
> *every time he wishes to disturb safe homes.*

Equal to which is:
> *The gods will be to blame made me too a sinner.*

Or:
> *Does it please you, gods, after you have decided to turn*
> *everything upside down, to blame it on our errors?*

Such an opinion does away with religion. For how can anyone love God and hate evil, when he believes God to be the generator of evil? The following words are therefore more realistic:
> *If gods do something evil, they are not gods.*

And in the words of Cleanthes:
> *Unless it is done by you, propitious deity, nothing happens*
>   *on the face of the earth,*
> *throughout the wide expanse of the sea, or in the realms of the thunder above,*
> *except what is deliberately done by wicked men in their wild madness.*

25 And yet these very evils, though not originating in God, are cured and regulated by Him, as sound reason and Christian religion teach. Religion, however, offers two things which it is highly useful for us to believe in: God's omniscience and His perfect goodness. His omniscience makes us stand in awe of His presence in all our most secret deeds and even thoughts. God's goodness makes us aim at being good ourselves too, in accordance with that Pythagorean saying "Follow God" and with Christ's words "Be perfect as your Father is perfect". To sum up all we have said about God: we have to admire Him for his perfect nature, honour Him for his boundless wisdom and love Him before everything for his exceptional goodness.

26 Now if you consider God not only as He is in Himself but also in His relations to other things, religion offers two aspects of God: that He is the creator as well as the ruler of everything. That He is the creator is evidenced by the same arguments by which His existence is proved, namely by the chain of causes which can only rest on one prime cause; and this, in addition, brings more honour to God and is more conducive to devotion. When, therefore, Plato thinks the world was born and Aristotle that it is eternal they certainly err, yet their arguments prove what Christians believe. For Plato was right in concluding that the world had a beginning at some point in time, and Aristotle was equally right in saying that it had not been born; from which we may conclude that it was made.

27 And when we say 'world' we do not only refer to visible things — including man — but also invisible, namely rational beings or natures inferior to God but superior to man, intelligent and active, who have been called gods or demons by many people. 'Demons' because of their superior intellect, but 'gods' on false grounds. For if polytheism has been rejected for sound reasons, it follows that they are not properly called 'gods' but because they share in some way in the divine majesty. It was with an eye to this point that the teachers of the Christians, in order to eradicate once and for all the error of those who by giving them the same honour as well as the same name had equated those creatures with their creator, abstained from using that name and preferred to call them angels, so that they might be seen as servants of God and not as His equals.

28 Now we are taught that God has made everything for His own sake, for, as we have said just now, not only the efficient cause but also the final cause of the creation has to be one and the same, though in a fixed order; in the sense that God, as the Stoics so correctly put it, made all other things for the sake of man, but man solely for the sake of God. That this is irrefutably true can be inferred from the fact that only he who is master of his own actions, i.e. he who has a free choice, can control other things. And of all creation only man and those beings we call rational spirits have this free choice. But the nature of these spirits is such that they have no need of things outside themselves. We may therefore conclude that it is for the sake of man that the earth and the sea have been created, as well as the air, fire, the beasts and the earth's produce, and finally heaven itself and the stars.

29 In saying that God is the ruler we do not only refute the doctrine of chance collisions held by the Epicureans, but also that of the power of fate held by the Stoics, doctrines which are equally detrimental to piety. For by his rule God does not destroy but preserves the natural order He created, and especially the free choice He gave to rational creatures. Which solves the question which for a very long time perplexed the minds of the philosophers: if good things come from God, whence the bad? No doubt from the possibilities offered by the freedom of choice, which, though certainly good in itself because given by God, can all the same lapse spontaneously into evil, even though God forbids and warns against it, without, however, preventing it by His power, so as not to remove the freedom which had once been rightly given and without which any reward would be impossible. Evil, therefore, or sin, proceeds from the absolutely free will of those inferior spirits and of men who of their own volition deviated from the law of their maker; and here we come across the Manicheans and those like them, who posit matter or some other

necessary principle of evil, and say that some people are by nature so conditioned that they cannot possibly either be or become good. Persuasions of this kind are an insult to God and prevent people from really repenting of their sins and from desiring a change of heart.

30   Let us now turn to the decrees with regard to man, some of which has already been touched upon before: that he consists of body and mind; that he has the faculty of free choice; that he is the finest and most worthy of all visible things, indeed master of other things. Let us add that beyond any doubt God made him good, for it is impossible for Him who is best to create evil, indeed, as some philosophers agreeing with the Christian doctrine have said, man is in a way the image of God, namely created after the likeness of God, and indeed that he has an aptitude for approaching this likeness more and more closely by making an effort; and that in the beginning one man, not several, was created by whom the others were begotten, a view which is the more plausible for being better and more conducive to mutual love and friendship, considering that lawyers also prove conclusively that "it is wicked for men to be after one another's blood," on the grounds that "nature has constituted some sort of kinship between us."

31   Christians, in contradistinction only to the Stoics but in agreement with other philosophical schools, opine with every justification that God has also endowed man with passions. This is demonstrated by the very nature of man, in which physicians too list certain members as sources and seats of the passions. This opinion, too, is highly conducive to piety whereas the contrary doctrine, unless we obstinately ascribe a meaning to the words which conflicts with their daily use, makes people unfeeling and uncharitable.

32   The relationship between man and God, as we have mentioned before, consists in man having been created in order to serve God. We have said that this was the view held by all philosophers, and some of them not ineptly draw the same conclusion from the very build of the human body, which is upright, eyes heavenward. This is why the Phoenician theologians of very long ago called man 'observer of the sky'.

33   And indeed how could it be that man should not have been created in the first place in order to do what he both could and above all should do? What he could do was to honour God, for to this end he had received the use of his mind. That he should do it was not only because of the perfect nature of God, but also because of the blessings received from Him, namely that he owed his very existence as a human being to God, that he was superior to other things, and finally because so much had been destined to serve his comfort. Honouring God implies all of the following points: loving, admiring and revering Him, the desire to please Him and

the fear to displease Him, aversion to the things that are contrary to His law. Since all these are names of passions, they prove what has been said before, namely that man should not be stripped of them. For it is not enough just to perform a prescribed task: you should do it wholeheartedly and with an all-round effort. In sum this is what man should be like.

34 Let us now turn to those principles which, in accordance with experience, define what man is in fact. Now it is an established fact that man is far from being what he ought to be: for he is ungrateful to God and truly bad. For although he should above all love and honour God with all the fervour of his heart and prefer Him to all else, and gratefully value His boundless gifts, everybody's conscience testifies to the contrary.

35 We should add that God, in keeping with His nature, wanted man to value his fellow-man more than anything else, since he is related to him by kinship and made in God's image. Indeed reason shows us both things, to wit that the highest kinship and relationship is that of common origin and blood, and that, if we want to be thankful, we should not only love Him who has showered us with the greatest benefactions, but also those who in some way are very close to Him. What we see, however, is a general situation fraught with hatred and dissension. Indeed a great many actions, even those that seem good to us, are bad, because everything that is deprived of some part of its goodness is bad. And nothing is good unless it is entirely good: "goodness is unqualified, but evil comes in many different ways." Wherever, therefore, the soul is not pure and unspoilt and the intention to serve God is not absolutely firm, there can be no perfect devotion to duty or right action.

36 In fact we should not be so very surprised at seeing man fallen into meaner actions, since it is clearly proved by the fact that innumerable practices exceeding the strength of man's inferior nature, to which the history of all peoples testifies that even some of those higher rational creatures have turned to evil, and consequently made all possible efforts to induce man too to become a partner in the conspiracy of their malice; which they could bring about more easily since man's faculties are just as susceptible to the lure of sin as inclined toward virtue. That this depravity has spread over the entire human species should be evident, if not from the repeated warnings of each individual's conscience, then from the shared misery in which mankind lives and from the fact that nature became no longer 'mother' but 'stepmother'. Nor would a benevolent God allow human life to be so exposed to tribulations if He did not deem all people answerable for their guilt.

37 There is, by the way, yet another error of the Stoics justly rejected by the Christians, namely that all sins are equal; that this is erroneous is loudly proclaimed by our very conscience, which accuses us more or less

severely according to the magnitude of our sins. Indeed the juridical laws vary according to the diversity of the offence, the one being more serious than the other. And the one deed is more remote from the same law than the other, just as is the case with oblique lines, which do not all have the same obliquity just because they proceed from a straight line. Nor should a guilty deed, even when compared with others it is of very minor importance, be considered as in itself not serious.

38 For this is inherent in every sin, that it insults the highest King, the perfect Father and the most generous Benefactor; indeed an insult from the very man to whom He gave the highest preference and whom He adorned with so many excellent gifts. Now since all men deviate from God's law, it follows first that all are slaves of their vices and consequently subject to the punishment which under the law has to be equivalent to the reward that awaits those who abide by the law.

39 Hence the first principle arises, that every vice leads to decline. "It is clearly a lack of intelligence", as Aristotle has it, "to overlook the fact that habits originate in activities with regard to individual cases", which he illustrates by two examples: that of the stone that has irrevocably been thrown; he who threw it held it in his hand before throwing it and while holding it could have not thrown it, but once it has been thrown he cannot afterwards call it back. Next, he gives the example of a man who has fallen ill as a result of his intemperance and because he did not heed the advice of the physicians; he could have avoided falling ill, but now he no longer can. And then he says in well-chosen words: "In the same way the unjust and the intemperate men were initially free not to become so; they became so therefore of their own free choice but once they have become like that they no longer have that choice." Seneca, too, worded it rather elegantly: "One of the frailties of the human condition is the obfuscation of the mind, which gives rise not only to inevitable error but even to an attachment to errors."

40 Moreover, God rightly withdraws His support, which is indispensable to man in his endeavours to live a correct life according to God's laws, from those who perfidiously deserted Him. Apart from that which already existed at the beginning of the history of mankind, later generations also had to cope with degenerate ancestry, inadequate education and bad examples all around.

41 This doctrine is by far the most salutary, for it both highlights God's goodness, namely that He has unfailingly loved mankind, even those who least deserve it, and it also effects in man the best safeguard, namely that it makes him unassuming, something we would wish for in virtually all philosophers. For none of them makes people so responsible for their deeds or stimulates modesty as does the Christian religion. An added

advantage is that it makes it easier for him who is aware of his own guilt to overlook other people's: In Seneca's words: "If we want to be just judges of everything, we should first convince ourselves that none of us is without guilt."

42   We therefore reject the doctrine of the the rivalry of the gods as propounded by the Stoics, one of whom, by the name of Sextius, denied that "Jove was more powerful than a good man"; and who taught that God "does not surpass a wise man in happiness, even if he does so in age". Indeed he even went so far in his folly that he declared that God is surpassed by the wise man, because God has no share in the suffering of misfortune, whereas the wise man transcends it. In the same breath we also condemn the arrogance of the Pharisees and of all those who think they can entirely of their own power escape punishment or obtain rewards.

43   Since, therefore, man, because of his failings, is prone to viciousness and liable to punishment, it follows that any religion has become obsolete which does not show the way to remission and reparation of sins. For he who deserves punishment cannot hope for a reward, and he who is sunk in vice cannot by himself rise up. But that religion has not been abolished can be deduced from the very fact that God both furthers the human race and for it prolongs the use of this world; and to what other end than that He be worshipped by man? There is, therefore, indeed a remission of sins as well as a restoration of fallen man; and it is not only necessary that there should be some forgiveness, but also that man's trust in God should become so firm that, certain of forgiveness, he sets himself to pleasing God. And this confidence is indeed a grace characteristic of the Christian religion, of which Zosimus, a non-Christian author, said in his discussion about it that it is "a promise of deliverance from all sin and all ungodliness." Elsewhere, he calls this religion "a faith that removes all sin and makes this promise that sinners on joining it, immediately become free from all guilt."

44   But very much depends on what is the basis of this confidence, for how dangerous an error on this point can be is demonstrated by Plato when he uncompromisingly condemns as corruptive to morality those religions which promise an easily obtainable forgiveness of sins by means of initiations. Aware of this pitfall, Plato's followers, among whom Porphyry, deny that there can be found any certain and universal means to purge souls, which they call a sacramental rite. And yet unless such a means is found there will be no religion at all. It must therefore be admitted that, had God not revealed it, men would never have reached any certainty on which they could base their confidence in forgiveness. All the same it is worthwhile examining how men, groping in the darkness but some more successfully than others, have approached the truth.

45 Firstly, almost all peoples agree that "forgiveness requires shedding of blood", because a sin committed against God cannot be expiated by any penalty less than that of death. But they should also have realized that beasts are of too lowly a value for them to qualify to act as a sacrificial substitute for man. For which reason some peoples have made human sacrifices, thereby firstly becoming homicides since they were in no way commanded to do so by someone authorized to give such a command. Secondly, they also erred in that they believed that someone who for his own sins has to pay the death penalty himself could become an expiatory sacrifice for others, because, even assuming they did find an innocent man — there was none —, he on his own would yet not be capable of expiating the sins of mankind in general or of a people in particular.

46 Now most peoples and philosophers are agreed that for man, especially as he is acknowledged to be somehow alienated from God through his own fault, a mediator should be sought who can take up a position somewhere between man and God. To this end they turned to the veneration of demons, whose nature they saw as something in between divine and human. But Porphyry denied that the sin of ignorance could be removed by any other means than "by the spirit of the Father." Now human perversity is closely tied up with the worst ignorance and blindness.

47 The Christian truth has brought all these elements together into one whole, so that it can teach that man has been given a mediator; not one who is neither man nor God but who is both, to wit the Word of the Father, who by the power of God was made true man, that he could expiate human sins by shedding his blood. For he had to be human in order to be able to die and he could not have given life to others had he himself not been God. The fruit of his death by far surpasses all other things. For in the first place it prevented men from underestimating the gravity of their sins, as is the custom of those who think they can set themselves free by sacrificing some petty animal or by making some trivial oblation. Now that on behalf of which God's true Son himself has been made the means of atonement must of necessity be a very serious sin. In the second place and viewed from another angle, it meets the desperate need of those whose conscience cannot find rest in other kinds of expiatory purges. This can only be effected in Christ's expiation, since man sees that the price matches his sins. Finally, nothing else can testify more convincingly to the love God feels towards men and stimulate us accordingly to love such a benevolent parent with a reciprocal love.

48 Famous is the story of Zaleucos, who, having enacted a law that an adulterer's eyes should be torn out, saved his son who was caught in this criminal act from blindness by having one of his own eyes and one of his son's torn out. "Thus", says Valerius Maximus, "punishment was

implemented according to the law and through his admirable fairness he showed himself a merciful father as well as a just legislator''. But still more was accomplished by Christ, who gave himself as a substitute in order to save us entirely from punishment. As we just said on a similar subject, the fact that we do not understand how God identified Himself with man does not make this less credible. For we do not even grasp what kind of bond and ties there are between our soul and body, and yet we do not doubt that both these things constitute one man.

49 We may add that most philosophers posit that God sometimes dwells in human minds. In this sense the Platonist Amelius quoted that well-known passage from John the Evangelist, ''in the beginning there was the Word'' and the next words, ''and the Word became flesh'', wrong though he was in his interpretation of these words as though they referred to 'dwelling in' in the sense that God is in all holy people. But this is immensely different from that extraordinary and ineffable state which is called 'substantial union'. Yet the former notion can lead to believing the latter. But the admirable works of Christ are more powerful than any other weapon in conquering the tardiness of human assent, they surpass all human power and that of created rational beings to such a degree that, taking everything into careful consideration, it would be far more difficult not to believe that it was God who did those things than to believe it; particularly because these very works, the time of Christ's birth, his ancestry and his country, his entire life and his death had been unanimously predicted by the prophets several centuries before.

50 We should now go into the question who has access to the forgiveness we spoke about. The Christian religion teaches that it is attainable for all mankind, as against the intolerance of the Jews who want to reserve that hope all for themselves to the exclusion of all other peoples. But not all people attain it as a matter of course, for this grace is offered on condition of penitence and belief, the first of which is always a requirement for any act of forgiveneness. Indeed no man in his right senses forgives the crime of somebody he knows does not repent; otherwise the evil of sinners would be encouraged by their impunity.
   By tolerating an old injustice, you would provoke a new one.
Now the second imperative, belief, is not only exacted by God's veracity, since it is an extreme insult to distrust His promises, but it is also necessary because there is no other way to accept individually what has been offered universally. And, as we said before, nobody can rise to the level of loving and worshipping God who did not previously conceive a firm confidence in the forgiveness of his earlier sins. This is wholly in agreement with sound reasoning. Someone once said, ''penitence is holy, wholly divine, and redeems all those who have sinned. The remaining

sufferings are removed by reason; repentance alone is produced by reason, which is consumed by shame and so works off its own punishment." And just as this repentance is extremely useful in correcting man, confidence in God is highly conducive to the glory of God Himself. That is why this forgiveness is actually what the philosophers say it is, "a grace not according to the law nor against the law but above the law and in place of the law."

51 The better to understand this, we must now turn to the restoration of man, which immediately follows in order after remission of sins. In order to achieve restoration remedies are required, the first of which is to remove ignorance; as long as this is left undone vices will inevitably remain. Now this ignorance has pride of place in man, as Aristotle said so well: "just as bats' eyes react to daylight, our mind and soul shrink from what in themselves are the most obvious things." This is not so much because things divine far surpass human comprehension as because the mind, obfuscated by sins and trammelled by material things, cannot raise itself to the point of seeing them for what they are. The only remedy for this is God's revelation of the divine truth. With peoples ignorant of Christ the gods used to speak about human matters and only the people talked about the gods, whereas it is much more consistent with God's nature to reveal His nature and His benefactions to man than to answer questions on the outcome of a war or matters of similar importance. It would, moreover, be extremely impudent of man to make rash pronouncements on such exalted matters without any authority. The Christian religion is therefore the only one to have the right to claim that all it hands down concerning God and divine matters was received from God himself, whose word was revealed through the holy prophets and ultimately through the Word of God himself; and in order that it would leave no room for doubt, it was also contained in the Holy Scriptures.

52 That these Scriptures reveal the truth is in the first place proved by the fact that, in their stories as well as in the rules they give, nothing is taught that is unworthy of God, nothing that is not conducive to the best conduct of life, whereas poets, philosophers and all those who claim to instruct others teach many things that are unworthy of God, absurd, and at variance with good morals. And all their stories, only dealing with other things, generally neglect the function which ought to be the most important. Add to this that books written by men, even those which belong to one sect, nowhere show such agreement. But the holy Scriptures of the Christians are not only coherent within themselves but can also adduce witnesses — even hostile — to many parts of their narrative.

53 Also their antiquity lends authority to their truth. For the antiquity of these books which form part of this volume goes farther back than that

of all human books, both as regards their argumentation and their composition. Varro, on the authority of the ancients, divided the whole past into three parts: the unknown, the mythical and the historical. The first age, he said, was that before the Flood, of which nothing can be known. The second period stretched from the Flood to the Trojan age, when myths prevailed. In the third period the light of history appeared at last. But that sacred and true history (contained in Scripture) connects both the period Varro calls mythical and that which he admits to be unknown into one running narrative. Moses, who was to Diodore the oldest legislator, was the first writer of this book, and nothing can be shown to have been written before his age; which is no matter for surprise, since the Greeks, from whom all literature developed among other peoples, acknowledged that they had adopted the alphabet as such from the Phoenicians; and the Phoenician alphabet being the same as that of the Hebrews, the Greeks gave their letters Phoenician or Hebrew names.

54 There is (in Scripture), moreover, a sublime simplicity of expression combined with majesty. The rhetorician Dionysius Longinus, who wrote about the sublime style, said that this sublimity, appropriate to divine matters, was best put into practice by the legislator of the Jews, whom he calls "an extraordinary man because he understood and explained the divine power in accordance with its dignity," writing, "right at the beginning of the laws: 'God said, "Let there be light", and there was light. "Let there be earth," and there was earth.'"

55 Now simplicity, apart from its being a major aspect of greatness, also enables all people, even the uneducated, to find out in a straightforward way enough to attain salvation. In this book man gains his knowledge of God not through knowledge of the laws of nature, or the theory of harmony, or mathematical lines and numbers like Pythagoras, Plato and others, in short by means of laborious subterfuges, but in plain words and at first glance He has made clear what is necessary to learn so that nobody is excluded from such an obvious truth by slow-wittedness, nor by a poverty which compels him to concern himself with the struggle for life nor by sex or age — as long as he is susceptible to reason. An eminent argument for all those other ways to gain knowledge of God not being the right ones is that they are not equally available to all people. For God, whom all people have in common and who is the same for everybody, has undoubtedly made the means to come to Him such that it is equally accessible and easy for everybody. This doctrine, that there is a dependable religious rule established by God, is both consistent with God's goodness and is highly conducive to preparing and leading our minds lest people fluctuate in uncertainty between so many philosophical statements and human institutions, or on this pretext abstain from religion.

56 What also restores man's strength is the perfect example set by Christ. It is in particular the Stoic philosophers who say that man is supported by examples no less than by words, if indeed often not more so. When we are in doubt as to what should be done in one situation or another, Epictetus refers us to Socrates, Seneca to Cato, some to Hercules and others to Ulysses; but it would be easy to point out many misdeeds committed by all of these people: lies, deceit, voluptuousness, arrogance, so much so that should one want to take their lives as an example, one would err very often indeed. Considering, furthermore, in what respects they sinned, it is questionable whether they acted rightly in other matters. Christians, however, take as their example him who can be accused of no crime at all; whose life, unlike that of Mohammed or the hoped-for Messiah of the Jews, is full not of violence and the din of arms, but of mercy, charity, gentleness and patience. And lest we be deterred by the sorrows usually to be endured by those who side with virtue, he offers us an example not only of suffering and virtue, but also of supreme reward and of happiness; after the most atrocious insults and torture and finally patiently accepting death, he was restored to life again, then exalted to heaven, and from this very heaven he manifested himself as king and ruler over everything by the power of his admirable deeds in order that all who want to follow in his steps could consider that they are going to share in such a magnificent glory. Anybody will easily understand how effective a means of moving people's hearts this is. And the Christian religion alone has this means.

57 The third and most important means is God's secret power, or Spirit, inciting the human heart to live a good life, urging, ruling and confirming it. Philosophers have wondered if it is by divine dispensation that one becomes good? The majority think that people become good by virtue of divine favour, for obvious reasons, because it is proper to God to give what is best and because man, having lapsed into vice of his own accord, needs help in attaining virtue. In Seneca's words: "God goes to men, or rather he enters into men. No one is good without God." Yet they usually do not emphasize this as strongly as they ought to. With the result that people do not request urgently enough from God what they need most. But the Christian religion with very salutary modesty renders unto God complete praise for the restoration of man, except that it is aware that a man cannot become good unwillingly, but only willingly. In this way two pitfalls are avoided: on the one hand despair over one's own weakness which is relieved by faith in God's support, so that in truth it can be said to those who give up in Seneca's words: "the real cause is unwillingness, impotency is just a pretext." On the other hand there is the danger of arrogance and recklessness, which are restrained by the fact

that man is faced with his helplessness, since he learns that he does not have virtue from himself — without which he on his own is nothing — but has received it as a gift from God; as against the arrogant Stoic statement: "It is stupid to ask for a good frame of mind, since you can obtain that by your own power." These are the principles about man as such.

58 As to human affairs one thing may suffice: apart from true virtue, to wit religion, all the rest is indifferent with regard to man's highest goal. Christians do not quibble over words; unlike the Stoics, they do not protest against calling life, health, learning, honour and wealth good things and death, illness, lack of education, shame and poverty bad. On the contrary, they feel that these words should keep their accepted meaning, the better to make man realize that for the former he has to be thankful to God, and that the latter, on the other hand, are either a penalty for his sins or a test of his endurance. For man to be thoroughly convinced of this, it is necessary both that he enjoys the former as being consistent with nature and deplore the latter as incompatible. But meanwhile we have to bear in mind that neither of the two categories has the power either to give or to take away the supreme and ultimate good, but that they can become instrumental in furthering our virtues or our vices, depending on whether we use them rightly or wrongly. So much for the principles.

IV

59 Now that we are about to pay attention to the rules, it will be worthwhile to examine what those who professed another religion thought of these things in general. Strabo calls those early Jews, whose tradition was passed on by the Christians who shared their doctrine, "God-fearing and virtuous", and about the successors of Moses he says "and their successors for some time adhered to the same institutions, truly pious and truly just". And Trogus Pompeius — or rather Justin, who excerpted his work —, talking about the same people, said that "their justice was permeated with religion". Pliny says of the Christians that "they bound themselves on oath not to committing some crime but to not committing theft, robbery or adultery, not to break promises, not, on being asked, to deny a deposit entrusted to them." And Ammianus Marcellinus says: "The Christian religion teaches only what is just and good." But these rules must be examined more closely in their various parts.

60 Now there are obligations toward God, toward people and in respect to human affairs. Of all duties those toward God should have pride of place, as is the case with Christians. In this respect we cannot sufficiently

reproach almost all authors from antiquity on the subject of duties and morals, who either passed this over in total silence even though this is the most important thing, or only enjoined it in so far as it is part of the obedience due to state institutions; to such an extent that Varro and others did not hesitate to write that religions should be maintained out of respect for the law, however false they and their gods were. Indeed the Roman Senate claimed the right to create gods at their own discretion. Is this any different from invalidating religion by turning it into an institution? Even the philosophers themselves felt differently from what they said, whereas truth should be more sacrosanct than anything else. Christian teaching for that reason easily surpasses all philosophers and legislators in that it impresses on people that it is necessary to worship, love and venerate God everywhere and at all times. This is its constant aim, this is what it is all about.

61 Duties toward God are partly interior, partly exterior. The interior duties are those we observe with the mind, two of which are the most important ones: to believe in God and to invoke him. To believe in God is certainly difficult for others who do not know God's Word, but for Christians who carefully observe God's very Word it is easy. We have already dealt with this.

62 Even invoking God's name is extremely hazardous, according to Plato, who admits that he would not know what to pray. And the poets show that many extremely unfortunate mishaps would befall people should all their prayers be answered. But Christians learn first to pray, as against the ungodliness of so-called philosophers who deny that God should be prayed to. Also in contradistinction to the prevailing ignorance, Christians learn what they should pray for, to wit those things that pertain to the glory and honour of God, in order that He may be worshipped and obeyed in all respects. And as regards themselves and indeed this earthly life, nothing above the necessities of nature, but in support of the life to come: forgiveness of sins and a safeguard against sins.

63 Of external actions with regard to God some are forbidden, others commanded. Some of the forbidden actions concern words, others deeds. As to words we are forbidden to speak about God in a profane, rash or irreverent way; this is indeed much more than others forbid, which is perjury only. But how far did a great part of humanity stray away from this in times past, considering that authors filled their books with the most acerbic accusations against the gods? As regards deeds, almost all peoples once thought that the chief prohibition was against portraying God by means of an image. Platonists argued among themselves about whether or not statues should be erected to the gods. This was vetoed by

Pythagoras among the philosophers and by Numa among the legislators. Also Euripides and Seneca condemned their use. And the emperor Hadrian had temples built without images. Tacitus, on the subject of Jewish institutions, gave a correct interpretation of the reason why: "The Egyptians venerate a great many animals and their effigies, whereas the Jews perceive one single God solely in the mind: they consider impious those people who depict God with man-like images made of perishable materials; for supreme and eternal is the divine majesty, constant and intransient. Therefore there are no effigies in their cities, still less in their temples." It is quite preposterous to compare the incomparable God with anything whatsoever, and man, in reflecting on God, should not only turn his eyes and sensory perceptions away from all material and sensory reality as best he can, but also his mind, in order to understand God's utterly simple and all-surpassing nature.

64   The Christian religion also refrains us from worshipping God with laborious and innumerable rites. In this respect it is superior not only to the religions of the peoples of antiquity who devised many rites which were not commanded by God and therefore were disagreeable to Him, but even to the Jewish religion, which is also replete with sumptuous and cumbersome ceremonies. Apart from the fact that it greatly enhances our freedom and is a extraordinary gift from God, it also reminds us that the cult of God principally takes place in the mind.

65   Among the external commands pertaining to the cult of God the most important one is that we frequent those gatherings that have been instituted for the worship of God, where God's words are set forth, people religiously stimulated and collective prayers said. For if Cicero was right in saying on philosophical grounds "that nothing in the entire world is more pleasing to the highest God who rules all of this world than the assemblies and gatherings of people who are joined together by the same law", how much more value should not then be attached to those gatherings which take place in order that many pious people worship God with equal devotion and shared love? Indeed if concord between people and the worship due to Himself are so dear to God, He must be even more pleased with concord between people in their worship of Him. And to facilitate this observance a fixed part of time has been reserved for divine worship, for meetings, to wit each seventh day of the week; a very wise compromise between frequent diversions from secular pursuits, and prolonged forgetfulness of religion. Had Seneca and others understood this, they would never have regarded the Jewish sabbath as a sign of laziness, for the debt to the time cannot be better squared than by offering it to the Creator of time. At this point we should also note that with the peoples who do not know Christ sacrificial gatherings, without any

instruction of the people, were held merely for the sake of the spectacle and with some external display or other, and it was not the high-priests but the philosophers who handed down the commands regarding divine matters and the (correct) mode of life. From which it is clear that their religion was void and to no avail. But when Christians meet, it is in the first place to hear God's will as it were through an interpreter.

66 And then, in the second place, signs have a part to play in the matter, which are few and simple, but extremely effective in moving hearts. And so it was fitting that God in every respect came to our support in our weakness, since mostly:

What is received through the ears is slower in exciting the mind
than what is reliably shown to the perception of the eyes.

In the first place, nearly all peoples use water for their lustrations.

You, father, accept the sacred vessels and the ancestral penates.
I, just back from such a terrible war and slaughter fresh in my mind,
am not allowed to touch them until I have cleansed
                                            myself with the life-bringing water.

Likewise, Christians too cleanse themselves with water, and in order that it may be certain that it will not be a ceremony devoid of meaning the quintessence of the entire religion is summarized in the fewest possible words by invoking the Father as the giver of life, the Son as the giver of forgiveness and the Spirit as the giver of sanctity. We read that in the Mithraic sacrifices bread and wine were used, and in the mysteries of the Greeks the most important rites were those of Ceres and Liber in token of bread and wine. Not surprisingly so, for these two are the most important gifts from God for daily use in this life. But just as religion teaches that this life leads to another life in the future, these gifts remind Christians of far greater gifts. Since the Word of God assumed the form of a human body and blood for our sake, so that he might become a sacrifice for us and we become united with him, it surely stands to reason that his body and blood are no less food for our souls than bread and wine are food for body and blood. How different this is from the secret rites of the peoples of old, many of which were obscene, most of them ludicrous and all of them such that not even the priests themselves could explain them satisfactorily.

67 At this point we must not fail to mention that widely prevalent error that the happiness of another life can be achieved by the sole performance of rites, the most effective way to ruin good morals. Sophocles expressed it thus:

Thrice blest are they
who having seen these mystic rites shall pass
to Hades' house; for them alone is life
beyond; for others all is evil there.

He is said to have filled many thousands of uninitiated with despair by these verses. Diogenes however, opposing someone who defended a similar statement, mentioned the case of Pataecio, a contemporary thief, and asked whether it was at all credible that Pataecio, merely because he had been initiated in the mysteries, would fare better in his future life than Epaminondas who had deserved extremely well of his country and his fellow citizens but had not been initiated. How different then are the Christians, who not only do not believe that ritual rules are in themselves sufficient, but are convinced that they rank second in importance to those rules which prescribe the duties of love. To which we now come.

68 Among the duties toward man there are some that concern the duties of man to others and others which concern himself. As to the duties toward others, he owes them either to humanity as such or to the institutions of society. Put briefly, to humanity he owes friendship on the ground of natural kinship in the image of God. In this respect Christian piety either requires more or at least gives clearer commandments than do other religions. For most of these only have an eye for observable actions but are blind to the soul. Indeed it was on this external flawlessness and the exact performance of rites that the Pharisees based their superstitious, indeed impudent faith in salvation. But Christians demand love that both comes from the heart and shows itself in deeds. Someone else's life, freedom, honour and wealth have to be cherished as though they were one's own. He who violates this commandment not only in deeds but also in words or even in thought is in God's eyes guilty of homicide and theft. This is what is referred to in that brief and famous rule, highly recommended by the emperor Hadrian: "Do not do unto someone else what you do not want done unto yourself."

69 The Christian therefore, unlike all other people, does not consider plundering justified on the excuse that it is called war, or theft because it passes under the name of interest. He judges things by their nature, not by what they are called or by the frequency of occurrence. He furthermore excludes nobody from his love, even though he acknowledges that there is a special bond between those who profess the same religion and for whom our love is for that reason bound to be greater and more spontaneous because there are more common ties. Nor does he, like Aristotle, set barbarians apart from Greeks as though they were a different species or subject them to injuries or even servitude. But nature persuades him that these people too are humans and therefore should be considered brothers. How fatally the Jews err now and erred in the past in this respect is clearly indicated by these verses of Juvenal:

Not to show the way to anybody but co-religionists,
to lead only the circumcised to the well they asked for.

And in the words of Tacitus: "among themselves there is a steadfast faithfulness and spontaneous compassion, but toward all others hostile hatred." What is more, the Christian realizes that even he by whom he has been injured is a human being. Aristotle and Cicero recommend revenge as being consistent with nature. Then preference is to be given to the Platonists and Stoics, who commanded not to retaliate for injustice. As Seneca put it: "there is only a difference in degree between vengeance and injury." Indeed the bond between God's image and nature is too strong for it be be torn apart by any (mis)deed of man.

70 Furthermore, man has to treat his fellow man as he himself wishes to be treated by God. Now, he wants God to be merciful and inclined to forgiveness. For which reason:

He who needs forgiveness should readily forgive.

On the basis of this religious principle it is not enough just to abstain from harm, unless you help whenever you can and unless you commiserate totally and wholeheartedly with the sufferings of others. Much has been written by philosophers about charitable acts, but they omitted the most important part, which commits some people to our care on the sole ground of their being miserable. Nakedness, hunger, thirst, illness, imprisonment, exile; these are the titles that demand from us a payment of natural debt. Hence the term compassion, passed over in silence or even criticized by some philosophers in their treatment of duties, but very dear to God and humanity. Surely the first thing it asks from us is that we should be kind when instructing those who err in respect of religion and morals. One of the things abominable to the Athenians was not to show the right way. How great a distance is there between this goodness and charity toward all people, including enemies, and the practices of many peoples like the Spartans of old, whose entire education was aimed at murder and plunder and not at the pursuit of peace!

71 The order on which human society is based has two elements: the family and the state. Christianity gives for either the best possible rules that can be said or thought. In the first place it forbids promiscuity, limiting sexual relations to matrimony, so that each head of family may take care of his own family, that the children be his, a far cry indeed from the insanity — totally unworthy of a philosopher — of Socrates and Plato, who have it that in an ideal state everything including wives should be common property. As though nature does not teach that personal and private things are better cared for individually than in an amorphous community, and the consensus on this, which prevails among all peoples except those few who have no civilized morals demonstrates conclusively how sacred an institution matrimony is.

72   Christians also condemn indiscriminate marriage, like the Persians with their mothers or the Asian kings and the Athenians with their sisters. But in order to avoid inbreeding they confine reverence for ancestral lineage and freedom of choice of matrimonial partners within certain bounds and spread the motives for love over several persons. Like the Romans, they also in this respect closely follow the rule of nature that one man should have one wife, from which norm most peoples for a long time and nowadays all Mohammedans have deviated. It has therefore very aptly been said about them:
> *Surely we know the Venus of the barbarians, who, blind after the fashion of wild animals, descrated innumerable laws and nuptial vows made by those united in marriage; and the secrets of concubinage have shown up among a thousand young women.*

But Euripides followed nature:
> *It is not right that one man rule over two women; whosoever wants to live a happy life should regard and be content with only one wedded love.*

Tacitus says about the Germans: "There is not one of their customs that could be praised more. For they are virtually the only ones among the barbarians who are content with one wife." Truly love, which in matrimony must be the strongest human affection, is bound to perish if divided, and the care of the household, which is a woman's prerogative, can only be exercised well by one.

73   Thus the Christian law demands indissoluble bonds of matrimony without divorce. Most of the Oriental peoples and even the Jews have acted contrary to this law, and it is virtually only the Romans who are to be praised because for six hundred years they preserved marital fidelity intact. For nothing can be more fatal to the highest form of friendship such as must exist between spouses than the possibility of its being broken off. Moreover, the shared task imposed by nature, to wit the bringing up of the children, has to be performed by both parents equally. And are those divorces anything other than adultery in disguise?
> *A woman who marries so frequently is an adulteress before the law;*
> *in my eyes a straightforward adulteress is less repulsive.*

The mutual duties of parents, children and spouses between them, a lenient leadership on the one hand and a lasting obedience on the other, must be confirmed by concord between all parties equally.

74   As regards the State, Christian laws are such that especially from the example set it should be clear that good people are at the same time the best citizens. For not only the tribunes of the people but anyone invested with authority is sacrosanct to Christians, since their power has been given to them by God. Under Christian laws, there is no question of the population being incited to hatred of kings and rulers by inflammatory

speeches of Stoics, no seditions are preached, but everybody is urged to be content with the polity he has received, to demand with votive offerings the best possible rulers and to tolerate them such as they may be, willingly to bear the burdens imposed and to accept commands even if they are difficult to accept, provided they do not run counter to God's commands — a tenet which is extremely serviceable in maintaining the *status quo* of the body-politic, especially since the rulers too are assiduously admonished never to forget that the highest authority which is closest to God is constantly being scrutinised by God.

75 Some of the duties man owes to himself concern himself directly, others concern matters associated with him. As regards the individual himself everybody is obliged to preserve as best he can his own life, safety and health. The Christian does not hesitate to contradict Cato on that long-debated issue raised by Plato, whether it is permitted to commit suicide. For it is natural to all living beings to protect themselves and man is not placed in this world by chance but by divine decree, and is thus not free to desert his post without being summoned. Better, therefore, to accept hardships and servitude than to testify to his inability to sustain life by committing homicide.

He who is able to cope with misery comes out the strongest.
When death presents itself he will not grudgingly part with his bodily dwelling, dear as it may be, but with every hope of a magnificent reward.
It is cowardice to give up a life, grudgingly
which is going to be restored to one.

76 Never shall the Christian consider death a greater evil than the sin of which he is guilty, nor should he bargain for his life at the expense of virtue, but rather than committing a deed forbidden by God he will bear his cross and not recoil from flames. One year under the yoke of enemies of this religion has often seen more examples of this true fortitude among Christians than all the centuries since creation have seen among people of other religions. And this is only to be expected, for only the Christian has a true consolation against death; and since philosophers do not have this they invent false consolations which for that reason do not reach the soul. Indeed what good is it to me when you tell me that after death there is nothing, since the very thought of being reduced from somebody to nothing is appalling and if anything contrary to nature? What is the use of saying that death is natural and no punishment, when evil, whatever its cause, will never stop being evil?

77 Associated with man there are matters, actions, words and thoughts; matters such as honour, wealth and pleasure. The Christian is bidden to suspect the craving for honour and glory of corrupting virtue, which perishes when he values anything more than God. If all the same he

obtains these matters he is not obliged to repudiate them but to render all honour to God, the Bestower of all goods; and, aware of his own weakness as regards evil, keep himself in check so as not to crash down. This humility, the jewel in the crown of all virtues, was, prior to the Christian teaching, so little known to most people that it is hardly ever mentioned in the lists of virtues.

78 As to wealth, we should be on our guard against the immoderate and endlessly increasing avarice which destroys the heart and ruins tranquillity. Everybody is commanded to acquire by honest work what is necessary for himself and his family. Should God give something on top of that the Christian should not, after the insane fashion of some philosophers, throw what is instrumental to life into the sea but relieve the destitution of others with his own affluence. On the other hand, should disgrace or poverty befall him, he should face it with courage, not so much because he would not be able to improve matters anyway — for this is inertia without solace —, nor because it should mean nothing to him — which would be unnatural —, but he should bear them as burdens imposed by God, so as to correct his faults by being aware of them, to practise virtuousness, just like medicines whose taste is bitter but whose effect is wholesome, or like hard contests which in the end allow him to win the prize.

79 Pleasure reigns supreme in food, drink and sexual love, to which we may add leisure and sleep. The Christian gratefully acknowledges food and drink as given by God for human use. For that reason he does not seek the Judaic servitude by abstaining from some sorts of food, nor, like the Mohammedans, condemn the Creator of wine by rejecting wine, but he takes the point that these things should be used moderately and prudently, not to satisfy his craving for luxury or his avarice but just so much as is required by nature, principally rejecting intoxication as a waste of good things and detrimental to clear thinking and health. And yet there have been instructions in this vice which were called orgies, once the most famous of Greek rites.

80 Over and above this everyday moderation in victuals the Christian has also learned another duty, for instance when his soul sours in prayer and his body tends in other directions he should diminish its weight and strength, and to that end practice fasting, not as a thing that in itself is pleasing to God but as a necessity for man, which was not mentioned by the philosophers but practiced in the rites of the barbarians, but only as a matter of tradition and not in such a way that it was explained satisfactorily.

81 Sexual intercourse out of wedlock is forbidden. In this respect the shortsightedness of all philosophers and legislators is amazing.

When a certain well-known man came out of a brothel, he said: well done!" in the hallowed words of Cato.
We had better listen to Epictetus: "abstain from sexual intercourse before marriage". And Dio Chrysostomus in one of his orations shows in an eminent way that promiscuity is only one step away from the brothel. If people would follow the lead of nature it would not be difficult to understand that sexuality has been instituted for the sake of progeny and that children should not be fathered without the intention to educate them well; and since this is incumbent on both parents, it requires that they should live constantly together. As to leisure and sleep, they should be enjoyed only in so far as it is proper and in the way that nature requires for relaxing body and mind.

82 As to deeds that law is taught to Christians to do or omit what is neither commanded nor forbidden, according as its being done or left undone can incite others to be virtuous or prevent them from being virtuous. This carefulness is in itself proper to Christian charity, a tradition such as is to be found nowhere else.

83 Words too have their own law, which is not to deviate from the truth. This is easy to defend, for instance against Plato, who in some case justifies people lying. But this is an inadmissible perversion. For God has given speech to man in order that human society should be more closely knit by people sharing their very thoughts. And once the license to lie has been given it is bound to overstep all limits and to remove that which is the most important in human relationships, namely mutual trust.

84 Closely connected with this command is the rule that promises must be kept. The Christian religion is much more stringent on this point than those who wrote about duties, such as Panaetius and, following his example, Cicero. According to these authors promises to a political enemy must be kept, but not those given to a robber or a tyrant, since, as they have it, there is no legally valid relationship with them. Now this is an utterly false argument. For there can be no one without any relationship whatever. Moreover, whether we adhere to our agreements is really a matter that concerns God rather than man; God loves truth so much that he wants us to say what we think and to do what we say. Everyone should therefore stick faithfully to all his covenants, unless you happen to have promised something forbidden by God, which was not within your power even before you gave the promise.

85 Our thoughts, too, are subject to a law. This law is not one made by man but by God, to whom we owe it to be good even without an outside witness. According to this law what is wrong to do is equally wrong to think. This means that the very source of evil is removed, its root cut off. For, as we say with Seneca: "A robber is a robber even before he defiles

86 What all commandments have in common is this commandment, that it is not sufficient to do what is commanded unless it is done because it is commanded. Many people carry out some command or other just to please others, or to make a good impression, people we very aptly call hypocrites, who pretend to be noble. They are not good but act as though they were. But a Christian shows by all his thoughts, words and deeds his solemn determination to obey God, which is much more than what most philosopers are agreed upon, namely to live in accordance with nature.

87 But because man in his weakness sins so frequently against the rules, whether commandments or prohibitions, since the remnants of our vices have not yet been fully conquered, there is one commandment that transcends all others: that we must let ourselves be led by repentance and beg for forgiveness. The rationale for this commandment has been systematically explained among the principles.

88 Having dealt with the commandments, it seems worthwhile to examine how much the world owes to the Christian religion. Most peoples, formerly barbarians, wild, uncivilized, practising the law of the jungle, have only come to accept morals and laws from this discipline. Indeed peoples thought to be very civilized used to expose their children before this religion was established, and held public games involving human bloodshed. And then there was discrimination between people, forcibly invented as an insult to nature, which led to some people being free and others slaves, which was unforcibly and gradually abolished by the Christian notion of equality. Nor are laws or punishments needed to force people into marrying against their will, but when libidinous license has been removed people marry of their own free will and produce enough offspring to maintain the State; not, as had been the case formerly, by means of a series of temporary marriages but thanks to indestructible marital fidelity. And if Christian life would answer to its name all over the world, we would live in a truly Golden Age, without wars, without quarrels, without poverty, in the greatest peace and harmony, an age of plenty for every single one of us.

EPILOGUE

89 When the venerable Patriarch had expounded the essentials of the Christian religion along these lines, he went on to say that it was amazing that people who agreed on so many points yet seemed so diverse and out of harmony. Wondering what could be the cause of this evil, he said, "It

seems to me that the principal cause is that the dogmas are declared to be the most essential part of the religion, whereas the ethical precepts are disregarded. Now this is altogether wrong, for dogmas generally subserve precepts and lead up to them." Indeed Seneca was right when he said, "everybody prefers discussing to living." And since ethical precepts are mostly plainer and less complicated, it stands to reason that most people readily agree on precepts. We therefore choose rather to think piety has to do with dogmas, for over dogmas we fight with others, while the battle over ethical rules takes place in ourselves. Now violating one's own conscience is more difficult than quarrelling with others. Because he is inclined to discharge his obligations as little as possible man has turned religion into a matter of controversy, and transferred to life what had been a matter for discussion in the schools.

90   Now when there is a fight over precepts, it hardly ever involves ethics — for these have definite and unequivocal rules — but deals with those matters which everybody establishes for himself for the sake of preserving order, and in which a short cut to concord is to leave every man to his own discretion. What could be more foolish than the Spartans and Athenians waging wars against Greek city-states, the former to impose their government by aristocracy, the latter to yield everything into the hands of the people. Among the Christians, there are similar occurrences. For how often did not at some time in the past dissensions arise from the fact that Easter was celebrated on different days by different people? Irenaeus sensibly wrote to the Roman bishop Victor: "What? Can we not live in concord even though they perform their rites while we do ours? Some fast on the fortieth day, others for a period of two days, some for four, or ten, or fifteen, or twenty, or forty days, and concord is preserved notwithstanding." Many controversies over dogmas are merely due to words which must be avoided for consensus to appear. With any further quarrels we have to check whether they concern matters which it is necessary to know. At this point we have, first of all, to correct the error that generally more dogmas are formulated than ethics require. Indeed it is impossible that everybody should agree about everything. Moreover, everybody sticks obstinately to what he has once learnt, however wrong. What as young people
   they learnt they do not as old people wish to consign to oblivion.
"So hard an evil to shake off", as Galenus says, "is the pride about one's sect, and of all things the most difficult to wash off, indeed more incurable than any scabies."

91   The remedy for this disease will therefore consist in limiting the number of necessary articles of faith to those few that are most self-evident; and to inquire into the other doctrinal points which lead to the

perfection of pious wisdom without prejudice, preserving charity and under the guidance of the Holy Scriptures. Finally, if people err even on matters of some importance, the only thing we can do is not to accuse them with hateful incriminations for the results of their unintended error, but to relieve the misery of their ignorance by a kindly explanation. For if we have to forgive sins committed against rules that are known and understood, there surely is no reason not to forgive a sin committed in spite of oneself? Salvianus gave a memorable statement on this matter when he wrote about the most odious error of his time; what better way to conclude this discourse than by quoting his words: "Granted they are heretics, but they are so unwittingly. That is to say that they are heretics in our eyes, but not in theirs. For they so much believe themselves to be Catholics that they bring us into disrepute by calling us heretics. So what they are in our eyes, we are in theirs. [...] We have the truth, but they presume they have it. We honour God, but they are convinced that their creed is the right way to honour God. They do not observe their religious duties, but to them this is the highest religious duty. They are impious, but they think theirs is the true piety. So they do err, but they do so in good faith, not out of hatred of God but out of love for him, convinced that they honour and love the Lord. Although they do not have the right faith, yet they consider this the perfect love for God. Nobody except the Judge can know in what way they are to be punished for this erroneous belief on Judgement Day. I think that until that time God is patient with them, since He sees that though they do not have the right belief, their error results from a sincere conviction."

COMMENTARY

COMMENTARY

The plan and intention of this commentary have been discussed in the Introduction (§ 8). In order not to overload the text I have as a rule limited references to *Ver.* and *Iur.*, editions of which are easily available.

As far as Grotius' theological works are concerned, references are throughout made to the edition of his *Opera Theologica* I-IV, Basil. 1732 (= *TMD* no. 921), as reprinted in recent years (Stuttgart 1972). When referring to this work, no title is given, but volume, page, column and line(s) are directly indicated, as, for instance, III 25a 3-7.

Title] The ms. contains the title twice; once on the cover in Grotius' own hand (= hand *c*), a second time (fo. 1ʳ) in the hand of copyist *a*. In the transcription Grotius has been followed; the copyist wrote '*his*' in stead of '*iis*'.

Meletius] i.e. Meletius Pegas, see above Introduction, 17ff.

epistola] Elswhere (*Mel.* 91.47) Grotius indicates his treatise as a '*sermo*' and in a letter to Walaeus (*App.* II no. 2.1) as a '*libellus*'. Walaeus (*App.* II no. 1.1) calls it a '*tractatus*', and Petrus Cunaeus (*App.* II no. 7.1) a '*dissertatio*'.

Mel. 1] Cf. the idea developed here with Michel de l'Hospital's statement in a harangue before the States-General of 13 December 1560 at Orleans, as cited by Albert Buisson, *Michel de l'Hospital (1503-1573)*, Paris [1950], (182): "C'est folie d'espérer paix, repos et amitié entre les personnes qui sont de diverses religions ... Nous l'expérimentons aujourd'hui, et voyons que deux, Français et Anglais, qui sont d'une même religion ont plus d'amitié entre eux que deux citoyens d'une même ville, sujets à un même Seigneur, qui seraient de diverses religions!" Grotius' and De l'Hospital's statements are typical examples of Renaissance political thought as defended, for instance, by Justus Lipsius in his *Politica* (1589). Grotius refers to this work in *Pietas* (IV 111b2-15). Cf. also *Mel.* 2.22 and 3.44. For more details, see G. Güldner, *Das Toleranz-Problem in den Niederlanden*, Lübeck/Hamburg 1968, 91-99, and G. Oestreich, *Neostoicism and the Early Modern State*, Cambridge 1981, 39-56; 76-89.

1.11 belli vixdum sopiti memoria] This is a reference to the war with Spain, interrupted by the Twelve-years Truce (1609-21).

1.12 Zelandosque] For Grotius' opinion about the situation in Zealand, see Introduction, 14ff.

2.18-22 Ex quo ... fuerant] This is an instance of the classical theme of 'Origin and Depravation', which was 'a cherished concept of Hellenistic historiography' (H. Erbse in *Rheinisches Museum* 94 (1951) 163). It was propagated in particular by Posidonius (cf. K. Reinhardt, *Poseidonios über Ursprung und Entartung*, Heidelberg 1928), from whom it was taken over notably by Sen. (cf. S. Blankert, *Seneca (Epistola 90) over natuur en cultuur en Posidonius als zijn bron*, thesis Utrecht, Amsterdam 1940). For more details about this 'Theory of Depravation' in an irenical context in the 16th and 17th centuries, see Dieter Wolf, *Die Irenik des Hugo Grotius*,[2] Hildesheim 1972, 91 ff.; for the period from the Middle Ages to the 18th century, E. Seeberg, *Gottfried Arnold. Die Wissenschaft und die Mystik seiner Zeit*. Studien zur Historiographie und zur Mystik, Meerane in Sachsen 1923 (reprint Darmstadt 1964), 257 ff. Speaking about Grotius (315-20), Seeberg observes (317): "... Grotius (stützt) seine Schilderung des Verfalls ganz wesentlich auf Ammianus Marcellinus." Many interesting observations on this topic are also to be found in Wilhelm Kühlmann, *Gelehrtenrepublik und Fürstenstaat. Entwicklung und Kritik des deutschen Späthumanismus in der Literatur des Barockzeitalters*, Tübingen 1982, 17-66.

2.22 morbus] Cf. *Or.* (IV 192b 50-58): "Publicarum ecclesiarum *morbi* politiam semper inficiunt et praeserim in eo statu, cuius praecipuum vinculum est religio. Solito enim semel hoc vinculo, consequitur necessario et concordiae, quae in ipso statu est dissolutio, tum hostilis provinciae in provinciam animus, civitatis in civitatem odium, in ipsis civitatibus factiones, imo vero intra privatos ipsos parietes intestina discordia." See also note to *Mel.* 1.

2.26 Indos] Grotius' *Mare liberum sive de iure quod Batavis competit ad Indicana commercia dissertatio* (= *TMD* no. 541) appeared in 1609.

2.28 Iudaeos] Grotius composed his treatise about the Jews, *Rem.* (ed. J. Meijer), in 1615. It was only published after the second World War. For Grotius as a hebraist and for his knowledge of Jewish affairs, see, besides the Introduction by J. Meijer to *Rem.* (55-70), Phyllis S. Lachs, 'Grotius' use of Jewish sources', *RQ* 30 (1977) 181-200, and A. Rosenberg, 'Hugo Grotius as a Hebraist', *SR* 12 (1978) 62-90.

2.29 necessitudinem] As very often in Cic., this term has here the meaning of: relationship, intimacy, friendship, bond. Cf. *Mel.* 35.182.

3.34 Magistro] Christus. Cf. the end of *Bewijs* (166):
"Wilt U niet scheurelyk van veele leeraers roemen,
maer laet U allegaer nae eenen leeraer noemen,
Gelyk gy alle zijt in eenen naem gedoopt."

3.43 minora ... utilia] Walaeus (*App.* II no. 1.12-14), while quoting verbatim *Mel.* 3.43, criticises this passage. See Introduction, 51. For the opinion expressed here see also Grotius to Casaubon (*BW* I no. 229, 200-01).

3.44 unius ... civitatis] See note to *Mel.* 1 and *Pietas* (IV 111b 12-15): "Quis adeo est ferreus qui non optet Christianos eadem sentire, praesertim qui propiori vinculo et Reformationis nomine inter se nectuntur, multoque magis τοὺς συμπολίτας *concives*?"

5.56 Patriarcham Meletium] See above, *Title*.

5.67 ὁμολογούμενα] = consensus. See Introduction, 24 ff., 61, and Grotius to Walaeus (*App.* II no. 2.66-67): "... si quid ultra addo, abiturum me a proposito manendi ἐν τοῖς ὁμολογουμένοις."

5.67 queis] Old form for '*quibus*', used frequently by Grotius, as in *AE* (= *Dichtwerken* I 1a, 209.62 & 241.225), and *Satisf.* X (IV 336a 24).

6.4 apostolus] St. Paul who was taken by Grotius for the author of Hebr. (11: 6). In his *Annot. in NT*, ad Hebr. 11: 6 (III 1053b 23-25) Grotius refers to *Iur.* II 20, 46 (518-20), where he develops the same argument much more elaborately, and concludes: "Hae notiones, numen aliquod esse (unum an plura sepono) et curari ab eo res hominum, maxime sunt universales et ad religionem sive veram sive falsam constituendam omnino necessariae."

6.5-7 Esse Deum ... testantur] Cf. *Ver.* I 2 "Deum esse" (IV 4a 7-b 25); I 7 "Deum esse causam omnium" (IV 5a 30-7a 9).

6.6. consensus hominum] In *Ver.* I 16 (IV 16a 4) he speaks again about the *consensus gentium*, cites many instances (annot. 22) and refers, moreover, to his exposition in *Iur.* II 20, 45 (516-18).

6.9 magis ... sentirent] Duplessis Mornay, *Ver.* (5 ff.) mentions in an analogous context Theodorus Cyrenaicus and Euhemerus, of whom he observes that they rather mocked at idolatry than denied the existence of God. The origin of this statement is Cic. *Nat.* I 63, as may be the case with Grotius, although he could also have been inspired by Lact. *Inst.* I 2, 1.

7.18 suprema causa] abl.

7.18 ratio Stoicos] Cf. v. Arnim *SVF* II no. 912 ff.

7.21 Translated by Cic. (*Div.* 2, 25) from an unknown Greek poet.

8.26-27 Epicureos excludimus] For Grotius' opinion about Epic. and his followers, see note to *Mel.* 29.120-122.

9.37 ζῷον λογικὸν καὶ προαιρετικόν] The phrase as such is not found in Aristot. or other philosophers from Antiquity. Grotius might have invented the formula himself, having possibly had in mind Aristot. *Eth. Nic.* 1111b 13.

9.40-42 Frustra ... auctorem] Cf. *AE* (= *Dichtwerken* I 1a 115.1106-10):

"Quicquid est, etiam bonum est:
Gratosque rebus singulis fines dedit
Natura cur sint, esse nil frustra jubens.
Rebus creatis si putes uti nefas
Hanc, quae cavenda fecit, accusas manum."

10.47-49 actio ... imperium] Walaeus (*App.* II no. 8.16 ff), quoting verbatim *Mel.* 10.47-49, criticises this passage. In his opinion Grotius restricts himself too much, since we should not forget that God also works in man through the Holy Ghost.

11.52 legem servanti praemium] Cf. *Ver.* II 9 "Praemii propositi excellentia" (IV 37 a 3-38a 31).

12.59-60 minus perfectis ... mosaica] Walaeus (*App.* II no. 8.22 ff) criticises this passage and states that Mosaic religion was perfect in its kind and promised to its adherents a no less real salvation than Christianity promises Christians. He thereby proves to be a true follower of Calvin. Cf. Calvin, *Institutio* II 11 (ed. Barth/Niesel II 423 ff.)

12.66 Ov. *Ars* 637.

Mel. 13] Cf. *Ver.* II 9-11 (IV 37a 3- 40b 12), where the same subject is treated much more elaborately.

13.5 inter philosophos ... certatum] Cf. *Ver.* II 9 (IV 37a 17- 38a 31): "Apud Graecos ... qui de vita post huius conspicuae vitae interitum spem habebant aliquam, valde de ea re haesitanter loquebantur, ut ex Socratis dissertationibus, ex scriptis Tullii, Senecae aliorumque apparet." An important passage with many evidences. Grotius clearly seems to follow Lact. *Inst.* VII 8.

13.7-8 frui eo qui ... est Deus] This is an Augustinian concept. Cf. Aug. *Conf.* VII 17, 23: "non stabam *frui Deo* meo'; *Doctr. chr.* I 5, 5: 'Res igitur quibus *fruendum* est, Pater et Filius et Spiritus Sanctus." Cf. G. Combès/J. Farges, *Le magistère chrétien. De catechizandis rudibus — De doctrine christiana.* Oeuvres de St. Augustin 11, 1e série: Opuscules, Paris 1949, note complémentaire (F. Cayré), 558-61.

14.9-10 Ut ... docet] See above, *Mel.* 6.5-7 and *Ver.* I 3 "Deum esse unum" (IV 4b 26-51).

14.12-13 beatitudo ... hominis] Grotius may have had Aristot. in mind (cf. *Mel.* 16.40 ff), but it is of course a general Christian tenet that beatitude concerns the whole man. See in this context Ragnar Holte, *Béatitude et sagesse. Saint Augustin et le problème de la fin de l'homme dans la philosophie ancienne*, Paris/Worcester 1962, reg. s.v. 'beata vita, beatitudo (inclut la sanctification du corps)'.

14.15 necesse ... removeri mala] Cf. *Ver.* II 9 annot. 11 (IV 37b 48-63), with reference to Plin. *Nat.* VII 7 and Lact. *Inst.* III 12, 7: "Virtus per se ipsam beata non est, quoniam in perferendis, ut dixi, malis tota vis eius est."

15.17 in ... fragili vita] See, for instance, Aristot. *Eth. Nic.* 1098a.

15.21-23 Errarunt ... quaesiverunt] The reference is to the philosophy of the Stoics. Cf. v. Arnim *SVF* III 38-48 and *Ver.* II 9 (IV 37b 12-18): "eo perducti sunt alii ut dicerent virtutem sibi esse praemium," with (annot. 10) references to Cic. *Tusc.* II 7, 17 & 18, and Lact. *Inst.* III 27, 4-5, who especially criticised the Stoics on this topic.

15.27 unde rectius alii] The same thought is expressed more clearly *Ver.* I 21 (IV 30b 20-24): "Cum Deus curet actiones, iustusque sit, et ita interim fiant, exspectandum est aliquod post hanc vitam iudicium, ne aut insignis improbitas sine poena aut magna virtus sine solatio praemioque maneat." For '*alii*' see *Ver.* I 22-25 (IV 30b 27-32b 20).

15.30-32 Sen. *Herc. f.* 526-28.

16.34-35 Iudaei ... Mahumetistae] Cf. *Ver.* II 9 (IV 38a 18-21): "Gaudia autem quae promittuntur non vilia sunt, ut epulae, quas post hanc vitam sperant crassiores Iudaei, et concubitus, quos sibi promittunt Mahumetistae."

16.36 τὸ δὲ εὐδαῖμον ἀνενδεές] Cf. Aristot. *Eth. Nic.* 1097b 5-11 and 1176b 3: οὐδενὸς γὰρ ἐνδεὴν ἡ εὐδαιμονία.

16.37 Pecudum ... bona sunt] Cf. Cic. *Ac. 2*, 6: "de vita et moribus et de expetendis fugiendisque rebus illi (Epicurei) simpliciter, *pecudis* enim et hominis idem *bonum* esse censent."

16.38 vera ... felicitas] Cf. *Ver.* I 25 (IV 32b 10-15): "Quod si animus et eius est naturae quae nullas habeat in se intereundi causas, et Deus multa nobis signa dedit quibus intelligi debeat, velle ipsum ut animus superstes sit corpori, non potest finis homini ullus proponi ipso dignior quam eius status *felicitas* ..."

16.39 σῶμα πνευματικόν] 1. Cor. 15: 43. Cf. *Annot. in NT*, ad 1. Cor. 15: 43-4 (III 825a 6-15) and *Ver.* II 9 (IV 38a 6-14).

16.41-46 Aristot. *Eth.Eud.* 1249b 16-23.

16.44 Grotius leaves ἢ δι' ἔνδειαν ἢ untranslated.

Mel. 17] In content as well as in terminology this passage resembles Cic. *Fin.* Cf. in particular *Fin.* II 13: "huic verbo (sc. voluptas) omnes ... duas res subiciunt, laetitiam in animo, commotionem suavem iucunditatis in corpore ... sed hoc interest, quod voluptas dicitur etiam in animo — vitiosa res, ut Stoici putant qui eam sic definiunt: sublationem animi sine ratione opinantis se magno bono frui —, non dicitur laetitia nec gaudium in corpore." II 19: "Multi enim et magni philosophi haec ultima bonorum iuncta fecerunt, ut Aristoteles virtutis usum vitae perfectae prosperitate coniunxit ... Illi (sc. Hieronymus et Aristippus) enim inter se dissentiunt. Propterea singulis finibus utuntur et, cum uterque Graece egregie loquatur, nec Aristippus, qui voluptatem summum bonum dicit, in voluptate ponit non dolere, neque Hieronymus qui summum bonum statuit non dolere, voluptatis nomine umquam utitur pro illa indolentia, quippe qui ne in expetendis quidem rebus numeret voluptatem." — The distinction between *voluptas in statu* and *in motu* is found in Cic. too. Cf. J. S. Reid, *M. Tulli Ciceronis De Finibus Bonorum et Malorum*, libr. I & II, Cambridge 1925, ad *Fin*. I 37 (*solam*), 57: "we have here the Epicurean doctrine of the two kinds of pleasure, the active and the passive, ἡδονή ἐν κινήσει and ἡδονή ἐν στάσει or καταστηματική (so named by Epicurus himself, quoted by Diog. L. 10, 136), which terms Cicero represents in II 16 by *in motu* and *in stabilitate*."

17.56 cum Hieronymo] This is the philosopher Hieronymus of Rhodos (290-230 BC) whose works were lost. See Reid, *o.c.* 112 n. 15 (113): "... the only tenet definitely attributed to him is this doctrine of ἀοχλησία = *indolentia* (Cic. Fin. II 19) = *vacuitas doloris* (5, 14; cf. 5, 73) = *vacare omni molestia* (*Ac. 1*, 131, 138)."

17.59 virtus placet] See above, note to *Mel*. 15.21-23.

17.60-61 addita ... prosperitate] Grotius quotes Aristot. *Eth.Nic.* 1098a 15, which was borrowed from Cic. *Fin*. II 19; see note to *Mel*. 17.

18.63 Epicureos ... Sadducaeos] Cf. *Ver*. II 9 annot. 2 (IV 37a 27-32), where Grotius refers to Mt. 22: 23; Act. 23: 8 and Ios. *Ant. Iud*. XVIII, I 4. See also *Annot. in NT*, ad Mt. 22: 23 (II 203b 32-35): "certum enim habeo errare eos qui ex Iosephi verbis male intellectis, *Sadducaeos Epicureis* aequant, quasi Deo res humanas curae esse negaverint."

18.66-67 Animum ... plerisque] Cf. *Ver*. I 22-25 (IV 30b 27- 32b 20).

18.67-68 Epicurei ... pictus homo] Negative statements about Epic. in Antiquity and in later times are, of course, frequent (see Wolfgang Schmid, s.v. 'Epikur' in *RAC* V (Bb IV) 'Abwertung E's gegenüber anderen Philosophen', 796-99). Grotius' statement is not found in Schmid, nor in H. Usener, *Epicurea*, Leipzig 1887. In fact, it is probably a free adaptation of Cic. *Fin*. V 80: "dicis eadem omnia et bona et mala quae dicunt ii, qui numquam *philosophum pictum*, ut dicitur, viderunt." The point of Cic.'s statement, which is also directed against Epic., is that it is stupid to ignore the conditions of life and to always take a wise man for a happy man. According to Cic. whoever asserts this looks like a man who has never seen the portrait of a philosopher, let alone a philosopher in person. That, it would seem, is the meaning of Grotius' phrase, which apparently was a current one, as can be seen in Walaeus (*Op. Omn*. II 263): "Epicureis exceptis, qui non aliter philosophi appellantur quam ignis *pictus* ignis appellandi sunt."

18.70-71 gentium ... expertem] With reference to this statement, Walaeus (*App*. II no. 8.32-39) suggests that Grotius wants to exphazise the immortality of the soul even more strongly, as being "*primum omnis religionis fundamentum.*"

18.71 mentem ... Dei imaginem] Cf. *Ver.* I 16 annot. 6 (IV 13b [49-50]).

19.4 δόγματα] = decreta. Cf. Cic. *Ac.1*, 27 & 29; Sen. *Epist.* 95, 10: "quae Graeci vocant *dogmata*, nobis ... *decreta* licet appellare'; *Epist.* 95, 60: '*decreta* sapientiae, id est *dogmata*."

19.4 παραινέσεις] = praecepta. Cf. Cic. *Off.* I 1; II 32: "benevolentiae *praecepta* videamus"; Sen. *Epist.* 94, 31: "inter *decreta* philosophiae et *praecepta*...". In *Iur.* II 20, 45, 1-3 (516-18) the distinction between '*decreta*' and '*praecepta*' is replaced by the analogous distinction between '*notiones contemplativae*' and '*activae*', which is also closely connected with Cic. and Sen. Cf. for instance, Sen *Epist.* 95, 10.

19.6 Decreta ... placita et scita] Cf. Sen. *Epist.* 95.10: ".. nulla ars contemplativa sine decretis suis est, quae Graeci vocant dogmata, nobis vel *decreta* licet appellare, vel *scita* vel *placita*."

19.9-10 cum religio ... intercedat] Cf. *Iur.* II 20, 44, 3-6 (513-16), with many references to authors from Antiquity.

Mel. 20] Cf. *Iur.* 20, 44 (513-16) and *Ver.* I 3 (IV 4b 27-34): "Evicto Numen esse aliquod, restat ad attributa eius veniamus, quorum primum hoc occurrit, non plures esse deos sed unum Deum. Hoc inde colligitur, quod Deus, ut supra [= *Ver.* I 2 (IV 4a 10)] iam dictum est, est id quod est necessario, sive per se; necessario autem sive per se quidquid est, non qua in genere consideratur, sed qua actu est; actu autem sunt res singulae." Thus, from God's 'esse' Grotius deduces God's 'unum esse'. See also Grotius' collection of translated texts from classical authors, *Sent. de fato* (IV 406a 62-63): "Quaecumque sunt per unum sunt. Nam et quod primo est ab uno primitus proficiscitur." The same reasoning was usual in contemporary Reformed dogmatic thinking, cf. H. Heppe/Ernst Bizer, *Die Dogmatik der evangelisch reformierten Kirche*, Neukirchen 1958, 41 ff.

Mel. 21] Cf. *Ver.* I 4-6 (IV 4b 52- 5a 28).

21.23 Plutarchus] Probably Grotius is alluding to Plut. *Mor.* 1051F: θεὸν τοίνυν νοοῦμεν ζῷον μακάριον καὶ ἄφθαρτον καὶ εὐποιητικὸν ἀνθρώπων. Cf. M. Stern, *Greek and Latin Authors on Jews and Judaism* I, Jerusalem 1974, no. 257 (550).

21.24 Tac. *Hist.* V 5. The quotation is a contamination of: "Iudaei mente sola *unum*que *numen* intelligunt", and: "*summum* illud *et aeternum neque* imitabile *neque interiturum*." Cited also Stob. *Dicta*, prol. (iii); *Iur.* II 20, 45, 1 (516) and *Ver.* I 16 annot. 101 (IV 27b 32-34).

Mel. 22] See Introduction, 53 ff., and Grotius to Walaeus (*App.* II no. 4 annot. 6-9).

22.28 νοῦν καὶ ἐνέργειαν] Probably Grotius refers to Aristot. *Metaph.* 1072b 21-23.

144   COMMENTARY

22.34 τρεῖς ὑποστάσεις] Cf. Stob. *Dicta* prol. [i ij^v]: "De hypostasium quoque distinctione, quanquam eo per se pertingere non potest humana ratio, aliquid ex traditione veteri hausisse putatur Plato et, ut quidam existimant, etiam Aristoteles." This statement is explained in more detail *Ver.* IV 12 annot. 10 (IV 71a 12-35). — The usage to speak about ὑποστάσεις in relation to the H. Trinity dates from an early period. See J. F. Bethune-Baker, *An Introduction to the Early History of Christian Doctrine to the Time of the Council of Chalcedon*, London [1962], 237: "It was at the Synod of Alexandria (362), presided over by Athanasius, that formal recognition was conceded to the usage of the word ὑποστάσις which made it possible to speak of the Trinity as τρεῖς ὑποστάσεις, while still being faithful to the definitions of the doctrine of Nicea." See also Grotius to Walaeus (*App.* II no. 4 33-51).

22.35 ὥστε ...νοητόν] Aristot. *Metaph*. 1072b 21. See Grotius to Walaeus (*App.* II no. 4.44-46).

23.38 assentit facile] Cf. Vives *Ver.* II 2 (214): "Anteaquam veritatem eam (sc. Trinitatis) Christus retegeret, neque veritatis neque rationum venisset ulli unquam in mentem. Sed postquam veritatem a coelesti, seu potius magistro Deo accepimus, ratione nobis coeperunt ostendere."

23.40-43 tria ... impartibilem] Cf. for his opinion on the Trinitarian and the Christological dogma's in general what he writes to his brother Willem about the intention of his *Bewijs* (= *Ver.*), (12 April 1620, *BW* II no. 600, 31): "Dogmata περὶ τοῦ Τριάδος, καὶ περὶ τῆς τοῦ Χριστοῦ θεότητος inter argumenta locum habere non potuerunt. Neminem enim ista ad Christianam doctrinam allicient adhuc alienum; imo operam ludunt qui ista aliter quam ex Sacris paginis demonstrare conantur. Sacrarum autem paginarum bene fundata auctoritate debent et ista probata censeri." As far as the doctrine of the H. Trinity is concerned, Grotius' attitude is always somewhat reserved (cf. Introduction, 53 ff.). In a letter written much later to G. J. Vossius (1. January 1639, *BW* X no. 3917, 12), he says: "Triados probationem in eo libro (sc. *Ver.*) directe aggressus non sum memor eius, quod a viro magno socero tuo (i.e. Franciscus Junius) audieram, peccasse Plessaeum (i.e. Duplessis Mornay in his *Ver.*) et alios, quod rationibus a natura petitis et Platonicis saepe non valde appositis testimoniis astruere voluissent rem, non ponendam in illa cum atheis, paganis, Iudaeis, Mahumetistis disputatione, qui omnes ad sacras literas ducendi sunt, ut inde talia hauriant, quae nisi Deo semet patefaciente cognosci nequeunt." To this he adds (14) that he had already expressed his thoughts about the H. Trinity in his *Annot. in NT* and in his *Poemata*. This suggests, for instance, *Annot. in NT*, ad Mt. 28: 19 (II 287a 15 ff.); ad Ioh. 1: 2 (II 475a 63- b 16) and, where his poetry is concerned, *Initium Evangelicae Historiae scriptore Iohanne παραφρασικῶς* (= *Dichtwerken* I 1a 205-07); *Onderwijsinge* (169) and *AE* (= *Dichtwerken* I 1a, 61-3):

"Est natus ipso patre ab aeterno satus,
Divina ratio, Mens patris: Lex omnium
Sermoque, cuius incomprehensa fuit
Virtute factum quod prius fuerat nihil:
Utrumque Sancti Spiritus Concordia
Amorque jungit: Tresque sunt Unus Deus."

The formulations used here are all in accordance with those employed in *Mel.* 23.41. For more details on his ideas on the H. Trinity, see Haentjens, *o.c.*, 69-70.

23.44 solus ... nomen] For this etymology, see Cic. *Nat.* III 54: "Cumque tu *solem* quia *solus* esset appellandum esse dicas."

24.47-48 Deum ... omniscium] Cf. *Ver.* I 6 (IV 5a 27) & I 10 (IV 7b 6).

24.51 Plato, Varro ... reprehenderunt] For Plato see *Rep.* 376c-381b; for Varro see his distinction between *tria genera theologiae*, as recorded by Aug. *Civ.* VI 5, 1: "Deinde ait (sc. Varro): "Mythicon appellant, quo maxime utuntur poetae; physicon, quo philosophi; civile, quo populi. Primum, inquit, quod dixi, in eo sunt multa contra dignitatem et naturam immortalium ficta. In hoc enim est, ut deus alius ex capite, alius ex femore sit, alius ex guttis sanguinis natus; in hoc, ut dii furati sint, ut adulterarint, ut servierint homini..." " Grotius may also have alluded to Max. Tyr. *Diss.* 10: Τίνες ἄμεινον περὶ θεῶν διέλαβον, ποιηταὶ ἢ φιλόσοφοι;

24.54-55 Eur. fragm. 841 Nauck[2], or originating from the lost *Chrysippus*, cited by Plut. *Mor.* 33E and 446A. In his ed. of Plut. *Aud.* (= *Mor.* 33E), incorporated in Stob. *Dicta* (65), Grotius translates these verses thus:

"Proh dolor ut illud caelitus missum est malum
Cum quis videt meliora non sequitur tamen."

Cited also in *Annot. in NT*, ad Rom. 7: 15 (III 715b 55-60).

24.59-60 Aeschyl. fragm. 156 Nauck[2], as originating from the lost *Niobe*. Cited in Plato *Rep.* 380a, Eus. *P.E.* 13, 3, 14 and Plut. *Aud.* (*Mor.* 17B). In his edition of Plut. *Aud.*, incorporated in Stob. *Dicta* (10), Grotius translates these verses, more happily, thus:

"culpam hominibus assignat Deus,
Eruere quoties funditus statuit domum."

24.64 Lucan. *Phars.* II 288. In 1614 Grotius published the first critical edition of this work (= *TMD* no. 423).

24.66-67 Lucan. *Phars.* VII 58-9. In his edition Grotius prefers the reading 'cum vobis' (303).

24.70 Eur. fragm. 292, 7 Nauck², as originating from the lost *Bellerophon*, cited by Plut. *Mor.* 21A and 1049E. Grotius omits to add a Latin translation. In his edition of Plut. *Aud.* (= *Mor.* 21A), incorporated in Stob. *Dicta* (22), he translates as follows:
"Si turpe patrant quid Dei, non sunt Dei."
These verses are cited also in *Excerpta* (378-79), where he translates:
"Si Di patrant quid turpe, iam non sunt Dei."

24.72-74 Cleanthes' Ὕμνος εἰς Δία, 15-17 (I.U. Powell, *Collectanea Alexandrina*, Oxon. 1925, 227).

25.83 ἕπου θεῷ] Diels *FV* I 58[45] 'Pyth. Schule', (466²⁰⁻²¹) fragm. c. 6: γλώσσης πρὸ τῶν ἄλλων κράτει θεοῖς ἑπόμενος.

25.84 Christi illud] Mt. 5: 48. Cf. *Annot. in NT*, ad Mt. 5: 48 (II 75a 30 ff.)

Mel 26] Cf. *Ver.* I 7, 'Deum esse causam omnium' (IV 5a 30- 7a 9).

26.93-97 Cum ... factus sit] Cf. *Ver.* I 7 annot. 3, with many references: "Sume de Platone mundi originem fuisse aliquam, ab Aristotele non esse genitum, et habebis ipsam Iudaeorum Christianorumque sententiam." (IV 7b 61-63).

Mel. 27] Cf. *Ver.* IV 2-3 (IV 63b 5- 64b 21).

27.98-99 quae videntur ... ἀόρατα] Cf. Col. 1: 16.

27.102 deos ... improprie] Cf. 1. Cor. 7: 5, 6.

27.107 non socii, sed ministri] *Ver.* IV 2 (IV 63b 23-25): "cum bonae mentes Dei summi ministrae sint, non possit eas non sibi addictas habere qui Deo utatur propitio", with reference to Arnob. *Adv. Nat.* III (annot. 3).

Mel. 28] Cf. *Ver.* I 7 (IV 5b 42- 6a 3).

28.112 Stoici dixere] See v. Arnim *SVF* II no. 1152 ff. *Ver* I 7 annot. 2 (IV 5b), with ref. to Cic. *Off.* I 22: *Nat.* II 37: "praeter mundum, cetera omnia aliorum causa esse generata."

Mel. 29] Cf. *Ver.* I 8-9 (IV 7a 11-42).

29.120-122 Epicureorum ... dogmata] For Grotius' judgement in general about Epicureans and Stoics, see *Annot. in NT*, ad Act. 17: 18 (II 630b 42-58): "Duo genera philosophorum nominat, maxime alienorum a christiana religione. Nam Epicurei neque mundum conditum a Deo credebant, neque Deo curam esse rerum humanarum, neque ulla praemia aut poenas post mortem, neque bonum aliud quam quod sensibus perciperetur...(Stoici) negabant *sapientem suum quicquam Iovi cedere; nihil eum Deo debere ob id quod saperet; Iovem diutius bonum esse, at sapientem nihilo minoris se aestimare, quod virtutes eius spatio breviori clauduntur;* quae habes apud Senecam Epistola LXXIII. *Manu quaerendam mortem* *potius quam ferendam servitutem, contumelias aut graves morbos.''* In his rejection of the Epicureans he seems to follow Cic. in particular, as may be seen from *Iur.* II 20, 46 (518-520). See also above, note to *Mel.* 31.150.

29.121 fortuitos concursus] Cf. Cic. *Nat.* I 66: "... ex his (sc. atomis) effectum esse caelum atque terram ... *concursu* quodam *fortuito.*''

29.124 quaestio] This question forms the title of Max. Tyr.'s *Diss.* 41. In his rendering Grotius wrote διδόντος in stead of ποιοῦντος.

29.131 Manichaeis] Cf. Grotius to Walaeus, *App.* II no. 4. 64-67, and Introduction, 57.

30.138 ante attigimus] *Mel.* 16.33-34; 9.37; 26.95 & 28.114.

30.142 philosophorum quidam] In *Ver.* I 16 annot. 6 (IV 13b) Grotius mentions Ekphantos' pronouncement, as transmitted by Clem. Al. (*Strom.* V 29, 2) and wrongly attributed to Eurysos: Τὸ δὲ σκᾶνος τοῖς λοιποῖς ὅμοιον, οἷα γεγονὸς ἐκ τᾶς αὐτᾶς ὕλας, ὑπὸ τεχνίτα δὲ εἰργασμένον λώστω, ὅς ἐτεχνίτευσεν αὐτὸ ἀρχετύπῳ χρώμενος, ἑαυτῳ. A detailed discussion of this passage may be found in: Clément d'Alexandrie, *Les Stromates*, Stromates V, t. II (ed. Alain Le Boulluec), Paris 1981 (Sources Chrétiennes 279), 125 ff.

30.143 effigiem ... Dei esse] Gn. 1: 26-27. *Vg.* uses the terms '*imaginem*' and '*similitudinem*'. Cf. *Satisf.* I (IV 302a 33-39).

30.145-146 non plures sed unum] Cf. *Ver.* I 7 (IV 6b 9-11): "(hominum genus) a certo tempore communem stirpi sumpsisse originem, evincunt inter alia artium progressus", with (annot. 3) many references; and *Iur.*, prol. 14 (11): "Sed et historia sacra, praeter id quod in praeceptis consistit, affectum illum socialem non parum etiam eo excitat, quod nos docet ab iisdem primis parentibus ortos homines omnes, ita ut eo quoque sensu dici recte possit, quod alio dixit Florentinus, *cognationem inter nos a natura constitutam*'' (see next note).

30.147-148 cum et iurisconsulti] This can only have been the Roman jurist Florentinus whose pronouncement (*Dig.* I 1, 3) is cited here, as in *Iur.*, prol. 14 (see preceding note), and I 3, 1 (31). Cf. also note to *Mel.* 63.53.

31.150 contra Stoicos] For Grotius' ideas on the affections, see for instance *Annot. in NT*, ad Mt. 5: 22 (II 41b 13-58), and particularly, ad Lc. 19: 41 (II 441a 52- b3). Referring to Lact. *Inst.* VI, he criticises here the doctrine of the affections of both Stoics and Aristotelians. Cf. also *Iur.* prol. 43 (22): "Inter caetera ... non sine causa videntur mihi ab Aristotele discedere, et Platonici nonnulli et Christiani veteres, in eo quod ille naturam ipsam virtutis in mediocritate affectuum actionumque posuerit; quod semel positum eo ipsum abduxit, ut et virtutes diversas ... in unam compingeret, et veritati daret opposita minime ex aequo respondentia ..." To "et Christiani veteres" he adds: "Late hoc persequitur Lact. *Inst.* VI 15-17.''

31.155 Rom. 1: 31.

31.156 ante attigimus] Grotius is mistaken; so far he has not spoken of God's intention in creating man.

32.160 hominem ... dixere] Cf. Eus. *P.E.* I 10, 2. After having given a description of the Phoenician theogonia (cited *Ver.* I 16 annot. 3 (IV 9b 40-50)) the fragment of Philo Bybl., handed down to us by Eus., continues: ἦν δέ τινα ζῷα οὐκ ἔχοντα αἴσθησιν, ἐξ ὧν ἐγένετο ζῷα νοερά, καὶ ἐκλήθη Ζοφασημίν, τοῦτ' ἔστιν οὐρανοῦ κατόπται.

33.162-166 Cf. Lact. *Inst.* III 9, 13-15: "non ergo ideo nascimur, ut ea quae sunt facta videamus, sed ut ipsum factorem rerum omnium contemplemur, id est mente cernamus. Quare si quis hominem qui vere sapiat interroget, cuius rei causa natus sit, respondebit intrepidus ac paratus *colendi se dei gratia natum*, qui nos ideo generavit, ut ei serviamus. Servire autem Deo nihil aliud est quam bonis operibus tueri et conservare iustitiam."

33.166-167 colere .. complectitur] Cf. *Ver.* II 11 (IV 40a 7-10): "At christiana religio Deum, ut mentem purissimam, pura mente colendum docet, et iis operibus quae suapte natura etiam citra praeceptum honestissima sunt", with (annot. 8 & 9) references to Ioh. 4: 24; Rom. 12: 1 & Phil. 4: 8.

33.169 ante dictum] *Mel.* 31.150.

35.180 atque] See A Szantyr, *Lateinische Grammatik II. Syntax und Stilistik*, München 1964, 478: "Nach einem Komparativ steht atque bis auf Hor. nur, wenn derselbe regiert ist."

35.181 imaginem suam] See note to *Mel.* 30.143.

35.181-182 communis originis] See note to *Mel* 30.145-146.

35.188-189 καλὸν .... κακόν] With minor variations (ἐσθλοὶ in stead of καλόν; κακοί in stead of κακόν) this quotation from an unknown poet has been borrowed from Aristot. *Eth. Nic.* 1106b 34-35. In his translation of *Eth. Nic.* (*Aristoteles' Werke in deutscher Übersetzung*, hrgb. v. E. Grumach, Bd. 6: *Nikomacheische Ethik*, übersetzt u. kommentiert v. Franz Dirlmeier,[5] Berlin 1969) Dirlmeier says, (310): "Der abschliessende 'Pentameter' ist von Diehl [*Anthologia lyrica Graeca*] unter die Fragmenta elegiaca adespota aufgenommen ([2] p. 138, Nr. 16)."

35.191 κατόρθωμα ... actio] Cf. Cic. *Off.* I 8: "Nam et medium quoddam *officium* dicitur et *perfectum*. Perfectum officium rectum, opinor, vocemus, quoniam Graeci κατόρθωμα, hoc autem commune officium καθῆκον vocant. Atque ea sic definiunt, ut, rectum quod sit, id officium perfectum esse definiant; medium autem officium id esse dicunt, quod cur factum sit, ratio probabilis reddi possit." Sen. *Epist.* 95, 57: "*Actio recta* non erit, nisi recta fuerit voluntas."

36.202 pro matre noverca] This echoes Plin. *Nat.* 7, 1, 1: "... non ut sit satis aestimare, parens melior homini an tristior *noverca* fuerit (sc. natura)." Cf. *AE* 1516-19 (= *Dichtwerken* I 1a, 145):

"Posteros omnes Hominum novercae
Ira Naturae sequitur, malique
Criminis seros amor in nepotes
Transit a primo comitatus ortu."

37.205 Stoicorum ... error] See v. Arnim *SVF* I no. 224: III no. 468. Cf. *Iur.* II 20, 20 (493 n. 6).

38.217 poena] For Grotius' ideas about punishment, see *Iur.* II 20-24 (493-96). Cf. W. C. L. van der Grinten, 'De opvatting van Grotius over straf', *Tijdschrift voor Strafrecht*, 51 (1941), 155-76.

38.218 κατὰ τὸ ἔννομον] A formula often used by Aristot., cf. Bonitz *Index Aristotelicus*, s.v. c. 252.

39.221-229 Aristot. *Eth. Nic.* 1114a 12-22.

39.231-233 Sen. *Ira* II 10, 1.

41.245-246 Sen. *Ira* II 28, 1.

42.247 Sextius] Q. Sextius, Roman philosopher in the time of Augustus, mainly known through Sen.

42.248-249 Sen. *Epist.* 73, 12 and 13.

42.249-250 ut Deum ... a viro sapiente] Cf. Sen. Epist. 73, 13: "Iuppiter quo antecedit virum bonum?"

42.250-251 quod ... patientiam] Free adaptation of Sen. *Epist.* 73, 14: "quod Iuppiter uti illis non potest, sapiens non vult."

42.252 καυχήματα] Cf. Rom. 4:2; 1. Cor. 9: 16; Gal. 6:4. See R. Bultmann s.v. καυχάομαι κτλ in *TW* III 646-54.

Mel. 43] See Introduction, 36 ff., and *App.* II no. 2.40-46.

43.264-269 Zos. *Hist.* IV 59, 1, and II 29, 3. Both quotations are slightly adapted. Zos. is also referred to in *Iur.* II 20, 49, 1 (524, n. 6).

Mel. 44] Cf. Eus. *P.E.* IV 9-23 and Aug. *Civ.* X 9, 2 & 26.

44.272 Plato] *Rep.* 365a.

44.275 Porphyrius] Cf. Aug. *Civ.* X 9, 2.

45.282-283 χωρίς...ἄφεσιν] Hebr. 9: 22. Cf. *Annot. in NT*, ad Hebr. 9: 22 (III 1044a 42-46): "Macrobius ex Trebatio *animalem hostiam* esse dicit, *in quo anima sola Deo sacretur*, eiusque causas explicari a Virgilio illo versu:

Hanc tibi, Eyrx, meliorem animam pro morte daretis" (*Aen.* V 483); also *Satisf.* X (IV 333a 19-21): "Commune est sacrificio expiatorio legali et sacrificio Christi illud, quod *sine sanguinis effusione non sit remissio*", and *Satisf.* X (IV 335a 29-31).

45.286 Quidam ... populi] In *Satisf.* X (IV 335a 42- 336a 24) all these are listed, with references.

46.298 Porphyrius] Cf. Aug. *Civ.* X 28: "Ignorantiam certe et propter eam multa vitia per nullas teletas purgari dicis (sc. Porphyrius), sed per solum πατρικὸν νοῦν, id est *paternam mentem* sive intellectum, qui paternae est conscius voluntatis." Cited also in *Satisf.* X (IV 335a 23-28).

47.303 μεσίτην] Cf. *Satisf.* VIII (IV 329b 18-39), where Grotius disputes Socinus' assertion that the term μεσίτης in the Scriptures meant nothing but "Dei interpres". Against this he sets texts like: 1. Tim. 2: 5; Hebr. 9: 15 and 12: 24. See also *Satisf.* X (IV 337a 58 ff.). Otherwise he leaves the controversy with Socinians undiscussed in *Mel.* See Introduction, 52.

47.305 δι' αἱματεκχυσίας] See above note to *Mel.* 45.282-283.

47.310 κάθαρμα] 'sin-offering'. Unusual theological term. Cf. *Annot. in NT.*, ad 1. Cor. 4: 13 (III 779a 59- b 38), with reference i.a. to Aristoph. *Plut.* 454 and *Equ.* 1133.

48.318-320 Val. Max. VI 5 Ext. 3. Also cited against Socinus, *Satisf.* IV (IV 315a 2-34) and V (316b 28-34).

48.322 in re simili] *Mel.* 23.40.

48.322-326 non ideo ... dubitamus] Cf. Symbolum 'Quicumque' ps.-Athanasianum — nowadays considered to be of Gallican origin from approximately A.D. 450: "Nam sicut anima rationalis et caro unus est homo, ita Deus et homo unus est Christus" (H. Denzinger/A. Schönmetzer, *Enchiridion Symbolorum*,33 Barcinone/Friburgi Brisgoviae/Romae/Neo Eboraci 1965, no. 76 (37) (p. 40).

49.328 Amelius Platonicus] Fragm. from Eus. *P.E.* XI 19, 1-4. Cited also in Stob. *Dicta*, prol [iijᵛ]; *Annot. in NT*, ad Ioh. 1: 1 (II 474b 16-21) and *Ver.* I 16 annot. 7 (IV 14a 31-35), where more references are given. See H. Dörrie, 'Une exégèse néoplatonicienne du Prologue de l'Evangile selon saint Jean (Amélius chez Eusèbe), in *Platonica Minora*, München 1976, 491-507.

49.329 Ioh. 1: 1, 14.

49.330-332 inhabitandi modo...immensum differt] Nestorius and the Antiochene theologians in general liked to explain the manner of God's indwelling in Christ "as being κατ' εὐδοκίαν, i.e. by way of favour or good-pleasure, *analogous to the way in which God dwells in His saints* (italics PM)." J. N. D. Kelly, *Early Christian Doctrines*, ³London [1965], 305, 314. Grotius is remarkably 'orthodox' in his rejection of the Antiochenes.

49.332 καθ' ἕνωσιν ὑποστατικήν] Reference to the early Christian discussions about the union of the divine and the human in Christ. Grotius probably quotes from memory, for the formula commonly used was: ἕνωσις καθ' ὑπόστασιν, which was authenticated notably by the council of Ephesus (431); see *Conciliorum Oecumenicorum Decreta*, ed. Centro di Documentazione Istituto per le Scienze Religiose — Bologna — (J.

Alberigo, P.-P. J. C. Leonardi (e.a.)), Basileae/ Barcinone/ Friburgi/ Romae/ Vindobonae 1962, 38¹⁶⁻¹⁷. Cf. Grotius to Walaeus (*App.* II no. 4.33-35).

50.340 Venia] Cf. *Satisf.* VI (IV 319b 60- 320a 1): "(Liberatio) circa poenam .. nomen proprium ... non habet, sed communi nomine vocatur gratia, *venia*, indulgentia, abolitio."

50.348 Publil. Syr. *Sent.* 645. Cited also in *Annot. in NT*, ad Mt. 5:39 (II 65a 8) and *Iur.* I 2, 8, 8 ann. 5 (68).

50.352 ante diximus] *Mel.* 43.254-256.

50.354-357 Apart from the first part, which I have been unable to locate, the quotation stems from Plut. *Mor.* 476F. Grotius repeatedly refers to it, for instance in Stob. *Dicta*, prol. [(u i)]; *Annot. in NT*, ad Lc. 15: 7 (II 418b 26-27); *Annot. in VT*, ad Eccl. 32: 24 (I 676b 40).

50.356 Grotius leaves τῆς ψυχῆς untranslated.

50.361-363 Theodoret of Cyrus, *Quaest. et resp. ad Orthod.* 104, formerly ascribed to Ps.-Iustin M.; see J. Quasten, *Patrology*, III, Utrecht 1952, 400 and 548 ff. The best text is found in *Iustini Opera* (ed. I. C. Th. Otto), III pars II, ³Ienae 1881, 166: Ἀγαθη μὲν οὖν ἐστιν ἡ συγγνώμη καὶ τῆς θείας χάριτος δῶρον, οὐκ ἔστι δὲ οὐδὲ κατὰ τὸν νόμον οὐδὲ κατὰ τοῦ νόμου, ἀλλ' ὑπὲρ τὸν νόμον καὶ ὑπὲρ τοῦ νόμου. ὑπὲρ τὸν νόμον μέν, ὅτι χάρις, ὑπὲρ τοῦ νόμου δέ, ὅτι διὰ μετανοίας ἄγει τοὺς ἁμαρτωλοὺς εἰς εὐπάθειαν τοῦ νόμου, καθάπερ καὶ τὸν Δαυΐδ. Cited also *Satisf.* V (IV 317a 24-31).

51.368-370 Aristot. *Metaph.* 993b 9. Also quoted in *Ver.* II 18 annot. 2 (IV 44b 61-45a 25). Cf. A. Walaeus, *Iudicium doctrinae et convocationem synodorum* (*Op. Omn.* II 62a): "Ideo etiam doctissimi ethnici fatebantur, quo plura de Deo cogitarent, eo minus sese de eo intelligere; et, in rebus divinis non plus posse ingenium humanum quam *oculos vespertilionis* in aspiciendo lumine solari. Hanc ethnicorum confessionem veram esse, apertis et planis verbis testatur Paulus, 1. Cor. 2: 14."

51.375-384 Apud gentes ... comprehensa est] Cf. *Ver.* II 18 "Probatur amplius praestantia christianae religionis ex praestantia ipsius Magistri" (IV 44b 30-48a 16).

Mel. 52-55] These paragraphs interrupt the exposition about the reparation of the relation between God and man, which is continued in par. 56-57. The argument in par. 52-55 about the reliability of the divine *Scriptures* was elicited in 51.383, where Grotius spoke about the Word of God as recorded in *Scriptures*.

52.385 evincat] sc. 'christiana religio' (51.381).

52.386 nihil non Deo dignum] Cf. *Ver.* III 6 (IV 51b 9-32).

52.391-392 in hominum libris ... consensio] Cf. *Ver.* III 13 (IV 54a29-55a2).

53.397-401 Varro] From Cens. *Dies.* 21, 1. Also quoted in *Ver.* I 16 annot. 48 (IV 18b 15-28.)

53.403-408 Scriptorum ... Hebraica] Cf. *Ver.* I 15 (IV 9b 1-7): "Accedit indubitata scriptorum Mosis antiquitas, cui nullum aliud scriptum possit contendere; cujus argumentum et hoc est, quod Graeci, unde omnis ad alias gentes fluxit eruditio, literas se aliunde accepisse fatentur, quae apud ipsos literae et ordinem et nomen et ductum quoque veterem non alium habent quam Syriacae sive Hebraicae," with (annot. 1 (IV 9a 54- b 20)) among others reference to J. J. Scaliger, *Animadversiones in Chronologica Eusebii*, in *Thesaurus temporum*, Lugd. Bat. 1606, 102 ff. Grotius owned this work, see Molhuysen, 'Bibliotheek', no. 26 (51). — From his youth onwards Grotius was interested in this subject. Cf. his 'Lectori' in *Sacra* (= *Dichtwerken* I 1a, 295), where he develops his scholarly plans and announces the following work: "Primum in sacris dialogus, cui Philarchaeo nomen, iam in manibus est, in quo Mosis sacra historia plurimis ethnicorum firmatur testimoniis, si tamen ita loquendum de re quae per se firma externo ad fidem auxilio non eget. In eo multa ex Aegyptia, Phoenicia, Orphica, Pythagorica theologia non contemnenda promerentur." *TMD*, addenda ad no. 944 (650), suggests that parts of this never published juvenile work were integrated in *Ver.* I 16 (IV 9b 12-28a 14). Would Grotius have suppressed the Philarcheus because his teacher Scaliger in the meantime had appeared with his famous *Animadversiones?*

53.404 Diodoro ... legislatorem] Diod. *Bibl. Hist.* I 94 and XL fragm. Sometimes Moses is represented by Diodorus as a law-giver from prehistoric times who received his instruction directly from God, like Minos, Lycurgus, Zarathustra and others, but he never calls Moses 'the oldest law-giver'. This theory stems from the early Christian Apologists (Theoph. Ant. *Autol.* III 23 for instance) who in their turn borrowed it from Jewish-Hellenistic Apologists, such as Ios. *Ap.* II §§ 154-156 and *Ant. Iud.* I § 16.

54.410-415 Dionysius Longinus] This is a slightly adapted quotation from Ps. Long. *Subl.* IX 9. The same fragm. also occurs in *Ver.* I 16 annot. 95 (IV 26b 26-39), to which Grotius refers *Annot. in VT*, ad Gn. 1: 3 (I 1a 40-42). — In a lecture delivered in 1923 and printed after his death ('Das Genesiszitat in der Schrift vom Erhabenen', *Abh. d. deutschen Akad. der Wiss. zu Berlin, Kl. f. Sprachen, Lit. u. Kunst*, 1954 1, Berlin 1955, 3-23) E. Norden tried to prove that Ps. Long. had his knowledge of Judaism from Philo. For this question see also John C. Gager, *Moses in Greco-Roman Paganism*, Nashville Tennessee 1972, 56-63, and M. Stern, *Greek and Latin Authors on Jews and Judaism* I, Jerusalem 1974, 361-65.

54.414 Grotius leaves τί untranslated.

Mel. 55] Cf. *Ver.* II 17 (IV 44a 35- b 29).

56.436-437 Philosophi Stoici ... saepe] As appears from *Annot. in*

NT, ad Ioh. 6: 53 (II 507b 56-57): "Duobus modis sapientiam ait doceri Seneca, *praeceptis* et *exemplis*...", Grotius would have had Sen. in mind, who says indeed (*Epist.* 6, 5): "...longum iter est per *praecepta*, breve et efficax per *exempla*."

56.437-439 Cf. *Rep.emend.* I 1, 5-6 (66); "ante oculos nobis ponunt Ulyssem poetae, Socratem Stoici, Catonem Romani."

56.437-438 Epictetus ... Socratem] *Ench.* 33, 12.

56.438-439 Seneca ... Catonem] Cf. Sen. *Epist.* 11, 10; 25, 6; 95, 72; 104, 21: "si velis vitiis exui ... ad meliores transi: cum Catonibus vive."

56.443-455 At Christiani ... nulla habet] The same matter is exposed more elaborately in *Ver.* II 18 "Probatur amplius praestantia christianae religionis ex praestantia ipsius Magistri" (IV 44b 30- 48a 16).

Mel. 57] See Introduction, 37.

57.458-459 εἰ γένοιτό...ἀγαθός] Title of Max. Tyr.'s *Diss.* 38. In Stob. *Dicta*, prol ([o ij^v] — o iij), when speaking of true piety which cannot exist without divine assistance, Grotius refers to Plato's *Phaedr.* and continues: "Sunt et similes alii ad Platonem loci, et insignis de hoc argumento diatriba Maximi Tyrii numero XXII (= 38). Seneca: *Bonus vir sine Deo nemo est. An potest aliquis supra fortunam nisi ab illo adjutus exsurgere* (*Epist.* 41, 2)? *In uno quoque virorum bonorum habitat Deus.* Mox: *Non potest res tanta sine adminiculo numinis stare* (*Epist.* 41, 5). Alibi: *Deus ad homines venit, imo quod propius est, in homines venit. Nulla sine Deo mens bona est* (*Epist.* 73, 16). Fide opus esse ad ea comprehendenda quae sub sensus non cadunt, docet sacra auctoritas."

57.462-463 Sen. *Epist.* 73, 16 (see preceding note).

57.466-468 Deo ... volentem] Walaeus (*App.* II no. 8.40-46) criticises this passage and cites *Mel.* 57.466-468 verbatim.

57.466 solidam laudem] Ciceronian term. Cf. Cic. *Sist.* 43, 93: "*solida* veraque *laus*"; *Vatin* 3, 8: "*solida laus* ac vera dignitas."

57.470 Sen. *Epist.* 116, 8.

57.473-474 Stoicorum vocem] Sen. *Epist.* 41, 1: "Facis rem optimam et tibi salutarem, si, ut scribis, perseveras ire ad *bonam mentem*, quam *stultum est optare, cum possis a te impetrare.*"

58.477-480 ἀδιάφορα... mala] Cf. Diog. Laert. VII 103.

58.484 indolere] Not in *TLL*. Grotius uses this term here, as he does in *Mel.* 70.174, in the sense of 'indolescere.'

Mel. 59] Cf. *Iur.* II 20, 44, 5 (515); II 20, 49, 1 (524); *Ver.* I 16 annot. 101 (IV 27b 18-29), where all these and other references are listed.

59.2-7 Strabo] XVI 2, 35-37.

59.8-9 Trogus Pompeius] Iust. 36, 2, 16.

59.10-12 Plinius] *Epist.* 10, 96, 7: "Adfirmabant autem hanc fuisse summam vel culpae suae vel erroris, quod essent *soliti* stato die ante lucem convenire carmenque Christo quasi deo dicere secum invicem, seque *sacramento non in scelus aliquod obstringere, sed ne furta, ne latrocinia, ne adulteria committerent, ne fidem fallerent, ne depositum appellati abnegarent...*'' Cited also *Annot. in NT*, ad Mt. 5: 34 (II 59a 38-41) and *Ver.* II 2 annot. 3 (IV 33b 31-38).

59.12-13 Ammianus Marcellinus] 22, 11, 5. Also cited *Iur.* II 20, 49, 1 (524).

Mel. 60] Cf. *Ver.* II 11 ''Praeceptorum eximia sanctitate circa Dei cultum'' (IV 39a 10- 40b 12).

60.21-22 Varronem ... reverentia] Cf. Aug. *Civ.* IV 27; 31; 32 and *Sent. Varr.* 99: ''Dum vulgus colat iustitiam, nil interest utrum vera praedices.''

60.23 senatus Romanus] It is not clear what Grotius is alluding to.

61.34 ante egimus] *Mel.* 51.380-384.

62.35 Invocare] Cf. Walaeus, *App.* II no. 8.47-51.

62.35-36 Plato ... orare] Plato *Alc.2* passim, in particular 141c-143b, and 150c.

62.35-36 fassus ... nescire] This is the whole tenor of *Alc.2*, 147a-150b.

62.36 poetae] Plato (*Alc.2* 138bc) refers for instance to the Oedipus-saga and (*Alc.2* 149de) to Homer. Cf. *Annot. in NT*, ad Mt. 6: 8 (II 78a 1-20), where Grotius refers to Plato without, however, mentioning *Alc*.

62.38 quorundam ... philosophorum] Max. Tyr. for instance who gives a negative answer in *Diss.* 11, entitled: Εἰ δεῖ εὔχεσθαι.

63.48 quod ... peierare] Cf. *Annot. in NT*, ad Mt. 5: 33 (II 56a 14-57a 24) and *Iur.* II 13, 10 (367-368).

63.52-53 εἰ ... θεοῖς ἱδρυτέον] Title of Max. Tyr.'s *Diss.* 8, where the question is answered negatively. Reference to this *Diss.* in *Annot. in VT*, ad Ex. 20: 4 (I 39a 58-59). See H. Funke s.v. 'Götterbild' in *RAC* XI, 659-828 (747). Cf. also Grotius to Walaeus, *App.* II no. 2.24-27, and *Rem.* (ed. Meijer, 110): ''Want alzoo een groot gedeelte van het Christendom den Goodtsdijenst heeft vermenght met affgodendijenst, ende namentlijck men den beeldendijenst, die expresselijck is verboden bij de onverbreeckelijcke Wet Goods, ... soo is het dan noodigh, om Goods wil nae te comen, dat de Joden mogen verkeeren onder Christenen, dije haer hebben affgesondert van de affgoden ende beeldendijenst, ende daerom wel te recht gereformeerden werden genoemt. T'geloof, twelck is boven de natuijr, neemt nijet wegh t'gunt dat is van de natuijre. *Cognationem quandam inter omnes homines natura constituit*, seggen de rechten.'' See above note to *Mel.* 30.147-148.

63.53-54 Pythagoras ... Numa] As appears from *Annot. in NT*, ad

Rom. 1: 23 (III 678a 35-36) Grotius has Plut. *Num.* 65 in mind, where Numa's and Pyth.'s opinions about this topic are qualified as 'kindred'. The same reference to Plut. occurs in *Iur.* II 20, 45, 2 (516-17) and *Annot. in VT*, ad Ex. 20: 4 (I 40b 29-30).

63.54 Euripides] As appears from *Annot. in NT*, ad Act. 7: 48 (II 597b 48-51), it concerns (ps.) Eur. fragm. 1130, Nauck²:

ποῖος δ'ἄν οἶκος τεκτόνων πλασθεὶς ὑπὸ
δέμας τὸ θεῖον περιβάλοι τοίχων πτυχαῖς;

Nauck *ad loc.*: "Christianus poeta haec scribere potuit, non potuit Euripides." It stems from Clem. Al. *Strom.* V 75, 1.

63.55 Seneca] As appears from *Annot. in VT*, ad Ex. 20: 4 (I 40a 63-b 1) Grotius refers to Sen. *Nat.* 8, 30: "Effugit oculos: cogitatione visendus est (sc. Deus)." Quoted also in *Ver.* IV 12 annot. 1 (IV 70a 29-35) with ref. to Lact. *Inst.* VI 25, 13: "quanto melius et verius Seneca *vultisne vos* inquit *deum cogitare magnum et placitum et maiestate leni verendum, amicum et semper in proximo, non immolationibus nec sanguine multo colendum — quae enim ex trucidatione immerentium voluptas est? — sed mente pura, bono honestoque proposito? non templa illi congestis in altitudinem saxis extruenda sunt: in suo cuique consecrandus est pectore.*"

63.56-60 Tac. *Hist.* V 5, 4. Also cited *Annot. in VT*, ad Ex. 20: 4 (I 40b 20-22); ad Deut. 4: 15 (I 84a 34-36). See above note to *Mel.* 21.25.

Mel. 64] References in *Ver.* IV 12 annot. 1 (IV 69a 42- 70a 40).

65.73 frequentare ... coetus] Hebr. 10: 25.

65.75-77 Cic. *Rep.* (= Somnium Scipionis) VI 13.

65.82-83 dies ... septima] Cf. *Iur.* II 20, 45, 2 (517); *Ver.* V 10 (IV 79a 1- b 20). See also next note.

65.85 Seneca, atque alii] Sen. *Epist.* 95, 47 and Rutil. Nam. *De reditu suo* 391-92, according to *Annot. in VT*, ad Ex. 20: 11 (I 46b 48- 47a 20):

"Septima quaeque dies turpi damnata veterno,
tamquam ut delassati mollis imago Dei."

For more details, see E. Lohse s.v. σάββατον κτλ, 'Die jüdische Sabbatfeier im Urteil der Nichtjuden', in *TW* VII 17-18.

65.86-87 cum nulli ... impenditur] Cf. *Iur.* II 20, 45, 2 (517): "... sabbati violatio ex instituto continebat abnegationem mundi a Deo creati."

66.97-98 Hor. *Ars* 180.

66.100-103 Verg. *Aen* II 717-20.

66.106-107 In Mithrae ... legimus] Grotius has Iust. M. *1. Apol.* 66, 4 in mind, but he is mistaken. What is being said is merely that in the service of Mithras bread and *water* are used. Archaeological evidence, however, does point to the use of wine, not of water. Cf. M. J. Vermaseren, *Mithras, de geheimzinnige god*, Amsterdam/Brussel 1959, 82.

66.108 Cereri ac Libero] Cf. *Ver.* II 11 (39b 7-12): "mysteria autem illa sanctissima sive Cereris sive Liberi patris plenissima fuere omnis obscoenitatis, ut apparuit postquam semel perrupta arcani religione evulgari coeperunt, quod late exsequuntur Clemens Alexandrinus (*Protr.* 20, 1-21, 1) et alii (Arnob. *Adv. nat.* 5, 25-26)."

66.112-115 Cf. Iust. M. *1. Apol.* 66, 2: "Οὐ γὰρ ὡς κοινὸν ἄρτον οὐδὲ κοινὸν πόμα ταῦτα λαμβάνομεν· ἀλλ' ὅν τρόπον διὰ λόγου θεοῦ σαρκοποιηθεὶς Ἰησοῦς Χριστὸς ὁ σωτὴρ ἡμῶν καὶ σάρκα καὶ αἷμα ὑπὲρ σωτηρίας ἡμῶν ἔσχεν, οὕτως καὶ τὴν δι' εὐχῆς λόγου τοῦ παρ' αὐτοῦ εὐχαριστηθεῖσαν τροφήν, ἐξ ἧς αἷμα καὶ σάρκες κατὰ μεταβολὴν τρέφονται ἡμῶν, ἐκείνου τοῦ σαρκοποιηθέντος Ἰησοῦ καὶ σάρκα καὶ αἷμα ἐδιδάχθημεν εἶναι."

67.120 caeremoniarum observatione] Cf. *Ver.* IV 12 annot. 1 (IV 69a 42- 70a 40).

67.122-132 There is an obvious connection between this whole passage and Plut. *Aud.* (= *Mor.* 21E). Cf. also Stob. *Dicta*, prol. ([o iij^v]).

67.122-125 Soph. fragm. no. 753 Nauck^2, transmitted by Plut. *Mor.* 21F. In his ed. of Plut. *Aud.* (= *Mor.* 21E), incorporated in Stob. *Dicta* (26), he translates as follows:

"Felices nimis,
Initia quotquot ista cum conspexerint
Eunt ad orcum. namque eos solos manet
Ibi vita; reliquos, miserias praeter, nihil."

Mel. 68] Cf. *Ver.* II 12 "Circa ea officia humanitatis quae proximo debemus, etiam laesi" (IV 40b 13- 42a 4).

68.148 quod tibi ... feceris] Verbatim quotation from Ael. L. *Alex. Sev.* § 51, incorporated in *Historia Augusta*. Cf. Stob. *Dicta*, prol. ([o iiij^v]): "Praecipuum caritatis praeceptum quod ubique Christus inculcat, Severus Imperator eisdem prope verbis extulit: *Quod tibi non vis, alteri ne feceris.*" Quoted also in *Annot. in NT*, ad Mt. 7: 12 (II 89b 56-58) and in *Ver.* II 16 annot. 12 (IV 44b 53-54). — For the history of this so-called 'Golden Rule', see Albrecht Dihle, *Die goldene Regel*, Göttingen 1962 (Studienhefte f. Altertumswiss. 7), and *JTS* N.S. 15 (1964) 384-88.

69.149-150 latrocinia] Cf. *Iur.* II 15, 5, 1-2 (391-392) and *Ver.* II 12 annot. 6 (IV 41a 26- b 22).

69.152-154 quamquam ... dilectio] Cf. Gal. 6: 10.

69.155 cum Aristotele] Cf. *Ver.* II 12 (IV 40b 22-23): "Sed idem (sc. Aristot.) in barbaros bellum dicit esse naturale." Probably is meant: Aristot. *Pol.* 1256b, as is the case *Iur.* II 15, 5, 2 (392).

69.160-161 Iuv. *Sat.* 14, 103-104. Cf. *Rem.* (108): "Een Roomsch poëet, der Joden maniere beschrijvende, seijt: dat sij noch wech noch fonteijn souden willen wijsen aan een onbesneden"; (followed by Iuv. *Sat.* 14, 103-104). Quoted also *Annot. in NT*, ad Mt. 5: 43 (II 71a 51-52).

69.162-163 Tac. *Hist.* V 5, 1. Also quoted in *Annot. in NT*, ad Mt. 5: 43 (II 71a 53-54), with reference to *Iur.* II 15, 9, 3 (396); and again in *Annot. in VT*, ad Deut. 7: 2 (I 85b 13-15).

69.164-165 Aristoteles et Cicero ... laudant ulcisci] Cf. Stob. *Dicta*, prol. ([oiiij^v]); "Ultionis privatae studium probare videntur Aristoteles et Cicero"; *Iur.* II 20, 8 (473-477); *Ver.* II 12 annot. 7 (IV 41b 22-36), with reference to Aristot. *Eth. Nic.* 1126a 7-9; Cic. *Inv.* 2, 27, 81, *Att.* 9, 12, 2 and others.

69.165 Platonici et Stoici] As in Stob. *Dicta*, prol. ([o iiij^v] - u) and *Annot. in NT*, ad Mt. 5: 39 (II 63a 20- b 37) Grotius refers notably to Plato *Crito* (49bc); Max. Tyr. *Diss.* 18: Εἰ τὸν ἀδικήσαντα ἀνταδικητέον; and Sen. (see next note). Cf. also *Iur.* II 20, 10, 6 (484) and *Ver.* IV 12 annot. 3 (IV 70a 50-63).

69.166-167 Sen. *Ira* 2, 32, 1. Also in *Annot. in NT*, ad Mt. 5: 39 (II 63b 19-21) in the following reading: "Immane verbum est ultio et ab iniuria tantum distans ordine. qui ulciscitur non nisi excusatius peccat." In Stob. *Dicta*, prol. (u), in this manner: "Inhumanum verbum est et quidem pro iusto receptum ultio, et a contumelia non differt nisi ordine. qui dolorem regerit, tantum excusatius peccat." Cf. also *Iur.* II 20, 5, 2 (469).

70.172 Sen. *Ag.* 267. Quoted also in *Annot. in NT*, ad Mt. 6: 14 (II 81b 20); ad Mt. 7: 3 (II 88a 21), and *Annot. in VT*, ad Eccl. 28: 2 (I 667b 43).

70.174 indoleas] Cf. note to *Mel.* 58.484.

70.179-180 culpatum ... ἐλεημοσύνη] See R. Bultmann s.v. ἔλεος κτλ in *TW* II 474 sqq. "... in der Stoa (wird) das ἔλεος unter die Krankheiten der Seele gerechnet; als πάθος und zwar als eine Art der λύπη ist es des Weisen nichtwürdig" (475) with many references.

70.181-182 In diris Atheniensium] Quotation from a fragment of Diphilus' comedy *Parasitus*, transmitted by Athen. (*Deipn.* VI 239 ff). See Th. Kock, *Comicorum Atticorum Fragmenta* II, Leipzig 1884, no. 62, 561. Grotius inserts this fragment in his *Excerpta* (793) and quotes it in *Annot. in NT*, ad Mt. 5: 43 (II 71a 39-42).

70.184-185 institutis ... Spartiatarum] The same, in more detail, *Ver.* II 12 (IV 40b 18-22): "Sic et Laconum instituta ... tota ad vim bellicam fuisse directa notat et in culpa ponit Aristoteles", with (annot. 1) reference to Aristot. *Pol.* (1333b 12-16) and Eur. *Andr.*

Mel. 71-74] The same, more copiously and with many references, *Iur.* II 5, 1-16 (231-250) and *Ver.* II 13 (IV 42a 6- 43a 10).

71.191 Socratis et Platonis insania] Plato *Rep.* 457d, cited *Ver.* II 13 annot. 5 (IV 42b -43). A frequent apologetic argument, cf. for instance Lact. *Inst.* III 21, and Eus. *P.E.* XIII 18, 18.

72.196-197 Persae ... Athenienses] As appears from *Iur.* II 5, 12, 3 (241) & II, 5, 9, 3 (237), Grotius had Phil. *Spec. leg.* n. 5 and Xen. *Apol.* in mind. Cf. also *Imp.* X (IV 214b 34).

72.200 cum Romanis] Cf. *Mel.* 72.219-220.

72.202 viri unius uxor] See *Ver.* IV 12 annot. 4 (IV 70b 8-20).

72.203-207 Lucan. *Phars.* 8, 397-401.

72.209-212 Eur. *Andr.* 177-180. Grotius omits a translation. Quoted also in Stob. *Dicta*, prol. ([ij^v]); *Iur.* II 5, 9, 2 (236 n. 2); *Excerpta* (232-33); *Ver.* II 13 annot. 14 (IV 43a 50-51) & IV 12 annot. 4 (IV 70b 11-18), where Grotius translates:

"...non etenim decet
Unum imperare feminis binis virum:
Contentus uno conjugis vivat toro,
Quicunque cupiet rite curatam domum."

72.213-214 Tac. *Germ.* 18, 1. Quoted also in *Iur.* II 4, 9, 4 (237 n. 2).

73.219-220 solis prope Romanis] Cf. *Ver.* IV 12 annot. 5 (IV 70b 21-24): "Foedus matrimonii debere esse perpetuum. Quale fuit apud Romanos ad annum Urbis vicesimum et quingentesimum, Valerio Maximo teste lib. II. cap. I"; again *Annot. in NT*, ad Mt. 5: 31 (II 51b 57-59): "Et Romani, cum nulla lex repudium vetaret, annos tamen quingentos et viginti sine exemplo repudii egerunt."

73.226-227 Martial. VI 7, 5-6. Cited Stob. *Dicta*, prol. ([u^v]), and *Annot. in NT*, ad Mt. 5: 32 (II 55b 60-61).

Mel. 74] See Introduction, 39.

74.233 tribuni ... plebis] Under the Roman Republic the tribunes of the people were sacrosanct, see for instance Liv. 3, 19; 3, 55, 6 ff. and 4, 3. The Emperors inherited this quality.

74.234 ut tradita a Deo] Rom. 13: 1. Cf. *Iur.* I 2, 7, 3 (62).

74.234-235 Stoicorum vocibus] Probably an allusion to the fact that the resistance against the Emperors very often was instigated by the Stoics who wanted the Republic back. Their ideal was Cato Minor. See note to *Mel.* 75.247.

75.246 Platonis controversia] Plato *Phaed.* 61d-64b.

75.247 Catonem] Cato Minor. After the battle of Thapsos he killed himself in order not to have to witness the decline of the Republic and the coming of Cesar. In his last hours he was reading Plato's *Phaed.* See for instance Cic. *Fin.* III 18, 60, 61 and Lact. *Inst.* III 18, 8-13.

75.247-249 Nam ... liceat] This argument against suicide agrees with Cic. *Rep.* (Somnium Scipionis) VI 15 (end): '... retinendus animus est in custodia corporis, nec iniussi eius a quo ille vobis est datus, ex hominum vita migrandum est ne munus humanum adsignatum a deo defugisse videamini."

75.248-249 divino ... statione] Cf. Epict. *Diss.* 1, 9, 24; 2, 15, 4-20; 3, 24, 99. For more details, see H. Chadwick s.v. 'Gewissen', II g. 'Selbstmord', in *RAC* X 1051 ff.

75.251 Mart. XI 56, 16.

75.254 Lucan. *Phars.* I 462. Grotius will have had the Dutch character in mind, as appears from *Par.* (III 78): "Lucanus egregie et, ut solet, significanter de gentibus locutus, quas Arctos despicit, *hoc est majoribus nostris*"; (followed by *Phars.* I 459-62).

76.262-263 nihil esse post mortem] View of Epic. Cf. for instance Cic. *Fin.* II 100.

76.264 naturae ... esse mortem] View of the Stoics. Cf. for instance Marc. Aur. II 17.

Mel. 77] Cf. *Ver.* II 14-16 (IV 43a 12- 44a 34).

77.267-268 honores ... voluptas] Cf. Cic. *Off.* III 10: "quae enim videntur utilia *honores, divitiae, voluptates.*"

77.273 ταπεινοφροσύνη] See W. Grundmann s.v. in *TW* VIII 22-24.

78.277 φιλοχρηματία] Cf. *Annot. in NT*, ad Mt. 6: 24 (II 84b 35).

78.279-280 insano ... philosophorum more] As appears from *Ver.* II 14 annot. 10 (IV 43-45), he had the philosophers Aristippus (Diog. L. II 77) and Crates of Thebe (cf. Philostr. *Vit. Apoll.* I 13, 15) in mind. See also *Annot. in NT*, ad Mt. 19: 21 (II 186b 22-24): "Narrantur alii in mare pecuniam proiecisse cum dicto: *Pereas, ne me perdas.* Tanti illis videbatur amovere recte sapiendi moras."

78.282 corrigere non possit] This is a Stoic argument. Cf. Epict. *Ench.* I 1.

78.283 ad se nihil pertinentia] Likewise a Stoic argument. Cf. Epict. *Ench.* I 15; III 26.

Mel. 79] Cf. *Ver.* II 11 (IV 38a9-40b12).

80.297 indictitiam] According to *LS 'indicticius'* or *'-tius'* means: declared, proclaimed.

80.298 ieiunium] Fasting, as a means of reinforcing prayer, is frequent in NT. See J. Behm s.v. νῆστις κτλ in *TW* IV 932-35. See also Grotius *Annot. in NT*, ad Mt. 17: 21 (II 170a 46-52): "Ieiunium ideo adiungit (sc. Christus), quia ad preces imprimis requiritur animus demissus, cui rei inservit ieiunium. Unde plerumque coniungi videmus νηστείαν [ieiunium] et δέησιν [orationem] sive προσευχήν [preces], Lc. 2: 37; Act. 10: 30; 14: 23; 1. Cor. 7: 5." In his younger years he translated into Dutch a number of Lenten Hymns: "*Audi benigne conditor*", "*Ex more festi mystico*", "*Iam Christe Sol iustitiae*" (*Bewijs*, 259-61).

81.302 Venus ... interdicta] Chastity was considered a proof of *temperantia.* Cf. for instance Plato *Rep.* 430e.

81.304-305] Hor. *Sat.* 1, 2, 31-32. Quoted also in *Annot. in NT*, ad Act. 15: 20 (II 621a 54).

81.306-308 Melius ... fieri] Epict. *Ench.* 33, 8: Περὶ ἀφροδίσια εἰς δύναμιν πρὸ γάμου καταρευτέον. Quoted also in Stob. *Dicta*, prol. (u) and *Annot. in NT*, ad Mt. 5: 27 (II 47b 33-43), where the quotation again is followed by a reference to Dio Chrys. (*Or.* 7, 139), who argues that the ever more shameless manifestation of adultery is the result of excessive licence in visiting brothels.

82.317 φιλανθρωπίας] Cf. *Annot. in NT*, ad Tit. 3: 4 (III 1003b 13-25); *Satisf.* I (IV 297a 26-27; 298b 48-49). In Plut.'s ethics this concept has a central place.

83.320 contra Platonem] Plato *Rep.* 382c. In *Annot. in NT*, ad Lc. 24: 28 (II 466a 20- 467b 61) and *Iur.* III 1, 17 (631-33) Grotius enters more deeply into the problem of the admissibility of lying, feigning etc.

83.321 Datus est autem sermo] Cf. Cic. *Off.* I 16, 50 (on the nature of human society): "Eius autem vinculum est ratio et oratio, quae docendo, discendo, communicando, disceptando, iudicando conciliat inter se homines coniungitque naturali quadam societate." *Iur.*, prol. 7 (8-9): "Homini vero perfectae aetatis cum circa similia similiter agere norit, cum societatis appetitu excellente, cuius peculiare solus inter animantes instrumentum habet *sermonem*..."

84.325 stare promissis] Cf. *Iur.*, prol. 8 (9): "promissorum implendorum obligatio"; III 19, 1 (813-15).

84.326-327 Panaetius ... Cicero] Cic. took Panaetius' Περὶ τοῦ καθήκοντος as a basis for his *Off.* See M. Pohlenz, *Antikes Führertum. Cicero De officiis und das Lebensideal des Panaitios*, Leipzig/Berlin 1934 (reprint Amsterdam 1967).

84.327 hosti publico servanda fides] Cic. *Off.* I 13, 39.

84.328 non est praedoni ... tyranno] Cic. *Off.* III 29, 107-08. Cf. *Iur.* II 13, 15, 1 (371), and III 19, 2, 1 (815), where Grotius also refers to Cic. *Off.* III 6, 32: "Nulla nobis societas cum tyrannis, sed potius summa distractio est", and Sen. *Benef.* 7, 19, 8: "Quicquid erat quo mihi cohaereret intercisa iuris humani societas abscidit."

85.335 Cogitationibus ... lex praescribitur] Cf. *Iur.* II 20, 45, 2 (517): "Tertio praecepto (sc. Decalogi) intelligitur cognitio et cura rerum humanarum, etiam *cogitationum*, nam id iurisiurandi fundamentum est. Deus enim testis etiam cordis, et si quis fallat vindex invocatur, quo ipso simul et iustitia Dei significatur et potentia."

85.338-340 Sen. *Benef.* 5, 14, 2: "Sic *latro est etiam antequam manus inquinet*, quia ad occidendum iam armatus est et habet spoliandi atque interficiendi voluntatem; *exercetur et aperitur opere* nequitia, *non incipit*."

86.341-345 Cf. Mt. 6:1-4.

86.343 ut famae imponant] "in order to mislead public opinion."

86.344 ὑποκριτάς] Cf. *Annot. in NT*, ad Mt. 22: 18 (II 202b 34-41).

86.348 ὁμολογουμένως τῇ φύσει ζῆν] the highest good as defined by the Stoics. See v. Arnim *SVF* III fr. 5 ff; 12 ff.

87.352 Cuius praecepti ratio] Cf. *Mel.* 50.

87.355 χειροδίκαι] The term stems from Hes. *Op.* 189.

88.357-358 liberos suos ... humano sanguine] The same argumentation is found, in reversed order, in *Ver.* II 12 (IV 41a 7-9): "Gladiatorum mutuae dilaniationes inter oblectamenta erant publica paganorum: exponere liberos quotidianum." With reference (annot. 8 & 9) *i.a.* to Lact. *Inst.* VI 20 & Tert. *Spec.* 19, resp. Tert. *Apol.* 9, 17 & Ter. *Hec.* 400. See also *Mel.* 8. 32.

88.364 christiana vita] Cf. *Iur.* I 2, 8, 1 (68): "certum autem est si omnes sint Christiani, et christiane vivant, nulla fore bella."

88.366 aureum ... saeculum] Allusion to the wide-spread notion of the Ancients that in its earliest period, the Golden Age, under the dominion of Kronos, mankind had experienced a life of abundance, freedom of care, and happiness. Since then a process of degeneration had started, which had brought about the Silver, Copper and Iron Ages. See B. Gatz, *Weltalter, goldene Zeit und sinnverwandte Vorstellungen*, (Spudasmata 16), Hildesheim 1967, and H. Levin, *The Myth of the Golden Age in the Renaissance*, London 1970. Cf. Vives, *Ver.* V, 9 (666): "Hoc est seculum aureum, non illud Saturno rege. Existit enim hoc ex abundantia et soluta rerum omnium licentia, ut olim fabulantur; sed ex animis puris, candidis, pulcherrima flamma incensis ad concordiam, pacem, hilaritatem, gratificationem et beneficentiam."

89.1 sanctissimus senex] i.e. Patriarch Meletius. His ideas about the relation between Ancient Philosophy and Christianity were shared by Grotius. See *Mel.* 5.

89.7-8 Sen. *Epist.* 95, 13: "simplex enim illa et aperta virtus in obscuram et sollertem scientiam versa est docemurque *disputare*, non *vivere*"; *Epist.* 108, 23: "sed aliquid praecipientium vitio peccatur, qui nos docent *disputare*, non *vivere*..." Cf. Walaeus' reaction (*App.* II no. 1.43-49).

89.13 scolarum ... vitam] A very common distinction made by all theologians, especially by those of a Christian-humanist persuasion. See for instance Erasmus, *Hyperaspistes* (*Ausgewählte Schriften* IV, Darmstadt 1969), 254, 258, 290, 300, 314, 324, 348, 356, 360, 392, 506, 554.

90.18 Lacedemonii et Athenienses] In *Iur.* III 15, 8 (794-95) Grotius defends the thesis that States must practice moderation in the extention of sovereignty, the restoration of peace being the principal objective. He then refers to the following instances: "Lacedaemonii et initio Athenienses in captas civitates nullum sibi vindicabant imperium: tantum eas republica uti volebant ad suam accomodata, Lacedaemonii quidem sub primorum potentia, Athenienses sub arbitrio populi, ut Thucydides (I 19), Isocrates (*Panathen.* 18), Demosthenes (*Orat. de Chers.* Did. XIII & XV) nos docent." In *Mel.* the same examples are presented to the disputing Christians, the point being that one party must not impose its will to an other.

90.21-26 Irenaeus ... retinetur] A very free allusion to Eus. *H.E.* V 24, 12. As a negative example also in quoted in *Def.* (IV 195a 22-27).

90.33 Hor. *Epist.* I 1, 85. Quoted also in *Annot. in NT,* ad Mt. 15: 10 (II 156a 25).

90.34-36 Gal. *Nat.Fac.* I 34.

91.38-39 credendorum numerum ... contrahere] A very common and characteristic recommendation of irenical theologians — criticised by Walaeus, (*App.* II no. 1.14-15). For Grotius, see *Or.* IV 178b 30- 179a 4); *Imp.* VI 9 (IV 231a63-b8): "Cautiones quae servandae unitati conducant, hae sunt potissimae. Prima, ut a definiendo abstineatur quantum fieri potest; hoc est salvis dogmatibus ad salutam necessariis, aut valde eo facientibus. Omnem in iure definitionem periculosam esse tradunt iuris auctores. De theologicis idem quis merito dixerit; vetus enim est sententia: *de Deo etiam vera dicere periculosum est.*" See for more details (*OT*) IV reg. s.v. 'dogmata'. Grotius honoured Erasmus as the man who had been the first to distinguish between essential and unessential articles of faith. Cf. *Par.* III 34: "Tu sacrosanctam theologiam, Augiae stabulo inquinatiorem, spurcissimis cavillationum argutiis repurgasti, et liberali manu asseruisti a crudeli sophistarum tyrannide. Tu primus (Erasme) humani ingenii instituta secreuisti ab ea necessitate, quae nobis divinis oraculis imponitur." Wolf, *o.c.* 89 ff. indicates analogous statements by Grotius' 16th-century predecessors; G. Brandt, *Historie der Reformatie* I, Amsterdam 1677 (aantek. 12), does so for some of his 17th-century contemporaries.

91.40-41 semotis studiis ... inquirere] Cf. Grotius to Walaeus (*App.* II no. 2.78-82).

91.48-59 Salv. *Gub.Dei* V 2.9-11 Cited also *Iur.* II 20, 50, 3 (526). For obvious reasons irenicists in the 16th and 17th centuries frequently referred to this text, see Brandt, *o.c.* I, aantek. 38 ff.

LIST OF MARGINALIA

6.1	religio
6.5	esse Deum
7.10	esse remuneratorem
7.11	Deus natura intelligens
7.15	Deus habet προαίρεσιν aut voluntatem
7.16	eamque liberam
8.25	Deus curat res coelestes et humanas
8.30	est omnipotens
8.32	est bonus
9.37	homo est animal ratione et vi praeelectiva praeditum
10.43	Deus legislator
11.53	Deus iustus
13.3	religionis finis
13.7	Deo frui, seu beatitudo
14.16	cum indolentia et immortalitate
19.1	religio in actione versatur
20.13	Deus unus
21.21	simplicissimus, infinitus, optimus
22.27	esse: ratio: virtus
22.32	seu Spiritus
23.40	tria unum
24.48	Deus omniscius
24.49	non est author mali, quia bonitas
26.90	factor omnium rerum
28.109	omnia sui causa fecit Deus
28.111	certo tamen ordine, omnia hominis causa, hominem sui
29.120	Deus rector omnium. Epicureorum fortuiti concursus et Stoicorum fatum ex aequo nocentia pietati dogmata
29.130	malum ex angelorum et hominum liberrima voluntate
30.140	homo a Deo bonus factus, et ad Dei imaginem
30.146	unus homo factus ab initio
31.150	πάθη homini indita
32.157	factus homo ut Deum colat
33.166	colere Deum, quid sit
33.172	qualis iam homo sit
34.175	ingratus adversus Deus et vere malus
35.184	debebat amare proximum
35.185	odit
35.187	plurimae actiones vitiosae
36.195	daemones quidam ad prava se verterunt
36.197	hominemque traxerunt ad suae malitiae consortium
36.200	pravitas sparsa per omne hominum genus
37.205	peccata tamen non omnia aequalia
38.217	homines mancipia vitiorum
39.220	1. quia omne vitium in praeceps ducit
40.234	2. Deus auxilium subtrahit
40.237	3. prava genitura, educatio, prava exempla
42.247	damnantur Stoici
42.251	Pharisaei
43.255	hinc religio intercidit, nisi sit remissio et reparatio
43.262	cuius rei debet fides fieri hominis

44.278	fidem eius rei facere Dei est
47.303	veritas christiana docet datum homini μεσίτην, Deum et hominem
50.340	cui pateat venia?
50.341	toti humano generi
50.344	sub lege poenitendi et credendi
51.364	reparatio
51.366	per ignorantiae purgationem
51.382	quae fit per verbum Dei
52.385	in scripturis, quae procul dubio a Deo sunt, quod probatur hinc: quod in illis nil non Deo dignum, nihil non ad optimos mores
52.391	quod magnus in illis consensus
53.395	antiquitas etiam dignitatem addit
54.411	sublimitatem dictionis
55.418	simplicitas in illis summa
56.435	alterum quod hominem restaurat est Christi exemplar
57.456	tertium arcana virtus seu Spiritus
59.1	praecepta
60.15	officia Deo debita
61.32	credere Deo
62.35	invocare Deum
63.47	non nominare Deum sine reverentia
63.52	non per imaginem exprimere
64.65	ne Deus operose et per innumeros ritus colatur
65.73	frequentare coetus qui Dei colendi causa instituuntur
66.104	baptismus
66.113	sacra coena
67.119	nota
68.138	quae humanitati debeantur
71.187	familia
72.190	coniugium
73.218	divortium
73.225	divortia adulteria colorata
74.231	respublica
74.233	magistratus
75.243	quod homo sibi debet

LIST OF UNDERLININGS

The underlined quotations and bibletexts are *not* recorded.

3.39-44	Itaque ... evincant	30.141	bonum
4.51-52	Graecos ... Maronitas	41.239	Dei bonitatem
4.52-54	etsi ... videba<n>tur	41.241	submisse
6.1	quod ... utitur	41.244	facilius aliis
7.10	remunerator	43.255-256	religionem ... via
7.11	intelligens natura	51.364	reparationem
7.14	voluntatem	51.366	purgatur ignorantia
7.16	libera	51.376	de ... humanis
8.30	omnipotentiam	51.376	de diis
8.32	bonus est	51.376-377	tantum homines
9.37	hominem ... λόγικον	55.430	aeque ... facilis
10.43	legislatorem	56.435	Alterum
11.53	Deus ... iustus	56.435-436	perfectissimum ... exemplar
12.58	principia ... christiana		
14.16	indolentia	57.456	arcana ... Spiritus
14.16	immortalitas	57.457	excitans, impellens
15.23-24	Nec ... uterentur	58.476-477	praeter ... ἀδιάφορα
17.55	voluptatem	60.15	erga Deum
17.56	indolentia	60.15	circa homines
17.59	virtus	60.15-16	circa humana
19.1	Religio	60.19	silentio ... praeterita
19.1	in actione versetur	60.20	est obedientiae
22.26	esse	60.27-28	Dei ... amorem
22.27	ratio divina	61.31-32	credere Deo
22.27	virtus	61.32	Deum invocare
22.32	Spiritus	63.56	institutis ... expressit
23.40	tria	64.65-66	ne ... colatur
23.40	unumque	66.106	Patre ... Spiritu
25.80-81	omniscientia ... bonitas	68.139-140	aut ... praecipit
24.85-87	naturam ... debeamus	73.220	sexcentos ... annos
26.90	Factorem	74.238-239	dum ... violent
29.121-122	ex ... dogmata	88.353-354	orbis ... debeat
29.122	servat	88.358-360	Illud ... sustulit
29.122	corrumpit	89.1	Hunc
29.123	praesertim ... προαίρεσιν	89.5-6	praeceptis ... statuitur
29.126-128	potest ... impediente	89.7	Seneca
29.129	Malum ... liberrima	90.26	multas ... faciunt
29.130	hominum voluntate	90.27-28	videamus ... necessariis
30.140	factum ... Deo	91.38-39	remedium ... contrahere

APPENDIX I

FROM THE PROLEGOMENA OF STOBAEUS' *DICTA POËTARUM* (e ij-sqq.)

Grotius published in 1623 his edition of Stobaeus (*TMD* no. 458). The fragment below has been discussed in the Introduction, 26 ff.

Utilitatem huius operis non est quod multis commendem. Constat enim cum omnes sententiae et scite dicta usum habeant maximum, tum ea quae versibus continentur et iucundius influere animo et in memoria firmius haerere. Hinc est quod antiquissimis saeculis sapientiae praecepta non nisi carminibus dabantur; quo et Homeri illud pertinet quod narrat Clytaemnestram ad vitium non prius flexisse quam cantorem amiserat.[1] Tantum monendi sunt iuvenes, non omnibus dictis adhibendum esse assensum, sed dilectu opus. Nam quia poetarum ars in movendis affectibus maxime illucescit, ideo fit ut dicta illorum non semper cum regulis congruant sapientiae, quae affectuum est moderatrix; quod in libris de republica allatis ex Homero exemplis probat Plato.[2] Accedit quod poetae ut pictores tam curva quam recta imitantur, et cuique personae pro ingenio ac moribus verba affingunt, quae habenda sunt ut lineamenta animi eius qui loquens inducitur, non ut poetae approbantis iudicium. His periculis sapientissime occurrit Plutarchus libello quem ad iuvenes scripsit de poetarum lectione, quem ea de causa huic operi praefigendum curavimus.[3] Optime enim docet poetarum dicta exigenda ad ea quae severiores professores, philosophi scilicet, dictant. Sed ne sic quidem vitatur periculum, nam et in his ipsis quae rationis ductu cognosci aliquatenus possunt, falli videmus philosophos, unde tanta inter ipsos placitorum discrepantia; et sunt quaedam res eius generis ut earum veritatem sola humana ratio per se indagare non possit. In quibus rebus cum alii philosophi saepe ab eo quod res est aberrant, tum ipse etiam in eo quem dixi libro Plutarchus, ut cum de providentia agit et de his quae post hanc vitam sunt exspectanda.

Multum ergo Deo Optimo Maximo debuerunt Hebraei veteres, plus eidem Christiani debemus, quibus omnia quae ad vitam recte instituendam momentum aliquod habent, ea certitudine sunt patefacta ut apud probos animos nullus dubitandi relinquatur locus. Nam a Deo profecta

---

[1] Hom. *Od.* 3, 265-72.
[2] Plato *Rep.* 590b-601b.
[3] Plut. *Aud.* See above, Introduction, 65 n. 169.

esse ea quae Prophetae et Apostoli nobis / prodiderunt constat, quo unico modo constare id potest et quantum potest, editis prodigiis et ipsorum testimonio, cui fidem adstruit vitae innocentia, nullum ex mendacio lucrum, et multa mala, interdum mors quoque, ob id testimonium tolerata. Quae autem a Deo dicuntur vera esse, inter enuntiata est primitivae lucis, quae lucem aliunde non foenerantur. Nam in ipso Dei nomine, ut omnis boni, ita et veracitatis inclusa est significatio. Sicut ergo a poetis ad philosophos, ita et a poetis et a philosophis ad tribunal tertium, hoc est ad Prophetas et Apostolos, nobis provocandum est; atque ea demum dicta rata habenda quae in hoc auditorio stare possunt.

APPENDIX II

THE CORRESPONDENCE OF GROTIUS AND HIS FRIENDS ABOUT THE *MELETIUS* (1611/1612)

Grotius showed the manuscript of his *Meletius* to four friends (see above, Introduction, 15,44 ff.). Three of them—Antonius Walaeus, Apollonius Schotte and Petrus Cunaeus—reported their views in writing. The one who wrote at greatest length was Walaeus. He devoted three letters to his reactions (see below, Letters 1, 3 and 8), and Grotius wrote two letters in reply (Letters 2 and 4). Otherwise three further letters concerning the *Meletius* have survived: one from Grotius to Schotte (Letter 5); one from Schotte to Cunaeus (Letter 6); and one from Cunaeus to Schotte (Letter 7).

Letters 1,2,3,4,5 and 8 are based on Molhuysen (ed.), *Briefwisseling van Hugo Grotius* I (= *BW* I); Letters 6 and 7 are taken from P. Burman (ed.), *Petri Cunaei...Epistolae*, Leiden 1725.

In establishing the text of the letters the same rules have been applied as in the *Meletius* (see Introduction, 71). Molhuysen's notes have sometimes been assimilated without further acknowledgement.

1. *Antonius Walaeus to Hugo Grotius*, 1 November 1611[1]

Aliquot abhinc dies est, clarissime atque amplissime vir, quod tractatum illum tuum, qui Meletius inscribitur, avide diligenterque perlegi. In quo equidem plurima deprehendi non laude solum sed etiam miratione digna, ita sententiis et crebris et egregiis confertus, authorem suum et vere doctum et sincere christianum ubique refert. Spero tamen libertati meae apud te veniam fore, si de nonnullis te paucis admonuero; non quo iudicio tuo a me praescribatur, cui me parem non agnosco, sed ut ne fructus, qui ex eo, si edatur, ubertim ad multos est proventurus, praeiudicio quodam adversus authorem concepto paulatim apud reliquos intercipiatur.

In primo, ut est postremo scripto tuo, videris controversias de quibus inter Christianos disceptatur plus nimio elevare, quum illa caeteris, de quibus consentiunt *minora et incertiora nec aeque utilia*[2] appellas, item scitu plaerumque non admodum necessaria, quumque *credendorum numerum in pauca et maxime evidentia contrahi*[3] postulas, etc. Quod ego quidem de nonnullis dici posse haud libenter diffitear, de omnibus tamen aut plaerisque idem pronunciare vehementer metuam; multa enim dogmata inter pontificios obtinent quae arcem verae fidei plane evertunt, ut iam omittam his nequiores Samosatenianos, Socinianos aliosque iis consentaneos, qui christianam fidem turcismo quam vero christianismo viciniorem edunt, quorum sententias te iuxta nobiscum abominari ego plene persuasus sum. Quae tamen verba, clarissime vir, facili flexu ita a te emolliri poterunt, ut iusta offensionum occasio omnibus plane adimatur.

De personarum sacra triade disertius quaedam exprimi a te etiam cupiam, nec solum voces usurpari quae ad naturales divinae naturae δυνάμεις restringi facile possint, sed quae divinas ὑποστάσεις paulo evidentius proponant.[4]

Postremo quae de arbitrii libertate post lapsum hominis ponis[5], benigne quidem interpretabuntur quicunque controversiis iam nuper motis implicati non sunt, reliqui vero novae suae sententiae te fautorem, etsi infirmo nixi argumento, temere iactitabunt; cuius sane gloriationis materiam ego haud libenter a te illis concedi velim, qui harum turbarum authores non satis auspicati sunt.

Haec sunt, amplissime vir, quae in doctissimo illo scripto tuo a multis fortasse desiderabuntur. Quemadmodum vero modus res hasce tradendi plane novus est, ita non dubitem si in lucem emittatur quin plurimum toti christianismo sit profuturum; inprimis apud illos qui ad christianam fidem paulatim sunt manuducendi aut qui theologorum quorundam rixis offensi omnem sacrae scripturae lectionem aversantur. Ad quam sacrae scripturae lectionem etiam aliquam adhortationem in fine scripti tui institui optem, ut qui in praecipuis decretis conveniunt, in reliquis quoque paulatim proficere cupiant, quia omnia scripta sunt ad nostram doctrinam.[6] Et licet morbus ille, ut eleganter mones[7], multorum animos obsideat, ut disputare de dogmatis christianis quam vivendo repraesentare verum Christianum malint, tamen hoc interim pro certo est habendum, quod nulla decreta in sacris literis contineantur, in quibus non utiliter laboretur et quae non etiam ad praeceptorum observationem paulatim nostros animos parent, modo sine contentione inquirantur, et inventa cum modestia et pietate examinentur. Datum Middelburgo, ipsis kalendis Novembris 1611.

---

[1] Printed in A. Walaeus, *Opera Omnia*, II, Lugd. Bat. 1647, 398, and taken over by Molhuysen, *BW* I no 214, 184-85.
[2] The words put in italics are quoted literally from *Mel.* 3.43.
[3] The words put in italics are quoted literally from *Mel.* 91.38-39.
[4] Cf. *Mel.* 22 and comment *ad loc.*
[5] Cf. *Mel.* 9, 10, 19, 28, 29.
[6] An allusion to 2 Tim. 3:16: Omnis scriptura ... utilis ad docendum.
[7] Cf. *Mel.* 89.

2. *Hugo Grotius to Antonius Walaeus*, 11 November 1611[1]

Quod et legeris libellum meum et tam amice iudicium mihi tuum perscribas, vir clarissime, debeo tibi plurimum. Nec profecto quicquam multo iam a tempore libentius legi quam literas tuas. Non quidem ob laudes, quas ut ab amico animo profectas agnosco, ita non deberi mihi scio, in isto praesertim opere rudi et subitario. Sed hoc me inprimis iuvit, quod meum iudicium, cui alioqui merito diffido, tuo, cui tribuo plurimum, multis in partibus confirmetur. Nam postquam misso in Zelandiam[2] exemplo, meum ipse scriptum relegere coepi, — et iam primus ille calor, qui nos a scriptione recentes ambit atque occupat, defervere inceperat —, notavi ferme eadem de quibus tu mones ut offensis obnoxia, his praesertim locis atque temporibus. Videbam non difficilem fore purgationem apud eos qui recte instituti mei rationem considerassent, attamen prudentius atque rectius fore si ita cuncta mollirentur, ut purgatione quam minimum indigerent; quod ipsum tamen cum esset difficile, — semper enim aut in hanc aut in illam partem impacturus videbar —, deliberare coepi an non rectius premerem foetum aut certe editionem in pacatiora tempora differrem.

Verum est omnino quod tu dicis, esse etiam inter ea quae cum papistis disceptantur, quae arcem verae fidei plane oppugnant. Attamen ipsa adhuc arcis fundamenta apud eos apparent, quae quidem necesse est maiora atque digniora esse, si comparatio instituatur, quam caetera quae superstruuntur, etiamsi fundamentis sint proxima, quanquam et inter haec sui gradus. Iunius[3] noster dicere solebat papistas ita in fundamentis errare, ut a fundamentis non aberrarent; cui ego plane assentio. Inter alia profanissimum morem Deum effingendi per simulachra ne scripto quidem meo dissimulare potui,[4] in quo tamen proposueram a controversiis abstinere, quia profecto spero etiam cordatos in ipsa romana ecclesia viros non posse illam impietatem approbare, ut nec crassas quorundam et pelagianas de libero arbitrio, quatenus gratiae opponitur, et de meritis opiniones. Ea autem ipsa quae apud pontificios sunt periculosissima, puto etiam ex illis principiis, quae ut confessa pono, posse convelli ac labefactari. Quo maior illorum esse debet auctoritas, quorum veritatem ne illi quidem negare audent, qui per ea ipsa falsitatis convincuntur. Ac ferme verum est quod quidam magni nominis theologi prodiderunt[5], omnia quae vera sunt et quae nos credimus eadem a papistis agnosci, sed addi insuper falsa alia, quorum quaedam sunt talia, ut cum primis illis agnitis veris non possint consistere. Unde sequitur, redacta religione ad ea in quae omnes christianae ecclesiae omnium temporum consentiunt, collabi papismum, ut qui conflatus sit ex privatis opinionibus.

Samosatenianos autem et si qui sunt similes[6], non modo Christianorum sed nec haereticorum nomine dignor; quae enim ipsi docent cum universali omnium aetatum atque gentium fide pugnant et christianitatem, quantum ego intelligo, nomine retinent, re destruunt; itaque hos a Mahumetistis non longe separo, qui ne ipsi quidem Iesu maledicunt. Quare non modo τοῦ λόγου ἀειθεότητα sed et veram satisfactionem extra τὰ ἀμφισβητούμενα posui; item praescientiam Dei et immensitatem.⁷

Ubi περὶ τριάδος loquor, haesisse me fateor, quia cum εἰσαγωγὴν quandam vellem scribere et me velut aptare iis quoque qui ad christianismum invitandi adhuc sunt, non inveni verba talia, quae cum meo instituto congruerent, hoc est aperta, plana, popularia. Nam ut ὑπόστασιν, quae vox in sacris literis hac in re usurpatur, intelligat, ὁ κατηχούμενος longo ambitu circumducendus est et humani ingenii captus, cui me in tradendis his principiis molliter insinuare volui, vix eo usque assurgit. Itaque tentabam an possem, qui modus de Deo loquendi tutissimus dicitur, ἀποφαντικῶς innuere id quod res est, addita insuper similitudine humanae mentis, quam inter veteres Augustino aliisque, et inter nostros Plessaeo⁸, etiam Iunio,⁹ prae caeteris placuisse memineram. Ad praecidendas haereses vox ὑποστάσεως plane necessaria est, maxime ut intelligantur λόγος καὶ πνεῦμα aliter Deo tribui quam veritas, bonitas, iustitia etc. Sed quae loquendi ratio meo isti instituto, quod plane intelligere te video, sit accommodatissima, velim cogites et hac in re vel maxime sudantem iuves.¹⁰

De arbitrii libertate usurpavi quantum potui phrases patrum, ne nostris quidem improbatas, et gaudeo videri tibi benigne haec interpretaturos, qui controversiis nuper motis impliciti non sint. Sed simul cogites velim, si quid ultra addo, abiturum me a proposito manendi ἐν τοῖς ὁμολογουμένοις¹¹ et sine dubio adversaturum me aperte patribus Graecis, si non et ipsi Augustino. Caeterum ad eos quod attinet qui apud nos hac de re et aliis quibusdam capitibus disputare nuper coeperunt, eorum ut ego sententiam, quippe haud dum plane mihi percognitam, damnare non ausim, ita vias quas insistunt aperte improbo. Si quid enim obscuri fuit, id in consessu eruditorum piorumque hominum inquiri oportuit, non aut apud indoctam plebem aut apud ipsos etiam magistratus tam odiose iactari. Et quotidie magis magisque suspectos se reddunt, qui ad fulciendam causam suam tales accersunt tibicines, qualis est D. Conradus Vorstius.¹²

De sacra scriptura meministi, ut puto, agere me in libello nec omnino perfunctorie, quantum quidem operis brevitas permittebat. Caeterum placet mihi tecum in fine scripti addere exhortationem, ut salva pace ac concordia diligenter quisque scrutetur omnem veritatem sacris libris abditam, non enim consistendum est ἐν τοῖς πρώτοις sed interius penetrandum, cum certissimum sit nihil frustra sacris literis esse traditum, quanquam multa sunt talia, ut in iis errantes tolerari debeant.

Haec ad te, vir doctissime, libere perscripsi ac rogo, ut occupationum tuarum rationes permittunt, mihi rescribas et consilio tuo, cuius apud me maxima est auctoritas, me iuves. Deus Optimus Maximus diu te ecclesiae servet incolumem, nobis autem graviter sane hic laborantibus medicinam afferat. 11. Novembris 1611.

---

[1] Printed in H. Grotius, *Epistolae quotquot reperiri potuerunt*, (= *Epistolae*) Amsterdam 1687, 4. Taken over by Molhuysen, *BW* I no. 215, 185-87. Reply to Letter 1.
[2] On the *Meletius* in connection with Zealand, see above, Introduction, 13 ff.
[3] The Leiden professor Franciscus Junius (François Dujon, 1545-1602), in whose house Grotius lodged as a student and whom he venerated throughout his life. Junius had defended the same thesis in his *De ecclesia libellus singularis*, in *Op. Theol.* II 997-1023. See also H. C. Rogge, *Joh. Wtenbogaert en zijn tijd* I, Amsterdam 1874, 215 ff.
[4] Cf. *Mel.* 63.
[5] Here Grotius is probably referring to George Cassander and other fellow Erasmians who had remained within the Church of Rome. See above, Introduction, 51.
[6] Antitrinitarians and kindred groups.
[7] See above, Introduction, 52.
[8] The Huguenot Philippe Duplessis-Mornay (1549-1623) in his *De veritate religionis christianae*, Lugd. Bat. 1587, ch. 5, 85-6.
[9] See n. 3.
[10] See above, Introduction, 52.
[11] Cf. *Mel.* 5.67.
[12] Conrad Vorstius (1569-1622), on whom see C. van der Woude in *BLGNP* I, 407-10.

3. *Antonius Walaeus to Hugo Grotius*, 1 December 1611[1]

Gratulor mihi, clarissime atque amplissime vir, quod scriptura mea et causa eius tibi ingrata non fuerit, nam ut ex eo animi tui in me studium ab una parte agnosco et amplector, ita ab altera parte iudicii tui candorem admiror, hoc enim vere magni est et christiani animi in rebus eius momenti non solum iudicia aliorum experiri sed etiam infirmiorum monita, si res ferat, non facile contemnere. Gaudeo insuper animo tuo iam antea tibi fuisse praeceptum, quod ego tibi amplius hoc quidem tempore cogitandum indicaram, nam ex eo facile erit suspicari aliorum animos in iis etiam nonnihil haesitaturos.

Caeterum ut ad argumentum epistolae tuae revertar, ego me iam satis defunctum arbitrabar, si literis meis ea breviter adnotassem quae offensae alicuius obnoxia futura metuebam, iam vero literis tuis aliquid etiam maius postulatur, quod ego mihi vendicare non ausim, nam scopulos ostendere ad quos nonnemo sit offensurus ingenii est non supra vulgus adsurgentis, sed modum ac rationem praestituere qua illi vitari possint in re tam lubrica et periculosa, ego sane supra vires meas esse agnosco, a te ipso igitur mutueris oportet quod in rem hanc fore iudicabis. Tamen ut occasionem aliquam praebeam meliora cogitandi, quoniam tibi ita lubet, sententiam meam de re ipsa paulo plenius adscribam. Editionem operis tui si premas[2] offensa quidem fateor vitabitur, sed et fructus omnis tam pulchri laboris peribit; talentum sub terra defossum, quia Domino suo cum lucro non redhibetur, graviorem offensam famulo apud Dominum parit.³ Edes ergo si me audis clarissime vir, adhibita ea προθεραπεία quam ipse facile ad offendicula lenienda pertinere cogitabis.

A papistis arcem verae fidei plane everti iudicabam, non quia verae fidei fundamenta ab iis quandoque non iaciantur, id enim libenter concedo, sed quia una manu struunt quod altera evertunt. Non ergo retento vero fundamento superficiem ei solum instruunt ex ligno foeno stipula,⁴ cuiusmodi plurimae ipsorum humanae traditiones ritusque censeri fortassis possunt, sed fundamento vero fundamenta alia conantur adiungere quae veri fundamenti vim omnino tollunt, adeo ut alterutrius damnum necessario illis sit faciendum, aut veri, si falsa retineant, aut falsorum, si verum retinere velint; exemplis rem illustro, Christum esse propitiationem pro peccatis nostris saepe recte asserunt, merita monachorum, confessorum, martyrum, quibus indulgentiae pontificum innituntur, pharisaica item opera sua ut salutis causas ita commendant, ut ea nullo pacto simul possint consistere; nam qui propriam iustitiam conantur statuere iustitiae Dei subiecti non sunt, et a gratia exciderunt quicunque ex lege iustificantur. Imo Christus iis inutilis est factus, testatur apostolus Galatis⁵, non quia Christum abiicerent, sed quia iustitiam legis ei conarentur adiungere. Dei veri invocationem per Christum intercessorem nonnunquam urgent; rursum tamen invocationem sanctorum cum fiducia in ipsos, artolatriam, imaginum cultum, ita praecipiunt, ut ab idololatria nunquam se sint expurgaturi, cui tamen a sacra scriptura ἀνάθεμα manifestum denunciatur.⁶ Licet ergo cibos salutares miserae plebi aliquando proponant, interim tamen venena praesentissima eis ita temperant, ut nisi Dei Spiritus per verbum suum in nonnullis efficiat ut salutaribus assumptis reliqua repudientur, — quod ego quandoque fieri agnosco experientia et scriptura teste —, omnibus illis necessario sit pereundum. Servantur ergo primi illi quidem in quibus hoc fit ὡς διὰ πυρὸς⁷, quia fundamento inhaerent, licet nonnulla superstitiosiora hominum commenta infirmitate quadam abrepti abiicere nondum possint.

De reliquis vero sententia diserta est pronunciata quod quicunque bestiae charactere notati sunt, aut eam adorant, locum in stagno ignis cum ipsa bestia sint habituri⁸, quemadmodum etiam de Pharisaeis Christus testatur quod sectatores suos fecerint gehennae filios, quos tamen iubet audiri in cathedra Mosis sedentes⁹. Quod vero addis ex illis principiis quae ut confessa ponis, reliqua quae pontificiis peculiaria sunt facile erroris convinci, ego etiam pro confesso habeo, nec inde tamen sequi videtur ea reliquis esse maiora. Quemadmodum ex reliquiis sanis et integris in humano corpore tabidae et morbidae partes facile arguuntur, imo earum etiam ope, si periti medici industria accedat, saepe restituuntur, non eo tamen tabidas et morbidas partes minoris esse momenti semper consequitur, et ut hoc consequatur ego tamen ea quae disceptantur nimium extenuari nolim ne, dum illis consultum volumus qui a religione aut omnino alieni, aut saltem de ea apud animum suum necdum satis certi sunt, aliis iam vere Christianis offendicula ponamus occasionemque praebeamus caetera omnia ut leviora contemnendi, atque adeo eorum animos in multis religione solvamus, in quibus se antehac, et merito quidem, solutos aestimare non sunt ausi. Ego ergo potius in hanc sententiam — ignosce libertati meae, clarissime vir — haec molliam, ut agnoscam non exigui ea esse momenti de quibus disceptatur inter Christianos et ab iis etiam qui plusculum profecerunt diligenter examinanda, sed tamen maxima ea et multa esse de quibus convenit inter eosdem et quae, si sola etiam sincereque retineantur, salutis, quam religio christiana promittit et exhibet, nobis esse causae queant; modo ab hoc consensu expresse separentur quos ipse quoque inter apostatas potius quam Christianos censendos putas, quia praecipua christianismi fundamenta e religione christiana tollunt, quod a pontificiis et Graecis — ut iam ostensum — semper non fit.

De sacra triade fateor ea a te proponi, quae ad ipsam doctrinam veram et salutarem manuductionis vicem esse possunt. Quia tamen hoc dogma caput quoddam est fidei nostrae, quaedam de eo paulo evidentius proponi optabam, praesertim cum in tota ecclesia id semper extra omnem controversiam sit habitum et adversus omnes surgentes haereses invicte defensum. Nam nisi Filius et Spiritus Sanctus sint unus ille et aeternus cum Patre Deus, omnes Christiani miseri sunt idololatrae, δουλεύοντες τοῖς μὴ φύσει οὖσι θεοῖς[10], cum unus tantum sit qui hunc cultum, natura et scriptura teste, sibi iure vendicat et, nisi vere ac reipsa a se sint distincti, tota oeconomia salutis nostrae, quemadmodum a Filio nobis tradita est, necessario intercidit. Quibus vero vocibus id ita exprimi possit ut ὁ κατηχούμενος aliqua saltem tenus intelligat, ego sane vix scio; scripturae voces usurpari tutissimum iudico, quia de Dei penitissima natura nemo quam ipse testari potest. Patres, quos haec quaestio ad lassitudinem usque exercuit, similitudinem nullam commodiorem adhibere potuerunt quam humanae mentis, ut ipse etiam notas, et lucis, splendorem suum ac calorem individuos traduces iugiter propagantis, quibus aliquo pacto mysterium hoc verius adumbratur quam exprimitur, in quibus ipsam etiam scripturam ducem habuerunt, quum Filium et λόγον, et σοφίαν, et εἰκόνα, et ἀπαύγασμα τῆς δόξης αὐτοῦ[11] appellat, etsi quidam ex iis exemplum humanae mentis etiam paulo aliter usurpent quam a te, si bene memini, sit explicatum: quemadmodum enim mens nostra si quando se ipsam plene intueatur et cogitet sui quandam imaginem ex se et in se gignit sibi per omnia aequalem, sic et Deum Patrem, *dum sese aeterno cogitat*

105 *usque animo* — ut Vidae[12] verbis utar — expressam sui imaginem ex se et in se gignere, utrumque vero producere et conspirare amorem mutuum ac reciprocum in eadem plane infinitate et natura divino modo consistentem; quae omnia ut rebus ipsis longe sint inferiora, aliquid tamen videntur exprimere cui mens humana haud aegre consensum
110 adiunget si se docilem praestare velit.

Quae de arbitrii libertate notaram illius fateor momenti non sunt cuius illa de quibus iam egi, diligenter tamen videndum ut duo scopuli vitentur, ecclesiae Christi et saluti hominum plane adversi. Primus ne virium suarum fiducia inflati sibi ipsi transcribant quod Dei solius dono accep-
115 tum ferendum, nam sententiae metuendae et tamen manifestae in hos extant. *Veni vocatum non iustos, sed peccatores ad resipiscentiam*[13]. Item, *Si caeci essetis, peccatum non haberetis, sed iam dicitis, Videmus, ideo peccatum vestrum manet* etc.[14] Secundus est ne ab altera parte ita in stoicismum inclinemus, ut homo iustam excusationem negligentiae aut perversitati suae possit
120 praetendere aut Deus ulla ex parte in culpae societatem trahatur. Hi duo scopuli si recte vitentur, disputationes pacatas quae intra hos fines consistunt, ego quidem tolerandas in ecclesia Dei iudico, quia (ha)ctenus de iis semper salva pace christiana disputatum fuit, licet hic nonnull(is) accidisse videatur, ut dum gratiae Dei patrocinati sunt, iustitiae eius pene
125 fuerint obliti, alii vero dum in solam eius iustitiam oculos converterunt, in gratiam eius iniurii fuisse deprehendantur. Si autem intra hos fines a me antea praestitutos Arminius[15] se continuisset, et si quid ab ipso in hanc rem observatum fuisset id omne piorum atque eruditorum examini subiecisset, aut etiamnum a discipulis eius ut aequum est subiiceretur,
130 sine dubio haud paulo pacatiores ecclesias haberemus; sed hanc rem Deus ille qui opus suum inter nos coepit ut spero ὡς ἀπὸ μηχανῆς restituet. Confido autem ea cautione etiam hac in re usurum te qua in patrum graecorum gratiam usum te fuisse scribis, nam quemadmodum ita temperasti stylum tuum, ut patribus illis aut Augustino adversari ne videre-
135 ris, ita etiam te operam daturum spero ut consensui ecclesiarum reformatarum hac in re praeiudicium non feras. Vale clarissime atque amplissime vir. Deum rogo ut te ecclesiae et reipublicae diu incolumem servet. Datum Middelburgo, kalendis Decembris 1611.

Tuae dignitatis studiosissimus
Antonius Walaeus

---

[1] Printed in Walaeus, *Opera Omnia*, II 400. Autograph in the Library of the Remonstrant Church in Rotterdam (nr.1829), on which *BW* I no. 216, 187-89 is based. Reply to Letter 2.
[2] Cf. Letter 2.16.
[3] An allusion to Mt. 25:14-30.
[4] An allusion to 1 Cor. 3:12.
[5] Gal. 5:2.

⁶ An echo of Gal. 5:20; 1 Cor. 10:7,14; 16:22.
⁷ 1 Cor. 3:15.
⁸ Ap.Ioh. 19:20.
⁹ Mt. 23:2,3.
¹⁰ Gal. 4:8.
¹¹ Ioh. 1:1; 1 Cor. 1:24; Col. 1:15; Hebr. 1:3.
¹² Marco Girolamo Vida (1490-1566), *Poemata*, pars III (Lond. 1732), Hymn 'Jesu Christo Opt. Max.', 55 line 24.
¹³ Mt. 9:13.
¹⁴ Ioh. 9:41.
¹⁵ Jacobus Arminius (1560-1609).

4. *Hugo Grotius to Antonius Walaeus*, 11 January 1612¹

Multum tibi debeo, Walaee doctissime, quod temporis tui occupatissimi partem tibi detraxeris, ut literis meis quam amice tam liberaliter responderes. Sed hoc consecutus es isto beneficio, ut iterum tibi molestus esse audeam. Remitto enim ad Borelium² libellum istum meum, iis in locis quos tu maxime salebrosos putabas nonnihil temperatum, quatenus scilicet et instituti ratio et scripti brevitas permittere videbantur. Hunc igitur rogo relegas, et si quid amplius mutandum aut adiungendum iudicas libere significes.

Atque ut tuis amicissimis literis aliquid respondeam, primum de papistis nulla inter nos dissensio est, etsi verbis forte utamur alius aliis, ut fieri solet. Accedo enim tibi esse in papismo communia quaedam cum caeteris ecclesiis, esse et peculiaria quaedam; illa christiana, haec magnam in partem antichristiana; illa per se salutifera, haec per se exitialia. Caeterum in eo quoque Deo habenda est gratia, quod qui inter papistas aequiores sunt, fateri cogantur non omnium de fide capitum eandem esse auctoritatem, ac proinde illa certa atque communia speciali quadam notitia apprehendi debere, caetera non item. Quapropter mihi, ad sanandos eos qui sanabiles sunt, videbatur haec ipsa quam insistebam via non esse incommoda, ut ea, quae saluti parandae sunt, indubitata habere docerentur, reliqua si ut pestifera exsecrari nondum possent, interim seponerent ut non necessaria. Quanquam autem ego ea quae inter Christianos controversa sunt, ac praecipue quae nos inter ac papistas agitantur, quam sint gravia atque conciliatu difficilia facile intelligo, tamen eam gravitatem atque difficultatem ante oculos ponere non erat eius instituti, in quo et Christianos, ob ea quae sunt inter ipsos communia, ad charitatem hortari volui et caeteris auctor esse, ut omissis quae disceptantur, ea quae inter Christianos confessa sunt ipsi quoque amplectantur, quos alioqui certum est offendi dissensionibus nostris, ita ut ferme putent praeter nomen nihil esse quod nobis conveniat.

In sacra trinitate malui, te auctore, aliquantum recedere a proposito tractandi modo, qui talis est ut in rebus christianis vocibus tamen communibus utatur, quam id quod religionis caput est a pravis erroribus non satis discernere. Quare et hic distinctionis ὑποστατικῆς³ et in Christi duabus naturis unitatis vicissim ὑποστατικῆς⁴ mentionem feci, non facturus forte, nisi incurrissem in tam petulans ac foetum prodigiosis quoque erroribus saeculum. Quod autem adfers de intellectu atque amore quodam velut reciprocante, scio multos veteres novosque existimasse hoc modo aeternam generationem Filii et processionem Spiritus non absurde explicari. Caeterum quominus id eo modo in libellum meum transtulerim, in causa fuit, quod non ut Filium σοφίαν καὶ λόγον, ita et Spiritum, qua nimirum est ὑπόστασις, amorem aut, ut alii loquuntur, voluntatem in sacris literis dici meminissem. Itaque cum Calvino⁵ et Confessione tum Gallica⁶ tum Belgica⁷ Spiritum appellare malui virtutem Dei atque efficaciam, qua voce illum sacra scriptura saepius indigetat. Et ut hoc in Deo discrimen ostenderem cum ratione non pugnare, Aristotelis ex Metaphysicis locum citavi.⁸ Et tamen, ne alterum illud πλατωνικώτατον damnare viderer, comparationem ad hoc induxi mentis humanae et intellectus et voluntatis,⁹ ut hoc velut gradu ad illam τριενότητα liceret ascendere. Lucis autem et caloris similitudo hoc magis placet, quod ὁ λόγος lux vocatur¹⁰ et Spiritus per ignem non raro designatur¹¹ in divinis oraculis.

Restat de libertate arbitrii difficultas, in qua sane parte, ut receptam patribus sententiam oppugnare per instituti mei rationem non potui, ita minime velim ecclesias nostras offendere. Quare si quid putas dici posse explicatius in harum ecclesiarum sententiam, atque ita tamen ut a veterum sensu atque locutionibus non exorbitet, rem mihi gratissimam feceris si suggeras. Neque enim spero me aliis duris hominibus satisfacere posse si tibi aequissimo iudici probare φράσεις meas non potero. Lapsum labemque humani generis et sub peccato servitutem, et tum ad remissionem peccatorum, tum ad vitae melioris originem profectumque, gratiae divinae necessitatem, breviter ita attigi, ut pelagianismum his finibus a me exclusum putem, saltem eum qui crassior est atque intolerabilior. Nam, ut dixi, omnibus omnino erroribus obviam ire, id vero istius non est tractationis. Vicissim puto eos, qui praedestinationis decretum rigidius urgent,¹² si quid a nobis adversum Stoicos aut Manichaeos necessario dicitur,¹³ non id continuo ut in se gravius interpretaturos, praesertim ubi hoc tantum agitur, quemadmodum tu sapientissime mones,¹⁴ ut neque peccati et perditionis causam ad Deum, neque salutis ad nos ipsos referamus. Sed, ut alteris literis scribebam,¹⁵ non est tanti qualecunque hoc opusculum, ut propterea quisquam, praecipue autem eae ecclesiae, quas ego omnium purissimas profiteor, offendi debeant, quare, si id aliter vitari non potest, prematur hic foetus, neque certa damna subeamus in spem fructus incertam. Vale vir ut doctissime ita religiosissime, et nos quaeso amare perge. 11. Ianuarii 1612.

---

¹ Printed in *Epistolae*, 5, on which *BW* I no. 221, 193-194 is based. Reply to Letter 3.
² Johan Boreel (1577-1629). See above, Introduction, 20.
³ Cf. *Mel.* 22.34.
⁴ Cf. *Mel.* 49.332.
⁵ Calvin, *Institutio*, I 18 (ed. Barth/Niesel, III 132): ...Patri principium agendi rerumque omnium fons et scaturigo attribuitur; Filio sapientia, consilium, ipsaque in rebus agendis dispensatio; at Spiritui *virtus et efficacia* assignatur actionis.
⁶ *Confessio Gallicana*, art. VI.
⁷ *Confessio Belgica*, art. VIII: Spiritus Sanctus *virtus* et potentia aeterna.
⁸ Cf. *Mel.* 22.35, comment *ad loc.*
⁹ Cf. *Mel.* 23.41, comment *ad loc.*
¹⁰ E.g. Ioh. 8:12; 9:5.
¹¹ E.g. Mt. 3:11: Lc. 3:16 and especially Act. 2:3.
¹² The Counter-Remonstrants.
¹³ E.g. *Mel.* 29.122 and 132.
¹⁴ Letter 3.111 ff.
¹⁵ Letter 2.116-117.

5. *Hugo Grotius to [Apollonius Schotte]*, [3 April 1612]¹

Amplissime domine. Verum esse comperi, quod tibi haud ita pridem metuere me dicebam, sequius quosdam interpretari institutum meum in conscribendo libello cui nomen Meletio feci. Quare te oro scribas ad Cunaeum, ut si ipsi transcurrere non vacat, libellum tibi remittat, quem ego aut premendum iudico aut certe mutandum hactenus, ut discutiantur suspiciones eiusmodi. Neque enim committendum mihi est, ut vel imprudens augeam huius saeculi mala.

Tuae dignitatis studiosissimus,
H. Grotius

---

¹ Printed in *BW* I no. 233, 205, on the basis of the autograph minute by Grotius (UL Amsterdam, [shelf-mark] III C 5). The letter is without address or date. Both addressee and date can be reconstructed from Letter 6.

6. *Apollonius Schotte to Petrus Cunaeus*, 3 April 1612¹

Grotius hodie mecum egit de sua dissertatione, mi Cunaee, quam a me habes. Et quoniam ab amicis commonitum se dicebat quorumdam theologorum — quod sane genus hominum admodum hodie irritabile est — iudicia de eo scripto huiusmodi esse quasi religionem christianam nimis latis terminis includat, rogabat me, ut eam quam primum per litteras a te vellem repetere; non tam quod aequitati tuae et prudentiae diffidat — scit enim mecum quam in huiusmodi rebus uti expertus, ita circumspectus sis —, quam quod crabronum istiusmodi impetum non alia ratione melius eludi posse existimet, quam si causa, qua irritati sunt, aliquandiu silentio prematur. Itaque, ne eius iustissimae voluntati deessem, has in ipso consessu senatus nostri subito ad te exaravi, quas uti scio pondus apud te habituras esse, ita ut festinanter et incuriose scriptis ignoscas propter necessitatem, qua expressae sunt, rogo. Bene vale, mi Cunaee, et nos amare perge. 3 Aprilis 1612.

---

[1] From P. Burman (ed.), *Petri Cunaei... Epistolae*, 11. In this letter Schotte is satisfying Grotius' request in Letter 5.

7. *Petrus Cunaeus to Apollonius Schotte*, 4 April 1612[1]

Vir amplissime, dissertationem Grotii, sive Meletium tibi remitto, in qua ego putidos theologos nostros quidquam reperisse miror quod reprehendant. Adeo enim erudite et pulchre rem totam pertractavit, ut, si operam una conferant omnes isti praeclari sacrorum antistites, nihil tale eos magnis laboribus et multa cura extrudere posse existimem. Qui profecto viri, dum leges suas et decreta sanciunt, fines theologiae paulo longius quam rei natura ferret protulerunt. Ego communis illius, quae inter Christianos esse debet, religionis multo pauciora capita posuissem eaque istiusmodi esse considerem, ut, qui nihil ultra inquireret, is et vir pius esse et bene de Deo Opt. Max. sentire videretur. Vale, vir amplissime. Lugd. Bat. 4 Aprilis 1612.

---

[1] From P. Burman (ed.), *Petri Cunaei... Epistolae*, 12. Reply to Letter 6.

8. *Antonius Walaeus to Hugo Grotius*, [April 1612][1]

Clarissime vir, quod literis tuis postremis ante aliquot menses non respondi in causa fuit partim morbus qui me tum aliquot septimanas graviter afflixit, cuius reliquias etiamnunc circumfero, iam vero occasionem praesentem nactus officio meo et postulato tuo amplius deesse nolui. Sententiam meam de editione huius tui qua docti qua pii scripti equidem non libenter pronuncio, quia fructum quidem, si eo, quo aequum est, studio excipiatur, non exiguum ecclesiae Christi ex eo oriturum plane mihi persuadeo; tamen nostrorum temporum et ecclesiarum ratio, medicam hanc manum, ut vereor, vix feret. Sed ab aegris ipsis faciendae medicinae consilium non est petendum. Quare pro prudentia tua quid hic agendum sit optime arbitraberis. Interim clarissime vir, ignosces ut spero audaciae meae, si de pauculis, quae aditerata lectione scripti tui adnotavi, te rursum commonefaciam. Nam quum semel prudentiae limites sim transgressus, ulterius etiam progrediendi animas mihi facit voluntas et aequitas tua.

Pag. 3. versa affirmatur, quod *actio superioris* προαιρετικοῦ *in inferius, qua tale, utcumque nihil aliud sit quam lex sive imperium.*² Quam sententiam veram esse agnosco, si aliae actiones Dei in arbitrium hominis non excludantur. Nam Deus non tantum legem fert humanae voluntati promissis suis et minis sancitam, sed etiam in bono *operatur* in nobis *velle et efficere, pro beneplacito*³ *suo*, per efficaciam Spiritus sui. Exclusiva ergo illa si tollatur sententia offensae minus obnoxia reddetur. Mosaica religio ibidem numeratur inter imperfectas, eodemque censu cum religione naturali aestimatur,⁴ quae tamen suo genere perfecta fuit et salutem veram, quam promisit cultoribus suis, non minus quam christiana exhibuit, etsi diverso modo et mensura; quod de naturali affirmari non potest, quia τὸ ἀδύνατον τοῦ νόμου⁵ propter carnis impotentiam in ea semper obtinuit, gratiae vero promissio ex ea plane exulavit, nisi per naturalem intelligatur illa gratiae dispensatio, quae ante legem per Mosen latam apud patriarchas viguit, quae a quibusdam quidem naturalis sed valde ἀκύρως appellatur.

Pag. 5. clarissime vir, argumenta duo immortalitatis animae, gentium namque consensus et natura perpessionum expers, obiter afferuntur.⁶ Quia vero animae immortalitas vel primum omnis religionis est fundamentum, iudicio tuo etiam atque etiam videndum relinquo, an non conducibile proposito tuo futurum sit, si fundamentum hoc paulo plenius et firmius stabilias, quo a religione alieniores animi facilius verae religionis sensum admittant quoque studiosius in eius inquisitionem incumbant.

Pag. 16. *Deo solidam laudem tribuis hominis reparati, ita tamen ut non sentias invitum quenquam bonum fieri volentem.*⁷ Quae sententia vera est, si de voluntate gratiam conversionis comitante, non antecedente, aut se cum gratia coniungente, intelligatur. Nam Deus reperitur ab iis qui illum non quaerunt, nec *est ea currentis aut volentis, sed miserentis Dei.*⁸ Voluntas ergo illa a gratia Dei est, ut ecclesia recte definivit adversus Pelagianos, qui ex nolentibus volentes facit.⁹

Pag. 18. ubi de invocatione Dei agitur,¹⁰ dogma, nisi me memoria fallit, a te omissum est, quod tamen invocationis verae fundamentum et inter omnes Christianos semper confessum fuit, nempe veri Dei invocationem intercessione mediatoris Christi niti; quia, nisi quae in nomine eius fiunt, preces acceptae Deo non sunt¹¹. Postrema lectione libelli tui haec paucula a me observata sunt, clarissime vir, quae fortassis accuratiore iudicii tui norma nonnihil dirigi queant. Deum rogo etc. Middelburgo.

¹ Printed in Walaeus, *Opera Omnia*, II 402. Taken over by Molhuysen, *BW* I no. 232, 203-04. This undated letter is probably the reply to Letter 4 which Walaeus says he received 'ante aliquot menses'. Molhuysen's suggestion that the letter can consequently be dated at the beginning of April seems plausible. The references in this letter to a couple of pages of the *Meletius*, concern a second (unknown) copy of this treatise. See above, Introduction, (10).
² The words put in italics are quoted literally from *Mel.* 10.47-49.
³ Philip. 2: 13.
⁴ Cf. *Mel.* 12.60. Walaeus' criticism echoes Calvin, *Institutio*, II 11 (ed. Barth/Niesel III 423 sq.).
⁵ Rom. 8: 3.
⁶ Cf. *Mel.* 18.
⁷ The words put in italics are quoted literally from *Mel.* 57.466-468.
⁸ Rom. 9: 16.
⁹ Walaeus probably intends to refer to can. 23 of the Council of Orange (529), (see H. Denzinger/A. Schönmetzer, *Enchiridion symbolorum, definitionum et declarationum de rebus fidei et morum*,³³ Barcinone/Friburgi Brisgoviae/Romae/Neo-Eboraci 1965, nr. 393 (196), 136), but he is actually quoting Aug., *Opus imperf.* II 157: operari Deum voluntates in mentibus hominum, non ut nolentes credunt, quod absurdissime dicitur, sed ut *volentes ex nolentibus* fiant.
¹⁰ Cf. *Mel.* 62.
¹¹ An echo of Calvin, *Institutio*, III 20, 18 (ed. Barth/Niesel IV 322).

INDEX OF BIBLICAL REFERENCES

Vetus Testamentum

Gn.	1:3	63n, 152	Deut.	4:15	155
	1:26-7	147		7:2	157
Ex.	20:4	154, 155	Eccl.	28:2	157
				32:24	151

Novum Testamentum

Mt.	3:11	179n	Act.	2:3	179n
	5-7	64n		7:48	155
	5:22	147		10:30	159
	5:27	160		14:23	159
	5:31	158		15:20	159
	5:32	158		17:18	146
	5:33	154		23:8	142
	5:34	154			
	5:39	151, 157	Rom.	1:23	155
	5:43	62n, 156, 157		1:31	148
	5:48	146		4:2	149
	6:1-4	160		7:15	145
	6:8	154		8:3	182n
	6:14	157		9:16	182n
	6:24	159		12:1	148
	7:3	157		13:1	158
	7:12	156			
	9:13	177n	1 Cor.	1:24	177n
	17:21	159		2:14	151
	19:21	159		3:12	176n
	22:18	160		3:15	177n
	22:23	142		4:13	150
	23:2-3	177n		7:5-6	146, 159
	25:14-30	176n		9:16	149
	28:19	144		10:7	177n
				10:14	177n
Lc.	2:37	159		15:43-44	141
	3:16	179n		16:22	177n
	15:7	151			
	24:28	160	Gal.	4:8	177n
				5:2	176n
Ioh.	1:1	150, 177n		5:20	177n
	1:2	144		6:4	149
	1:14	150		6:10	156
	4:24	148			
	6:53	153	Phil.	2:3	182n
	8:12	179n		4:8	148
	9:5	179n	Col.	1:15	177n
	9:41	177n		1:16	146

1.Tim. 2:5	150	9:15	150
		9:22	149
2.Tim. 3:16	170n	10:25	155
		11:6	31, 62n, 139
Tit. 3:4	160	12:24	150
Hebr. 1:3	177n	Ap.Ioh. 19:20	177n

INDEX OF PROPER NAMES

Actuarius   18
Aelius Lampridius   156
Aelianus   66n
Aeschylus   145
Alexander Severus   34n, 156
Amelius   88, 117, 150
Ammianus Marcellinus   92, 122, 138, 154
Aristippus   108, 141, 159
Aristophanes   66n, 150
Aristoteles   29, 34, 39, 55, 66n, 67, 68, 79-82, 85, 89, 96, 108, 110, 111, 115, 119, 127, 139-44, 146-49, 151, 156, 157, 178
Arminius, J.   46, 56, 176, 177n
Arnobius   146
Athanasius   144
Athenaeus   66n
Athenagoras   66n
Augustinus   32, 54, 56, 69, 140, 145, 149, 154, 172, 182

Barton, E.   17, 18n
Basilius Magnus   65
Bertius, P.   7
Bèze, Th. de   46, 64n
Bignon, J.   70n
Boreel, J.   14, 15, 20, 22, 23, 41, 45, 104, 177, 179n
Brandt, C.   1

Calvin, J.   13n, 55, 64n, 140, 178, 179n, 182
Canter, Th.   65n
Casaubonus, I.   53n, 64n, 70n, 139
Cassander, G.   46n, 51, 173n
Cassius Dio   34
Cato Minor   91, 98, 121, 129, 131, 158
Cattenburgh, A. van   5
Censorinus   151
Ceres   95, 125, 156
Cicero   33, 34, 36, 67, 68, 80, 94, 96, 100, 109, 124, 127, 131, 138-43, 145-48, 153, 155, 157-60
Cleanthes   82, 111, 146
Clemens Alexandrinus   64n, 66n, 147, 155, 156
Colomiés, P.   20n
Commodus, Emperor   69
Crates of Thebe   159

Cunaeus, P.   10n, 15, 45, 48n, 58, 59, 137, 169, 179, 180

Demosthenes   162
Dio Chrysostomus   99, 131, 160
Diodorus Siculus   90, 120, 152
Diogenes Laertius   153, 159
Diogenes of Sinope   95, 126
Diphilus   157
Dousa Jr., J.   18
Dousa Sr., J.   17, 18
Dousa, G.   17, 18, 20
Drusius, J.   64n
Dumaurier, Aubéry   33, 34, 67
Dumoulin, P.   13n, 68
Duplessis Mornay, Ph.   54, 70, 139, 144, 172, 173n

Ekphantos   147
Epaminondas of Thebe   95, 126
Epictetus   91, 98, 121, 131, 153, 159, 160
Epicurus   34, 80, 139, 141, 142, 159
Epiphanius   64n
Episcopius, S.   7
Erasmus, D.   64n, 161, 162
Euhemerus   139
Euripides   34, 93, 97, 124, 128, 145, 146, 155, 157, 158
Eurysos   147
Eusebius of Caesarea   28, 64n, 68, 69, 148-50, 152, 157, 162

Florentinus   147

Galenus   102, 133, 162
Gomarus, F.   46
Groot, P. de   7
Groot, W. de   144

Hadrian, Emperor   93, 96, 124, 126
Haggenmacher, P.   62n
Heinsius, D.   69
Henri IV, King of France   51n, 52n
Hercules   91, 121
Hesiodus   161
Hieronymus of Rhodos   80, 108, 141, 142
Hogerbeets, R.   48, 49
Homerus   27, 167, 168n
Horatius   34, 155, 159, 162
Hospital, M. de l'   137

Iosephus 152
Irenaeus 101, 133
Isocrates 162
Iustinus 93, 122, 153
Iustinus Martyr 28, 32, 66, 69, 155, 156
Iuvenalis 96, 126, 156

James I, King 25n
Jeannin, P. 14
Jeremias II, Patriarch 17
Jesus Sirach 34
Junius, Fr. 46, 47, 51, 54, 69, 144, 171, 172, 173n

Kristeller, P. O. 69n

Lactantius 67n, 69, 139, 140, 147, 148, 155, 157, 158, 161
Liber 95, 125, 156
Limborch, Ph. van 6, 7
Lipsius, J. 137

Livius 158
Lucanus 145, 146, 158, 159
Lukaris, Cyrillus 17
Lycurgus 152

Macrobius 149
Marcus Aurelius 159
Martialis 158
Maurice, Prince 49
Maximus, Archidiakonus Alex. 18n
Maximus Tyrius 68, 69, 145, 147, 153-54, 157
Melanchthon, Ph. 59n
Meletius of Antioch 4n
Meletius of Lycopolis 4n
Meletius Pegas, Patriarch 17, 18, 20-24, 40, 41, 44, 76, 101, 104, 105, 132, 137, 161
Mendes da Costa, M. B. 6
Minos 152
Mithras 91, 125, 155
Molhuysen, P. C. 1, 3-5, 15, 169
Moses 90-2, 120-22, 152

Navarra, Queen of 18n
Nestorius 150
Numa 93, 124, 154-55

Oldenbarnevelt, J. van 48, 49
Ovidius 140

Panaetius 100, 131, 160
Paraeus, D. 13n
Pataecion 95, 126

Perkins, W. 13n
Perrot, Ch. 46
Petrus Galathinus 70n
Philo Alexandrinus 66n, 158
Philo of Byblos 148
Philostratus 159
Piscator, J. 13n
Plato 27, 29, 39, 66n, 68, 81, 82, 87, 90, 93, 94, 97, 98, 100, 110, 111, 116, 120, 123, 127, 129, 131, 144, 145, 149, 153, 154, 157-60, 167, 168n
Plinius Maior 140, 148
Plinius Minor 92, 122, 153
Plutarchus 27, 34, 64n, 65, 66n, 67, 68, 81, 110, 143, 145, 146, 151, 155, 156, 160, 167, 168n
Polyander, J. 46
Polybius 34
Pompeius Trogus 92, 122, 153
Porphyrius 87, 116-17, 149-50
Posidonius 138
Pseudo-Iustinus 151
Pseudo-Longinus 90, 120, 152
Publilius Syrus 151
Pythagoras 34, 90, 93, 120, 124, 146, 154-55

Raimundus Martini 70n
Raimundus of Sabund 70
Reigersberch, M. van 13, 15, 49
Rutilius Namatianus 155

Sallustius 34
Salvianus 102, 134, 162
Sassen, F. 68
Scaliger, J. J. 18n, 26, 70n, 152
Scheltema, P. 5, 6
Schotte, A. 10n, 15, 45-8, 58, 59, 159, 179, 180
Schotte, J. 15, 46, 48
Schottus, A. 31n, 66n
Seneca 33, 34, 36, 67, 68, 80, 86, 91, 93, 96, 100-01, 109, 115, 116, 121, 124, 127, 131, 133, 138, 140, 141, 143, 148-49, 153, 155, 157, 160-61
Sextius, Q. 86, 116, 149
Sextus Empyricus 66n
Socinus, F. 35, 64, 150
Socrates 91, 97, 121, 127, 140, 157
Solomon 34
Stobaeus 65
Sophocles 95, 125, 156
Strabo 92, 122, 153

Tacitus 81, 93, 96-7, 110, 124, 127, 128, 143, 155, 157-58

Terentius 34, 161
Tertullianus 64n, 161
Theodoretus of Cyrus 151
Theodorus Cyrenaicus 139
Theophilus Antiochenus 66n, 152
Theophrastus 34
Thomas Aquinas 34n
Tideman, J. H. 6
Thucydides 162
Trelcatius, L. 46

Ulysses 91, 121

Valerius Maximus 88, 117, 150, 158
Varro 38, 81, 90, 92, 110, 120, 123, 145, 151, 154
Velserus, M. 18n
Vergilius 149, 155
Victor, bishop 101, 133
Vida, M. G. 176, 177n

Vives, L. 70, 144, 161
Vollenhoven, C. van 3
Vorstius, C. 46, 172, 173n
Vosbergen, C. van 49
Vossius, G. J. 63n, 64n, 144
Vulcanius, B. 18n

Walaeus, A. 1, 10, 15, 45-53, 55, 57, 58n, 59, 137-38, 140, 142, 143-44, 151, 153-54, 162, 169-79, 180-82
Waszink, J. H. 69n
Whitaker, W. 13n
Wtenbogaert, J. 20n, 48n

Xenophon 158

Zaleucos 88, 117
Zarathustra 152
Zosimus 86, 116, 149

INDEX OF SUBJECT MATTERS AND TERMS

The following index refers to the text of the *Meletius* and the Commentary only. References to the Latin text are marked by the letter *M*, followed by paragraph- and linenumbers; those to the Commentary by the letter *C*, equally followed by paragraph- and linenumbers. In some cases the Commentary will give further references to the Introduction or to the Appendices.

actio (see also Rules, concerning actions) – *M* 10.47; 19.1; 35.186, *C* 10.47-49
ἀδιάφορα– see Ethics (General)
Affects – see Man
Age, Golden – *M* 88.366, *C* 88.366
amicitia – *M* 30.147; 68.138
Angels (and Demons) – *M* 27.101; 27.107
Articles of faith – see Dogma
Atheism – *M* 6.3, *C* 6.9
Baptism – *M* 66.99; 66.104
barbarus – *M* 5.66; 69.155-156, *C* 69.155
Beatitude – see Religion (General)
Charity – *M* 56.445-446; 68.144; 70.183
Christ / Christology (see also Trinity, H.) – *M* 25.84; 48.320, *C* 25.84
—, Example – *M* 56.435-436
—, καθ' ἕνωσιν ὑποστατικήν – *M* 49.332, *C* 49.322
—, λόγος θέου – *M* 51.383; 66.112
—, *magister* – *M* 3.34, *C* 3.34
—, Mediator (μεσίτης) – *M* 46.295; 47.303, *C* 47.303
—, Son of God – *M* 47.311
Christianity (*Christianitas*) – see Religion (Christian)
civitas (see also *respublica*) – *M* 3.44, *C* 1; 3.44
cogitatio – see Rules (concerning thoughts)
colere / cultus – *M* 32.157; 33.162; 33.166; 34.176, *C* 33.162-167; 60; 60.21-22; 63.55
concordia – *M* 3.37-38; 65.79; 88.365; 90.16-17, *C* 2.22; 23.40-43
conscientia – *M* 10.50; 34.178; 36.201; 37.206
consensus / ὁμολογούμενα – *M* 5.67; 6.6; 52.392; 71.195; 90.27, *C* 5.67; 6.6; 52.391-392
culpa – *M* 24.61; 37.211; 41.246; 45.283; 46.294, *C* 24.59-60

cultus – see *colere / cultus*
Death (*mors*) – *M* 76.255; 76.260-261; 76.264, *C* 76.262-263; 76.264
decretum – see Dogma
Demons – see Angels (and Demons)
disciplina christiana – see Ethics (General)
divortium – *M* 73.218; 73.224
Dogma / δόγμα (*decretum*) (see also God, Christ / Christology, Trinity, H.) – *M* 19.4; 19.6, *C* 19.4; 19.6; 91.38-39
—, Articles of faith (necessary and not necessary) – *M* 3.43; 90.27; 91.38-39, *C* 3.43; 91.38-39
—, Dogma's concerning:
  God in relation to Himself – *M* 20-25
  God in relation to the Creation – *M* 26-29
  Man and his evil nature – (see also Man, Evil, Sin) – *M* 30-40
  God's goodness and forgiveness – (see also Penitence) – *M* 40-45
  Christ – *M* 46-50
  Reparation of the relationship between God and man – *M* 51-58
Dutch character – *C* 75.254
ἐλεημοσύνη – *M* 70.180
Epicureans – *M* 8.26; 18.63; 18.67; 29.120, *C* 16.37; 17; 18.63; 18.67-68; 29.120-122
epistola – *M* Title; *C* Title
Ethics (*praeceptum / officium*), General (see also Religion (General), Rules, Stoics) – *M* 19.4, *C* 19.4; 68
—, ἀδιάφορα – *M* 58.477, *C* 58.477-480
—, *disciplina christiana* – *M* 60.26
—, κατόρθωμα – *M* 35.191, *C* 35.191
—, Precepts:
  regarding God – *M* 60-67
  regarding humanity in general – *M* 68-69

INDEX OF SUBJECT MATTERS AND TERMS

regarding one's neighbour - *M* 70
regarding oneself - *M* 75-81
regarding society - *M* 71-74
—, virtue (see also Stoics) - *M* 15.22; 15.25-26; 17.60
Eucharist (*coena, Pascha*) - *M* 66.112-115; 90.21, *C* 66.112-115
Evil (*malum*) - *M* 14.15; 24.48; 24.56; 24.69; 25.78; 29.125; 29.129; 34.175; 40.237; 76.265, *C* 14.15; 24.34-35; 24.70; 29.124
experientia - *M* 9.37; 18.66; 34.178
Faith / Piety -
—, *fides* - *M* 50.351
—, *fiducia* - *M* 44.271; 44.279
—, *pietas* - *M* 24.49; 29.122; 31.154; 56.445; 89.10, *C* 57.458-459
familia - *M* 71.187, *C* 71.191; 72.202
Fasting (*ieiunium*) - *M* 80.298, *C* 80.298
felicitas - see Religion (General)
Forgiveness - see Penitence / Forgiveness
God (see also Trinity, H.) -
—, Absolute, Eternal, Highest Being - *M* 21.21
—, *causa effectrix* - *M* 14.9; 28.110
—, Creator - *M* 26.89-90
—, *esse* - *M* 6.4; 6.5; 20.14, *C* 6.5
—, Good - *M* 8.32; 25.81-82; 41.239
—, *iustus* - *M* 11.53
—, King- *M* 38.213
—, Legislator - *M* 10.43; 11.53
—, *natura intelligens* - *M* 7.11
—, *omnipotens* - *M* 8.30
—, *omnisciens* - *M* 24.48; 25.80-81, *C* 24.47-48
—, One - *M* 20.13; 23.40, *C* 14.9-10; 20
—, *rector* - *M* 8.34; 12.68; 26.90; 29.120
—, *remunerator* - *M* 7.10; 9.36
—, Will (προαίρεσις) - *M* 7.15; 7.16; 8.29; 10.43-50; 13.1
Ghost, H. - see Trinity, H.
History - *C* 2.18-22
Honour - (see also Ethics) *M* 77.267
Ignorance - see Man
immortalitas - see Religion (General)
indictitius - *M* 80.297, *C* 80.297
Indies - *M* 2.26, *C* 2.26
indolentia - *M* 14.16; 17.56, *C* 17.56
indolere (= *indolescere*) - *M* 58.484; 70.174, *C* 58.484

invocare Deum - see Rites / Ceremonies
Jews - see Religion (Jewish)
lex humana - *M* 12.63
lex Dei - *M* 38.216
liberi - *M* 8.32; 71.190; 73.223; 73.228; 88.357, *C* 88.357-358
Lust - *M* 79.287, *C* 79
Lying - *C* 83.320
Magi - *M* 8.22
magistratus - see *respublica*
Man - (see also Dogma, Ethics, Sin, Stoics) -
—, Affects - *M* 31.150; 31.153; 33.169
—, Body - *M* 16.38-39; 18.64
—, Created good - *M* 30.141
—, Ignorance - *M* 3.35; 46.300; 51.366; 91.44, *C* 46.298
—, *imago Dei* - *M* 18.71; 30.143; 35.181, *C* 18.71; 35.181
—, Logical and deliberative being (ζῶον λόγικον καὶ προαιρετικόν) - *M* 9.37, *C* 9.37
—, One origin - *M* 30.146; 35.181-182, *C* 30.146; 35.181-182
—, Sinful - *M* 36.193-204
—, σῶμα πνευματικόν - *M* 16.39, *C* 16.39
—, Soul (*animus / mens*) - *M* 14.12; 16.39; 18.65-66; 18.71, *C* 18.71
—, *vis deliberativa* - *M* 9.39-40
—, Will (προαίρεσις) - *M* 10.43-50; 28.115; 29.123
—, World, created for - *M* 27.98; 28.118-119
Manicheism - *M* 29.131, *C* 29.131
matrimonium - *M* 71.195; 72.198-199; 88.361, *C* 73.219-220
Muslims - see Religion (Muslim)
mysteria - see Rites / Ceremonies
natura - *M* 9.42; 18.63, *C* 9.40-42; 30.145-146; 63.52-53
—, *impatiens* - *M* 14.9-10
—, *mater noverca* - *M* 36.202, *C* 36.202
necessitudo - *M* 2.29; 35.183-184, *C* 2.29
officia - see Ethics
ὁμολογούμενα - see *consensus*
orare - see Rites / Ceremonies
Paganism - see Religion (Natural)
pax (see also *amicitia, concordia*) *M* 2.26; 5.64; 70.185; 88.365
pecunia - *C* 78.279-280

Penitence / Forgiveness –
—, *ignoscere* – *M* 70.170; 91.44
—, *poenitentia* – *M* 50.344; 50.359; 87.351
—, συγγνώμη – *M* 50.361, *C* 50.361-363
—, *venia* – *M* 43.262; 44.274; 50.340; 50.353; 50.361, *C* 50.340; 50.361-363; 87.352
Perjury – *M* 63.48, *C* 63.48
Pharisees – *M* 42.251
Philanthropy – *M* 36.203; 82.317, *C* 82.317
Philarcheus – *C* 53.403-408
Philosophy (Ancient) – see Epicureans, Magi, Manicheism, Stoics
Piety – see Faith / Piety
poena – *M* 11.52; 38.217; 42.252; 42.254-256; 45.289; 48.321; 76.265
Polytheism (see also Religion, Natural) – *M* 20.17; 27.112
Poverty – see Richness / Poverty
praeceptum (παραίνεσις) – see Ethics
praemium – *M* 11.52; 29.128; 38.218; 42.253; 42.256; 78.286, *C* 11.52
Praying – see Rites / Ceremonies
Promise – see Rules (concerning promises)
ratio – *M* 7.18; 15.25; 35.181, *C* 22.38
—, *divina* – see Trinity, H.
—, *humana* – *M* 23.37
—, *recta* – *M* 13.6; 25.79
—, *sana* – *M* 50.354
Religion (General) – *M* 2.18; 6.3; 19.1; 19.9, *C* 19.9-10
—, *beatitudo* – *M* 13.4; 14.12, *C* 14.12-13
—, *felicitas* – *M* 14.16; 16.38; 67.120, *C* 16.38
—, *finis* – *M* 13.2-3; 18.70-71
—, *frui Deo* – *M* 13.7; 14.11; 15.19, *C* 13.7-8
—, *immortalitas* – *M* 14.16; *C* 18.70-71
—, *summum bonum* – *M* 13.4; 13.6-7; 15.17-18; 17.54; 18.62
—, *virtus est religio* – *M* 58.476-477
—, *vita altera* – *M* 15.28; 66.110; 67.120; 67.130, *C* 15.27
—, *vita beata* – *M* 16.36, *C* 16.36
Religion (Christian) (*Christianitas*) – *M* 2.18; 3.32; 6.1; 12.53; 13.5-6; 18.69; 21.20; 25.79; 41.243; 50.341; 51.381; 56.454; 64.65, *C* 2.22; 51.375-384; 56.443-455

—, fruits of – *M* 88.353-366
—, non-Christian authors on – *M* 59.1-14
Religion (Egyptian) – *C* 53.403-408
—, (Jewish) – *M* 2.28; 12.60; 16.34; 18.63; 50.342; 56.445; 64.68; 69.158; 79.289, *C* 2.28; 12.60; 16.34-35; 63.52-55; 69.160-161
—, (Muslim) – *M* 16.35; 56.445; 72.201; 79.290, *C* 16.31-35
—, (Natural) – *M* 12.60
—, (Phoenician) – *C* 53.403-408
remissio / reparatio (see also Christ / Christology) *M* 43.261; 51.364-365; 56.435
remuneratio – see God, *remunerator*
respublica / magistratus – *M* 71.187; 74.231; 74.233, *C* 74.234
Revelation – see God, Christ / Christology, H. Trinity)
Richness / Poverty (see also Ethics) *M* 78.276-286
Rites / Ceremonies (see also Baptism, Eucharist) *M* 64.66; 64.69; 67.120
—, *coetus frequentare* – *M* 65.73, *C* 65.73
—, *invocare Deum* – *M* 62.35, *C* 62.35
—, *mysteria* – *M* 66.116, *C* 66.108
—, *orare* – *M* 62.36, *C* 62.35-36; 62.38
—, Sabbath – *M* 65.85, *C* 65.85; 65.86-87
Rules – (see also Ethics)
—, concerning actions – *M* 82
—, concerning matters – *M* 77-81
—, concerning promises – *M* 84, *C* 84.325; 84.327
—, concerning thoughts – *M* 85, *C* 85.335
—, concerning words / speech – *M* 83
—, Golden Rule – *M* 68.148, *C* 68.148
Sabbath – see Rites / Ceremonies
Sacraments – see Baptism, Eucharist, Rites / Ceremonies
Sadducees – *M* 18.63, *C* 18.63
schola / vita – *M* 89.13, *C* 89.7-8
Scripture, H. – *M* 51.384; 52.392, *C* 52-55; 53.403-408
—, antiquity of – *M* 53.395
—, simplicity of – *M* 54.409; 55.418
—, truth of *M* 52.385
Sexuality (see also Ethics) – *M* 81.302, *C* 81.302; 81.306-308
simulachra – *M* 63.53, *C* 63.53
Sin (see also Man)

INDEX OF SUBJECT MATTERS AND TERMS

—, *peccare* - *M* 36.199
—, *peccatum* - *M* 37.205; 38.213; 47.308; 51.372
societas - *M* 84.329-330, *C* 83.321; 84.328
Stoics (see also Ethics, Man, Sin) - *M* 7.18; 9.38; 15.21; 17.59; 28.112; 29.121; 42.247; 56.436; 58.478, *C* 7.18; 29.120-122; 70.179-180
—, affects - *M* 31.150, *C* 31.150
—, *fatum* - *M* 7.19; 9.38; 29.121
—, ὁμολογουμένως τῇ φύσει ζῆν - *M* 86.348, *C* 86.348
—, *peccata aequalia* - *M* 37.205-206, *C* 37.205
—, Precepts and Examples (see also Ethics) - *C* 56. 436-437
—, *virtus* - *M* 15.22; 17.59, *C* 15.21-23
Suicide - *M* 75.243-254, *C* 75.247-249
summum bonum - see Religion (General)
Sun - *M* 23.43-44, *C* 23.44
symbolum 'Quicumque' - *C* 48.322-326
ταπεινοφροσύνη (see also Ethics) - *M* 41.243; 77.273, *C* 77.273
Tolerance - see *pax, amicitia, concordia*

tribuni plebis - *M* 74.233, *C* 74.233
Trinity, Holy - *M* 23.40, *C* 23.40-43
—, Hypostasis (ὑπόστασις) - *M* 22.34, *C* 22.34
—, *intellectus, voluntas* - *M* 23.40-41; 24.46
—, λόγος / σοφία - *M* 22.29
—, νοῦς / ἐνέργεια - *M* 22.28, *C* 22.28
—, νοῦς / νοητόν - *M* 22.35, *C* 22.35
—, νοῦς πατρικός - *M* 46.299, *C* 46.298
—, *ratio divina* - *M* 22.27, *C* 23.40-43
—, *Spiritus* - *M* 22.32; 57.456, *C* 10.47-49
—, *virtus divina* - *M* 22.27; 22.31; 24.47-48; 57.456
ulcisci, ultio - *M* 69.165, *C* 69.164-165; 69.166-167
venia - see Penitence / Forgiveness
Virtue - see Ethics (General), Stoics
vita - see *schola / vita*
voluptas - see Lust
War - *M* 1.11; 2.25; 88.364; 90.18, *C* 1.11
World - see Man
Zealand - *M* 1.12, *C* 1.12
Ζοφασημίν - *M* 32.160, *C* 32.160

DATE DUE

HIGHSMITH   #LO-45220